Cyber Recon

My Life in Cyber Espionage and Ransomware Negotiation

Kurtis Minder

WILEY

Copyright 2025 by John Wiley & Sons, Inc. All rights reserved. All rights reserved, including rights for text and data mining and training of artificial intelligence technologies or similar technologies.

Published by John Wiley & Sons, Inc., Hoboken, New Jersey.
Published simultaneously in Canada.

No part of this publication may be reproduced, stored in a retrieval system, or transmitted in any form or by any means, electronic, mechanical, photocopying, recording, scanning, or otherwise, except as permitted under Section 107 or 108 of the 1976 United States Copyright Act, without either the prior written permission of the Publisher, or authorization through payment of the appropriate per-copy fee to the Copyright Clearance Center, Inc., 222 Rosewood Drive, Danvers, MA 01923, (978) 750-8400, fax (978) 750-4470, or on the web at www.copyright.com. Requests to the Publisher for permission should be addressed to the Permissions Department, John Wiley & Sons, Inc., 111 River Street, Hoboken, NJ 07030, (201) 748-6011, fax (201) 748-6008, or online at http://www.wiley.com/go/permission.

The manufacturer's authorized representative according to the EU General Product Safety Regulation is Wiley-VCH GmbH, Boschstr. 12, 69469 Weinheim, Germany, e-mail: Product_Safety@wiley.com.

Trademarks: Wiley and the Wiley logo are trademarks or registered trademarks of John Wiley & Sons, Inc. and/or its affiliates in the United States and other countries and may not be used without written permission. All other trademarks are the property of their respective owners. John Wiley & Sons, Inc. is not associated with any product or vendor mentioned in this book.

Limit of Liability/Disclaimer of Warranty: While the publisher and author have used their best efforts in preparing this book, they make no representations or warranties with respect to the accuracy or completeness of the contents of this book and specifically disclaim any implied warranties of merchantability or fitness for a particular purpose. No warranty may be created or extended by sales representatives or written sales materials. The advice and strategies contained herein may not be suitable for your situation. You should consult with a professional where appropriate. Further, readers should be aware that websites listed in this work may have changed or disappeared between when this work was written and when it is read. Neither the publisher nor authors shall be liable for any loss of profit or any other commercial damages, including but not limited to special, incidental, consequential, or other damages.

For general information on our other products and services or for technical support, please contact our Customer Care Department within the United States at (800) 762-2974, outside the United States at (317) 572-3993 or fax (317) 572-4002.

Wiley also publishes its books in a variety of electronic formats. Some content that appears in print may not be available in electronic formats. For more information about Wiley products, visit our web site at www.wiley.com.

Library of Congress Control Number: 2025911131

ISBN: 9781394334612 (Hardback)
ISBN: 9781394334636 (ePDF)
ISBN: 9781394334629 (epub)
ISBN: 9781394334643 (oBook)

Cover Design: Wiley
Cover Image: © Feng Yu/stock.adobe.com

SKY10117559_061625

*To my parents, Floyd and Brenda,
who molded me into the person I am today.*

Contents

Foreword vii
About the Author xi
Acknowledgments xiii

        Introduction 1
Chapter 1 Why Spy on Bad Guys? 11
Chapter 2 FFS DNM 33
Chapter 3 Cyber Espionage 101 61
Chapter 4 Whodat? 83
Chapter 5 OPSEC or Die 107
Chapter 6 How Not to Go to Jail, Hell, or Worse 137
Chapter 7 Negotiating with the Enemy 161

Chapter 8	You Don't Have to Be a Doctor to Know How Not to Die	191
Chapter 9	Robots, Digital Money, and Teleportation	213
Chapter 10	Digital Novichok	229
Index		245

Foreword

Thinking back, it is appropriate that my first meeting with Kurtis Minder took place in the lounge of the National Press Club in Washington, DC. Neither of us expected that 11 years later Kurtis would become an author and I would have the great privilege of introducing what surely is the first of many works.

While Kurtis is deeply technical and immersed in the world of cybersecurity, this book paints a much larger picture than the details of ransomware, attack methods, and building of bots to eavesdrop and record conversations in illicit dark web groups. It exposes us to the universe of criminal online activity and may arm the reader to prepare for their own cyber incidents.

Reading *Cyber Recon* has been an eye-opener for me. While my career in cybersecurity has exposed me to plenty of hackers, most of my conversations with them have been after they faced the consequences of their actions. Most had experienced the "knock on the door" when the FBI tracked them down. Because they were often under age, they were able to mend their ways and go on to have successful careers as consultants, founders, and even authors.

But Kurtis brings us a wealth of experience engaging with threat actors in the here and now. Mostly Russian or Eastern European, they are engaged in ransomware and extortion as a business.

You will recognize in Kurtis's descriptions of his interactions with these nefarious characters somebody whose EQ (emotional quotient) is off the charts. He describes a "worldview that we must understand to put ourselves in the heads and walk in the shoes of foreign cybercriminals in order to better protect ourselves." That level of empathy explains his success as the top-performing telecom salesperson at Fortinet and then as co-founder and CEO of GroupSense.

As an illustration of his ability to sway people, Kurtis once had to respond to a crisis at a primary OEM partner of GroupSense. This well-known brand had its own threat intelligence product, but the sales team at the company had much more success selling GroupSense's service. After a couple of years the partner copied the GroupSense product and switched it out at all of their customers. Kurtis went into high gear and paid visits to all of those customers and won them back from the partner.

So it should be no surprise that Kurtis had the innate ability to negotiate with threat actors demanding ransoms for data they had encrypted. In these pages you will receive a master class in the inner-workings of the ransomware economy. If you are unfortunate enough to be caught up in a data hostage negotiation, you will know what to expect and what to do.

Ever since a feature-length article in the *New Yorker* titled "How to Negotiate with Ransomware Hackers" (www.newyorker.com/magazine/2021/06/07/how-to-negotiate-with-ransomware-hackers), Kurtis has been in high demand as a speaker. He is also the first person you need to call if an organization succumbs to ransomware. The two vocations even collided onstage one day as he was presenting and he had to respond to incoming messages from the threat actor in an intense negotiation. His audience was happy to stand by as he dealt with the situation.

As you read these pages, you will be transported into a William Gibson novel—only none of the conversations are fictional. You will learn about initial access brokers, infostealer logs for sale, and the popular dark web marketplaces. You will come away with a new understanding of the constant dance between the bad guys and the 570+ vendors of threat intelligence products and services, not to mention the law enforcement agencies that camp out on cybercrime forums.

You will also be schooled in negotiation techniques from a diligent student of such. When he found himself in the role of negotiator, Kurtis dove deep into the techniques practiced by FBI hostage negotiators. He has applied those techniques and offers his firsthand experience, thus contributing back to the body of knowledge he took from.

Kurtis offers guidance on how to avoid becoming a victim of a cyberattack. Rather than promoting huge investments in tools, he promotes some simple steps, including the use of strong authentication and taking steps to improve cyber hygiene. I know he takes this message on the road to small businesses, healthcare providers, and school systems, some of the most common victims of ransomware. He also describes incident response and crisis communication plans. One of his clients could not access their incident response plan because it had been encrypted by the attackers!

If you want to become sufficiently paranoid, just read what Kurtis has to say about OpSec, the practice of keeping your personal life and activities from prying eyes. You may think you have nothing to hide, but Kurtis will change your mind and provide guidance on how to improve your security stance.

This book is an enthralling read and should earn a place in your reference library next to Cliff Stoll's *Cuckoo's Egg*, where you can turn to it for the trove of insights that Kurtis has compiled from his years of keyboard to keyboard interactions with threat actors.

Richard Stiennon,
Chief Research Analyst, IT-Harvest,
and Author of Surviving Cyberwar
(Government Institutes, 2010)
Birmingham, Michigan
March 29, 2025

About the Author

Kurtis Minder is a globally recognized authority in cyber espionage, ransomware negotiation, and digital risk intelligence. As the CEO and co-founder of GroupSense, he has developed one of the most sophisticated cyber reconnaissance operations worldwide, safeguarding Fortune 500 companies, government agencies, and critical infrastructure from nation-state adversaries and cybercriminal syndicates.

With over 30 years of frontline experience, Kurtis has led some of the most complex cyber investigations and ransomware negotiations, successfully mitigating high-profile breaches and multimillion-dollar extortion attempts. His unique expertise in cyberthreat actor engagement has made him a trusted adviser to corporations, law enforcement agencies, and policymakers.

Beyond his professional endeavors, Kurtis is deeply committed to community service. He founded GoodSense, a nonprofit organization dedicated to assisting small businesses and individuals with cybersecurity and cryptocurrency safety. He is also championing the RAPIDS project, aiming to modernize the management systems of the Colorado River with a focus on advanced cybersecurity measures.

Kurtis is an avid motorcyclist and outdoor enthusiast who finds balance through mountain biking, hiking, camping, and overlanding. These pursuits fuel his passion for adventure and resilience, which permeate his professional life.

Kurtis is a sought-after keynote speaker at leading cybersecurity and intelligence conferences, including DEF CON, Black Hat, and the NYPD Counterterrorism and Cyber Intelligence Conference. His insights have been featured in the *New York Times* and the *Wall Street Journal* as well as on CNN and Bloomberg, where he provides expert commentary on cyber warfare, ransomware trends, and digital defense strategies.

In *Cyber Recon*, Kurtis takes readers behind the curtain of the cyber underworld, revealing the strategies, psychology, and operations of today's most dangerous threat actors. His groundbreaking work in cyber intelligence has reshaped how organizations defend against modern cyberthreats and has underscored the urgent need for a proactive, intelligence-driven approach to cybersecurity.

Acknowledgments

For years, I did this gratitude exercise while I was hiking. On a long hike alone, I would imagine I wrote a book and think of all the people to whom I owe a debt of gratitude. I would walk through their contributions and support to my life and how I would thank them. Ultimately, I ran out of trail before I ran out of people to thank. Often, I would be in tears. I have had a remarkable and amazing life and career. The best thing about that life, and the reason my career has been so fruitful, is other people who have seen me through it. I have had some dark moments, difficult times, and some huge wins. I was never alone. As with the hike, this book would be a book of thank-yous if I named everyone I am grateful to and for. I will try my best...

I am blessed to have Brenda and Floyd Minder as loving parents. I wouldn't be who I am without your guidance and direction. And Breah, for being my first and favorite partner in crime. Thank you to my nieces Haley and Alexa for reminding me what it is like to be young. You girls help me look at the world with fresh eyes. I love you with all my heart.

ACKNOWLEDGMENTS

Respect and love to Carl and Dorothy Schmedeke for instilling in me a strong sense of right and wrong, pride in my work, and strength to overcome adversity.

Thank you to my wonderful family for the support, love, and encouragement.

I want to thank Lucia. Lucia. Your commitment to greatness, yours and mine, is unwavering, and it is the only reason I have the will to write. You are my motivation; I love you.

Bryan Clay, you have been my best friend since first grade. We have hung on and confided in each other for over 40 years. I know you are there when my world is falling apart, and I can't express how much that means to me. I love you.

Curtis and Marleine, thank you for being a part of my family. I appreciate you both.

Robin Mayes, you will always be my other dad; I love you, and thank you for sticking with me.

Dave and Val Leonatti, your love and encouragement kept me going through some of the most difficult times in my life. Lauren and Alena, my spirit sisters, I love you.

Gratitude in remembrance of Ralph Faught, who saw my potential and took a chance by giving me access to education and systems that propelled me forward.

I want to thank Randy Maxey for those weeknights showing me how to use a Toshiba Libretto to program circuit boards from radiology machines. Because of you, I saw what it meant to apply technology for good.

Greg White. We had coffee in a hotel lobby decades ago when a customer blew us off. At that moment, I knew what kind of human you were. I love you, brother; thanks for listening to my shit for decades and being so patient and kind.

To Paul Whittenburg, whose single idea started the journey that became GroupSense.

Adam Bregenzer, Taylor Banks, Beau Woods. You dudes changed my life. I don't know what I did to win your favor, but there is no fucking way I would be where I am today without you. I am forever grateful, and I love all of you.

Acknowledgments

Mike Potter and Taylor Larimore. This book can help you sleep in your tents on your next motorcycle journey. Taylor, thanks for letting me turn your house into a tech incubator. Mike, thanks for the motorcycle maintenance sessions.

Steve Ocepek, I knew when we started hacking the Mirage product to make it work for customers, we were 1. Dangerous, and 2. Besties. I got your back, brother.

Jon DiMaggio, when Yasir said we should get to know each other, I was skeptical. But you won my heart and my loyalty on the first call. You are first-class, my friend.

Richard Steinnon, when we first met, I was starstruck. I was dumbfounded when you suggested that you join my (non-existent) advisory board. Thank you.

Special thanks to Wes Fleming, who assisted with editing this book. He lives in the Venn diagram of my life and career: friendship, music, motorcycles, writing, and cyber.

Thank you to Rachel Monroe. Your interest in my work has changed my life and put me in a position to help others. I am grateful.

Thanks to the leaders who helped me sharpen my tools:
Tim Simons, Carlos Avila, Eric Clelland, Grant Hartline, Trent Fitz, Greg Stock, Robert Rounsevall, Tom Cirone, Peter Ruijters, Michael Ayers, Maureen Kaplan, Carlos Otal, Andrew Rubin, Dan Reckmeyer, Bob Henig, Steve Minder, Bac Tran, Shawn Carpenter, Paul Garrett, Steve Horrighs, Joel Christner, Karl Gumtow, Mike Kostoff, Wade Alt, Wayne Petersen, Tony Prince, Bill Tyndall, Bob Tkach, Caleb Barlow, Joanna Burkey, Jonathan Nguyen-Duy.

To my friends and colleagues who have been instrumental in my growth and success:
Terry and Mary-Jo Hackney, Jim and Tiffany Taft, Bill Fehring, Todd Vorhauer, Heather Antoinetti, Kurtis and Melissa Hale, Amy Faught, Chuka Eze, Greg Johns, James Cambrey, Jason Ingalls, Jay Seaton, Anna Stout, Yasir Ali, Anthony Solazzo, Michael Springer, Kathleen Alcorn, Chris Mizera, Carlos Cardero-Loza,

Jack Graziano, Tracy Lonstein, Cody Kennedy, Drew Alexander, Todd Dibell, Kermit Jackson, Paul Marrinan, France-Lee Griggs, Ted LoScalzo, Max Bevilaqua, Dave Canning, Rob Wells, David Lutz, Erin West, Mark Swain, Grant Sewell, Tim Grossner, David Gibson, Jibran Ilyas, Chris Voss, Scotty Keohler, Santiago Holley, Amy Lett, Richard Rushing, Dee Muran, Lester Godsey, Jax Scott, Mark Towner, CJ Taylor, Matt Hargett, Angel Ventling, Chan and Tina Swallow, Tamar Tesler, Lt. Colonel Sarah Frater, Boon Lowry, Doug Novak, Kelly Moan, Roger Shepard, Ryan Peat, Horace Jones, Ted Wong, Daniel and Natasha Lauer, John Holland, Rob Shavell, John Marshall, Rob Eggbrecht, Robin Brown, Scott Lindquist, Allyn Lynd, Josh Dann, Jason Graun, Dhimant Patel, Elizabeth Gozzer and Stefano Calvetti, Rob and Berni Neal, Kira Potter, Tara Secor, Tara Cormier, Josh Lowry, Kristin McGee, Salvador Camacho, Jay Gamble, Michael and Teri Austin, Joe Corso, Michael Sutton, Shauna Reckmeyer, Dr. Yan Chen, Barb and Clark Germann, Tim and Lena Germann, Hans and Denitta Germann, Carl and Jillian Germann, Linda Miller, Zack Armstrong, Hillary Zelnick, Neil Ballentine, Phil Bandy, Lee Bentch, John Flores, Frank Gugliuzza, Chase and Corey Hinderstein, Mark Hogan, Scott Keimig, Lindy Kyzer, Curtis Meins, Charles Menzes, Jonathan Nguyen-Duy, Will Nuland, Peter and Amanda Snelgrove, Cyrus Robinson, Debbie Runaldo, Robin Dean, Dave Rucco, Adry Schiffer, Geoff Shively, Andy Murphy, Tonya Silvio, Andy Simons, Meghan Locke, Shannon Smith, Wendy Starland, Michael Tanji, Rich Tyson, Jason Valdez, Amy Ruckes, Seth Rosenblatt, Greg and Shannon Krammes, Jeremy Brown, Dave Ladley, Joe Meadows, Ed Lutz, Bill Vrettos, Ravi Satkalmi, Melissa Smith, Ron Faltin, Sparkles Smith, Brian Shear, Sarah Jones, AJ Sigh, Paul DiBello, Clint Laskowski, Renee Dudley, Ron Schiltz, Kevin Boe, Maria Lipana, John DeLoche, Ping Chen, Bill Sadlick, Pete Nicoletti, Jack McKenna, Lonnie Schilling, Damon Fleury, Steve Rivera, Brandon Wood, Monty St. John, Rusty Chomiak, Chad Mayfield, Adam Ford, Alan Currie, David Carrion, Diana Pan, Dancho Danchev, Matt Shaker, Chris Boyd, Neil Sullivan, Angela Padalecki, Rick Taggart, Spencer Cobb, Bilal Shebaro, Mario Garcia, Dominic Vogel, Bill Butler.

Acknowledgments

Thank you to the GroupSense team, past and present. This team has been part of my life for over a decade and has contributed to my life and success in immeasurable ways. For OPSEC reasons, I will not mention you by name, but you all know who you are. We have built the most fantastic community, continuing to punch above our weight class!

Thank you for being you. Go Recon!

Introduction

Kudos to the security researcher who tricked me into giving up this access.

– Bassterlord

The first time I engaged a cybercriminal, it was because I noticed unusual logins on a router in a nearby town where the ISP I worked for had a point of presence (POP). Closer inspection indicated the alleged perpetrator had pivoted from that system to one of our systems primarily used to make backups. I engaged that first threat actor in a short but important dialogue: "Boss, I know it's you. I don't know what you are doing, but you are putting my job at risk. Please log out and do not return. Next time, I will report this."

Now, 30 years later, I find myself faced on a daily basis with the startling knowledge that there are dozens of private companies providing spying-as-a-service to commercial and public organizations around the world. These companies have privatized espionage and established prying eyes in some of the seediest parts of the Internet. My company, GroupSense, is one of the best, and we found ourselves specializing in engaging in an often misunderstood and unique part of this business: talking to cybercriminals in the Internet underground.

For decades, a small set of Internet espionage practitioners have quietly infiltrated and interacted with cybercriminals. Cyber intelligence companies were formed to do this at scale, some with more success than others. The criminals, knowing this was occurring, adapted over time and attempted to thwart the Internet spies. Thus, a spy versus spy, cloak-and-dagger game began to formulate across a multitude of channels, websites, forums, and Internet chat tools.

Governments organized stings, bought their way into forums, and occasionally disrupted criminal activity. The FBI would semi-annually announce the dismantling of a particular forum or group's activities, only to have a proverbial mole pop out of another dark hole on the Internet, awaiting the next attempted digital whack.

The cycle accelerated around 2010 when BTC and blockchain technology, coupled with the dark web and the Onion Router (TOR), afforded the bad actors a new platform for anonymity and the ability to transfer seemingly unlimited amounts of capital across international borders with impunity. This technology shift fostered an exponential growth in Internet crime, state-sponsored activity, and new forms of extortion, ransoms, data theft, and espionage.

Nation-states took advantage; the likes of North Korea, Iran, and Russia used this underground platform and the crime war it facilitated to bolster their digital warfare capabilities. North Korea took a chapter from the criminal playbook and weaponized cyber ransom activities. Iran did something similar, while simultaneously using these digital mediums to threaten their enemies abroad. Russia, affording an unofficial amnesty to the cybercriminals within its borders, used plausible deniability at the nation-state level to wage full-on cyber war against the United States and others. Other Russian-friendly states engaged in similar activity.

I inadvertently became a key player in this cyber landscape, starting small but quickly growing into a global voice for policy change, personal cyber hygiene responsibility, and a voice for the victim, especially individuals or small businesses. My interactions with Internet criminals and bad actors started early in my career, in the early 1990s, and like gravity, an invisible force continued to pull me back into the realm to lead and fight Internet evil.

The Internet was once a budding landscape for most people, and there really was no concept of a cybercriminal. But I found one in those early days and engaged him.

My father worked in a flour mill for Pillsbury in central Illinois. I once visited his workplace as a young boy. It was 110 degrees, a haze of gooey flour, and the air perfumed heavily with sweat and musty yeast. Everything my dad touched—his car, his La-Z-Boy recliner, every shirt he owned—smelled like it. He had a white crust seemingly permanently cemented into any wrinkle of his body, his elbows, and even around his eyelids. During that visit, I watched him move 100-pound sacks of flour from one conveyor belt to another, deafened by the sound of the machines. "This sucks," I thought.

I also made a number of visits to my mom's place of work. She worked for the state of Illinois in some accounting capacity. I never understood what she did, but I took note of this: It was quiet and climate-controlled, and she had a cup of fresh coffee in front of her. She typed away on a typewriter and occasionally pecked one-handed on a calculator so fast you could barely make her fingers out, tape mechanically rolling out of the top of it. "I want to work like this," I thought.

As a result, I took every typing, keyboarding, or business-related class I could find. After taking everything my high school offered, I enrolled part-time in a vocational school to take data processing classes, and there I fell in love with Unix. I fell hard, the way a young man falls for the only girl who ever paid any attention to him. Microsoft was a thing then, and Windows was the standard for what would soon be known as "desktop computing." Yet I had never used a Windows machine. I had used DOS here and there and Macintosh a bit, primarily to play *Oregon Trail* in the library. Unix was different and intoxicating for me. I ordered books about it, and when I finished my classroom assignments, I would poke around the systems. I even conspired with some other students to write some code that stole the other students' passwords. We got caught. No bueno.

One day my mom threw a folded newspaper in front of me at breakfast, a job ad highlighted in yellow. It seemed fortuitous: "TECH SUPPORT ENGINEER WANTED . . . typing . . . Internet . . . Unix experience is a plus."

I was a shoo-in for the job at CenCom Internet, one of central Illinois's first dial-up Internet providers. I quickly became a favorite of the systems administrator, who would invite me to join him on the weekends rebuilding Sun Microsystems servers, standing up new terminal servers, and loading some 20-plus floppy disks to build new Slackware Linux machines to provide domain name resolution to our customers. I ate it up.

It only made sense, then, when politics ensued and the systems administrator was hastily fired, that the company's president asked me to "keep things running" until they found a replacement. While outwardly I radiated confidence, on the inside I was terrified and angry at my mentor for his lack of restraint. Still, I moved my things from the tiny desk in the tech support area, which consistently screamed like a nest of baby pterodactyls because of the garage shelves with hundreds of US Robotics and Hayes clamshell modems, volume on, receiving calls.

My mentor's desk was a mess of papers, floppy disks, a few cards from *Magic: The Gathering*, and two large Sun Microsystems CRT monitors. Two glass mousepads with a grid and corresponding three-button laser mice rested on the strewn papers. I sat in his chair across from the crappy wicker chair I usually occupied when I was patiently waiting for an answer to a technical question and discovered how strange it was to be on *this* side of the desk. My mentor had a protocol for handling anyone who came in asking a technical question. If you spoke before he acknowledged you, you would be ignored. We learned to sit in that wicker chair, silent until he looked up or spoke; it seemed that each time you spoke prior to his acknowledgment, the longer you would have to wait. It was an effective method of making sure the prospective question was something that needed asking. This forced many of us to RTFM (Read the F*cking Manual) before we demanded his assistance.

My first move was to log in to the Sun Sparc10s underneath the monitors. I pulled up an X-Windows terminal and began to issue commands to populate my screens with terminals of various colors and titles in the title bars.

```
xterm-color -r -fg rgb:20D0C0 -bg rgb:303050 -cr wheat -fn rom14 -T "Decatur-Router" &
```

I repeated this step for every terminal server, router, and critical system. I then connected each terminal to the corresponding system and executed a tail command on the critical system logs.

```
tail -f /var/log/syslog
```

The result was CRT monitors full of colorful text-filled system log windows, scrolling as things changed and errors occurred on each system. While largely unmanageable, this was the only way I felt safe until I had my administrator legs under me.

The book *The Cuckoo's Egg*, a true story by Clifford Stoll, was fresh in my mind as I sat behind two massive Sun Microsystems 30-inch monitors. Clifford was an engineer at Berkeley Labs; while doing his day job, he noticed a discrepancy in some of the usage logs of their computing system. He turned digital detective and tracked down his foreign adversaries remotely, accessing the systems and stealing confidential data. I was so inspired by this book that I wrote a short story about an African American person who found a white supremacist online bulletin board and joined the community. The other members believed he was one of them. Later in my story, the protagonist befriended and taught a clichéd lesson to the BBS members: "You are colorblind online." This was a roadmap to building a persona or sock puppet. The book inspired me to pay close attention to the system logs, where through sheer luck, given the volume of information on my screen, I found something suspicious and began to investigate.

What I found were unusual logins on a router in a nearby town where we provided service. Closer inspection indicated that the alleged perpetrator had pivoted from that system to one of our BSD systems that were primarily used to make backups of the NIS network. It was on those BSD systems that I engaged my first threat actor in a short but important dialogue, letting the intruder know

I knew he was my recently fired boss and letting him know in no uncertain terms that should I catch him again, I'd report him to the authorities.

If he returned, I never knew it. His experience eclipsed mine by more than a decade, and if he had wanted, he could have pulled the digital rug out from under CenCom and me any time he wanted. Eventually, he hired me at his new venture as his "Chief Technician," and we launched a competitive Internet company together, where, among other tasks, I found and chased bad guys online.

Back then, the bad actors were unlikely to be nation-states or financially motivated cybercriminals. They were often kids like me, testing their skills and inflating their egos. If you had explained to me the world we live in now and that I, Kurtis Minder, would be involved in some of the most effective cyber espionage and cyber warfare in history, I would have no doubt spewed Mountain Dew from my nose.

My entire career in tech has been peppered with what we now call *threat actor engagement*. When working for Ameritech in Chicago, I built a lab in my bedroom to conduct cybersecurity experiments. I didn't know it when I built a honeynet and honeypot network, enticing bad actors on IRC to exploit my vulnerable Windows box while watching every Internet packet and every Ethernet frame in between in an effort to learn their tactics, but I was pioneering something that would one day become fundamental to protecting some of the largest companies and government organizations in the world.

Today, I am humbled to be surrounded by some of the best talent in cybersecurity. On a daily basis, we engage in clandestine conversations with ransomware gangs, Russian organized criminals, lone-wolf actors, and even nation-state adversaries. Years of experience have aided in creating a playbook of best practices in operational security (OPSEC), cryptocurrency logistics, compliance adherence, and, of course, the psychology of transacting or negotiating with those who occupy the internet's seedy underground.

As I started writing, I consistently returned to this place where I questioned why I was the right person to document this fascinating industry. After all, I am surrounded by great thinkers and leaders who are as qualified as I am to do so. In an attempt to balance my responsibility with humility, I have decided to profile some of these professionals throughout the book. In each chapter, you will find a profile of someone I respect and admire whose work has directly impacted me or the industry as a whole. Each profile will (somewhat ironically) provide a QR code that directs the reader to a YouTube video where I interview that professional.

This book is intended to entertain but to also serve as a sort of field guide to those who want to fight the good fight. It is for those who want to fight the bad guys, learn their methods, become their confidants, and turn the tide. It will also serve as a primer for the less technical person who wants to familiarize themself with the cyber risk landscape. After all, even in this supremely connected, computer-driven, AI-crazy world, our adversaries are still human.

This book is not a tell-all, biography, or tactical how-to guide, nor is it a condemnation of the threat actors or a glorification of their craft. Further, this book does not detail the actual tactics currently in use, as doing so could compromise operations on the ground. If you are interested in that level of detail, there are ways of obtaining it. This book does contain real stories of cyber espionage, threat actor conversations, example negotiations, and all sorts of cyber spy activity. In that, it can be entertaining for anyone who likes spycraft or is curious about what this cyber underworld looks like.

My people—the nerds—will no doubt find some problems with my book. That is what nerds do. Nerds will find oversimplified technical jargon; they will accuse me of not adequately explaining a particular function or system. They will strongly dislike—dare I say hate—the way I reference a method or process. Good for you, Mr. or Ms. Geek. You are likely right!

My hacker friends, I am trying my best not to misuse the label. I recognize that the descriptor "hacker" is not a derogatory term; it references a whole community of people who like to tinker with, take apart, rebuild, and better understand all things. When a reference to a "hacker" in any other sense is made, it is in context with how the reader or the media would have positioned it, right or wrong. I assume you will call me out if I dishonor this.

The entrepreneurial reader will find anecdotes of building a business in the cyber market. Many of the stories occur in that context. Expectations for a business strategy book will fall hopelessly short. Considering this book does not have a business strategy focus, I will not be inventorying clichéd mistakes or promoting or correcting business decisions. That is another book, perhaps one which has already been written more than once.

When my publisher informed me this book may be printed in Russian, I was a bit uneasy. Given that the majority of my threat actor engagements involve someone from Russia or a Russia-friendly country such as Belarus, Moldova, or parts of Ukraine, I wasn't sure I wanted them reading this manuscript. Perhaps, though, it is positive that those sitting on the other side of the proverbial table understand where we are coming from. It is possible they will see that we are only trying to defend what is ours and do so in a scientific and professional manner. Further still, maybe they can see that we are human and want what is best for our families and our country, just like they do for theirs.

To the best of my ability, I have changed the names of people, places, channels, sites, and indicators in order to (1) honor any nondisclosure agreements, and (2) protect myself and others from incrimination or harm. If there are screenshots, I have done my best to maintain proper OPSEC, a discipline to which I have dedicated an entire chapter. This means details of the screenshots are blurred out to conceal how they were obtained and by whom.

I did not change my company's name, but this book is not intended to be an advertisement for GroupSense. It is more of an advertisement of the discipline, the practice, and the behaviors contained within. In some cases, I chose to use the real names of people I admire, respect, or feel deserve recognition. I do so only when I feel the content does not cause harm.

I am grateful you have chosen to pick this book up or download it. I welcome any feedback, corrections, or affirmations you may have. Please reach out to me at www.kurtisminder.com or www.groupsense.io.

INTRODUCTION

Cyber Recon Leader Profile:

Jax Scott

Current Role: VP Cybersecurity, Pearson

Other Affiliations: CyberSecurity Warrant Officer, 75th U.S. Army Reserve; Member of the Counter-Terrorism Project, Atlantic Council; President, Outpost Gray; Podcast Host, "2 Cyber Chicks"

Jax's Bio

Jaclyn "Jax" Scott is a cybersecurity trailblazer and decorated Special Operations Warrant Officer with over 20 years of military service. A master of electronic warfare and cybersecurity, she has led global cyber operations, strengthened NATO security initiatives, and safeguarded digital infrastructure against emerging threats.

Beyond her military career, Jax is an influential thought leader, author, and content creator. She founded Outpost Gray, mentors cybersecurity professionals, and co-hosts the award-winning podcast "2 Cyber Chicks." She also authored the *Cybersecurity Career Master Plan*, a key resource for breaking into the field.

Jax is a member of the Counter-Terrorism Project at the Atlantic Council, shaping policy on emerging threats. As a board member for the Special Operations Association of America, she advocates for female combat veterans, spearheading the Jax Act for improved healthcare access.

Jax's Impact

I believe in forging our own paths, not waiting for the world to hand us anything. I stand for supporting others, holding space for different perspectives, and giving a voice to those who are afraid to speak their truth. Fear is normal, but pushing through it—embracing vulnerability as a strength—is how we grow. I challenge the status quo, rock the boat, and believe that true leadership means lifting others up. A team is only as strong as its weakest member, and everyone has the potential to grow if they're willing. It's okay to move on when things no longer serve you, but never burn a bridge—you never know when you may need to walk across it again.

YouTube URL: https://www.youtube.com/watch?v=pSv1SlovhVc

YouTube, LLC

Chapter 1
Why Spy on Bad Guys?

I am sure you are wondering why the *hell* a commercial cyber espionage operation is necessary. I assure you that it is not because doing so is fun. Don't get me wrong—it is—but that isn't why we do it. We do it because the industry needs us; our clients need to know what the bad guys are doing so they can plan a defense. It was a rough evolution to get here, though.

I once consulted for a chief information security officer (CISO) in the retail space. He had informed me of his investment in a software-as-a-service (SaaS) cyber-intelligence vendor. I inquired if I could ask a few questions about his program. Even though it was clear the word *program* confused him, he agreed.

> "Okay, so you have some very specific use cases for intelligence—is that why you licensed this platform?"
> "Um, not specific, more general."
> "Okay, but you know what specific data your company needs to turn into intelligence and for whom inside the organization?"
> "I think so..."
> "Okay, so you are hiring a full-time intelligence professional to sit in front of this thing?"
> "No."

"Oh, so you are taking one of your existing staff, training them on intelligence process and production, and putting them on this full time?"

"No."

"So you are taking the person that reads your EDR [endpoint detection and response] events all day and letting them query this platform when they have time?"

"Kurtis, you are making this sound like it's not a good idea . . ."

"That's the point. But let's say this all works well—it won't—but hypothetically, let's say it does. And your EDR person runs a query one day and finds a bad actor on the dark web talking about a backdoor into your online system where they can change the prices. They are selling the price change as a service to anyone who wants to purchase products from you—that is, someone pays them a small amount in Bitcoin, and then they change the price of a very expensive product to $1."

"Yes! Yes! This is exactly the kind of intelligence I am looking for!"

"That isn't intelligence, but I see. Okay, next question. What do you do next?"

"Um . . ."

"You see, there are many bad actors on the dark web. Most of them are full of shit. How do you validate this before you start ringing alarm bells? My guess is you have *a lot* of APIs. Which one is it? What is the vulnerability that was exploited? Is this bad actor credible? Can you see if they have already received payments? Can you talk to them?"

"I don't know . . ."

"Then what good is this platform? If it just sends you data or information that you cannot validate and cannot act on, that sounds like a terrible investment."

This is how it goes, and so it is with intelligence platforms at the enterprise level. So many of the suppliers and vendors are selling a tool that produces data for organizations that need intelligence. Further, most organizations cannot act on the data, information, or intelligence they receive. This is why it is critical not to look at cyber intelligence as a product but rather as a program. It is a supporting business operation and requires process and talent like any other business function.

This chapter aims to baseline what cyberthreat intelligence is and *why* we do it. We will delve into a bit of the *how*, but the details of *how* are covered in Chapter 3, "Cyber Espionage 101." Chapter 4, "Whodat?" will cover *where*.

The evolution of the cybersecurity product and service market has been largely unbalanced, its offerings primarily reactive in nature and typically from a defensive position. Over the decades, the cyber adversaries' sophistication, motivation, and collaborative nature have increased considerably, and the vendors have responded with more defense tools, technologies, and service offerings. The defense-in-depth cyber stack has begun to overwhelm even the largest and most forward-thinking organizations. CISOs are inundated with new gizmos and coerced into buying the newest thing to defend against the threat.

What are the real threats? Who is targeting your organization and why? What are their motives and capabilities? What tools do they have? What data about you do they have? How successful have they been attacking similar organizations in the past? Are they script kiddies or nation-state cyber armies?

The U.S. federal government has the largest military defense budget of any country globally by a significant margin, but it isn't limitless. How does the government decide how to allocate that budget? The U.S. federal government uses intelligence to inform them of their adversaries' motives and capabilities. The Central Intelligence Agency (CIA) is the tip of the spear for defining the nation's defensive (read: "offensive") strategy and budget allocation. Instead of guessing and trying to defend ourselves against virtually anything, which would be a poor strategy for our tax dollars, the CIA gives our military the information necessary to focus their capabilities. The CIA uses myriad sources to gather this information. These include signals intelligence (SIGINT), open source intelligence (OSINT), and the one we watch movies about, human intelligence (HUMINT). The CIA correlates this information in Langley, Virginia; validates; adds context; assesses the impact; and produces intelligence. Of all the sources, HUMINT is one of the most impactful, as it is the most tangible and most easily validated source. After all, our nation-state adversaries are also human.

Likewise, CISOs have limited resources. For most of the history of the cybersecurity market, they have been building digital walls and response systems to defend against unknown attacks and ghostly attackers. Gathering information about the threat to a specific organization and its would-be opponents helps CISOs focus their spending.

To do this effectively, one has to take the fight to the bad actors. Not unlike with a CIA asset or field operative, this invaluable information has to be gathered from the trenches, the chatrooms, the dark web forums, and the private chats of those who would do us harm. It is, in fact, cyber espionage.

As a result, an ecosystem and extensive market providing such services has burgeoned. Companies have been integrating and maturing a practice to keep watch on adversaries for over a decade. Many of these companies fall under the cyberthreat intelligence (CTI) or threat intelligence (TI) umbrella. Unfortunately, there is no litmus test on how to deliver these services well, nor has there been a quantitative method for measuring success. The net result is that many of these programs serve as a box for a CISO's security program checklist, and business outcomes are elusive. One of the key reasons this continues to be a challenge is the focus on providing raw data rather than real intelligence.

Some of the earliest versions of TI were simply feeds of known bad digital indicators. There were seemingly independent operators, like Spamhaus and the SANS Internet Storm Center, who supplied lists of known bad IP addresses and domains. The security vendors jumped in around the same time in the late 1990s, often crowdsourcing their threat data from their software and appliances on their customer sites. If Firewall A at Company A detected an attack or malware from IP X.X.X.X, they would tell companies B–Z to automatically block any traffic from X.X.X.X. This was immensely valuable, and versions of this kind of threat intel feed exist today. In fact, most EDR vendors like CrowdStrike and SentinelOne share their threat telemetry data across customer installations in a similar manner.

The next iteration in threat intelligence is thought by many to have been pioneered by iDefense, a company founded by James Adams and later run by John Watters; they are credited with pioneering the next phase of the cyberthreat intelligence industry. iDefense began providing threat actor profiles, advanced persistent threat (APT) monitoring, and data on zero-day development and activity.

John Watters' next company, iSIGHT Partners, took the iDefense playbook and advanced it iteratively. By employing hundreds of analysts across the globe, iSIGHT infiltrated and interacted with the threat actor community. They delivered detailed "ThreatScape" reports with a particular vertical or cyber domain focus to their high-paying customers. FireEye acquired iSIGHT in 2016, and remnants of the iSIGHT intelligence practice remain inside what is now Mandiant, a Google Cloud company.

By 2013, even iSIGHT's army of analysts couldn't scale to deliver what customers were beginning to ask for. Customers wanted tailored cyber intelligence for their business and their brand. What's more, they didn't want it in report form; they wanted it in as close to real time as possible.

In 2014, when two partners and I launched the company that would become GroupSense, we knew the benefits of what we were doing. The original use case was simple and narrow, with just three pillars:

1. Find the customer-specific data being pilfered by the bad guys on the Internet before they monetize it, and let the customers know about it.
2. Find bad guys talking about specific customers and tell the customers about it.
3. Find infrastructure that bad guys set up to attack specific customers—and tell the customers about it.

We worked long and hard to develop avatars or personas trusted by the underground Internet community. We were successfully invited to participate in the forums and channels where the illicit activity occurred. We had a platform that was capturing those conversations via our personas and analyzing them at scale for customers. Jackpot, right?

Not exactly. We were lucky to have landed a couple of the largest brands in the world as early-adopting customers. Our platform was successfully identifying digital artifacts that, in the wrong hands, could cause material damage to their businesses. The software was successfully alerting them to those digital artifacts. "ALERT! Bad Guy on Bad Channel is offering to sell this Intellectual Property of yours!" The customer was disturbed but pleased with the platform's effectiveness. Yet, only weeks into their use of our product, they had begun calling us. "Hey, we firmly believe the data you sent us about the bad guy is . . . well, bad. We just don't know what to do next." This is a challenge companies all over the world struggle with when it comes to cyber intelligence and dark web monitoring programs. How does a cyber organization take action on or operationalize that data or information?

We knew what the answer was. Someone had to talk to the bad guy to determine if the intellectual property was indeed stolen, if it was real, and if it was truly a threat. The customer couldn't do that. Not only did they not have a tenured, trusted avatar on the dark web, but this advertisement was made by a Russian actor in a Russian forum, where they speak—well, Russian. To make things worse, even if they had a Russian-speaking staffer with access to a tenured sock puppet in the relevant forum, their legal department would not allow them to engage.

We had to ask ourselves if we spent all that time creating a poor product, delivering a solution that kept people up at night, and sending alerts that could not be verified or acted on.

Driven by a sense of duty and purpose, we did what we had to do. We talked to the bad actor, got sample data, verified where the leak was, weighed the potential risks of not acting, and sent a custom alert to the client explaining the situation, the context of the forum, intel on the actor and their credibility, screenshots of the sample data, and a recommended course of action based on that information. We sent them actionable intelligence in a report we later renamed an "advisory."

Much has been written about the difference between data, information, and intelligence. Data is a single artifact, information is a collection of them, and intelligence is a combination of those things, combined with context, predictive analysis, and a recommendation on how to proceed.

The GroupSense Managed Security Intelligence Center (MSIC) was born from these early lessons, and we have since made a name for ourselves in the cybersecurity industry for driving outcomes with cyber intelligence, also sometimes referred to as *digital risk*. Today, our MSIC recruits, trains, and hires some of the top cyber espionage practitioners on the planet. They speak more than a dozen languages natively and manage more than 4,000 avatars and personas across thousands of dark net, social, and chat channels, as well as private groups—even the metaverse. Graduates of MSIC have gone on to run cyber, CTI, and response programs at companies like eBay, American Express, Trend Micro, Xerox, and Google.

Cyberattackers are most successful when they have illicit access to some information, data, systems, or personnel. These digital artifacts sometimes surface because some threat actor gained unauthorized access and shared it illicitly. In other cases, though, it is simply because the rank-and-file staff have done something not malicious but silly. A mature security program utilizes digital risk and CTI to find those digital artifacts surfacing in places they shouldn't be and to mitigate the risk. This is often done by removing the artifact altogether, negotiating for its removal, or paying for its removal. In other cases, it is accomplished by implementing changes within the organization, such as new processes, procedures, or fraud playbooks, to get in front of the potential threat.

To do this well, one has to be "invited to the party," so to speak. The "party" is where threat actors, organized criminals, and nation-state agents do their business and collaborate. The "party" is often ephemeral and difficult to pin down, and doing so typically requires a massive investment in HUMINT operations. Researchers trying to find where the real dirt is being done are multilingual, context-aware espionage experts. They employ a combination of cyber know-how, personal networking, and psychology to achieve their goals.

Versions of HUMINT practices have been used since ancient times. Examples of using human intelligence in warfare date back to the Egyptians, Greeks, and Romans, all of whose armies used spies and informants to gather information. Similarly, the Byzantine Empire famously had a large network of spies to monitor its interests, and even Sun Tzu's famous *The Art of War* emphasizes the importance of spies and human intelligence sources in war. It wasn't until after World War I that modern nation-states began formalizing this practice. The United States formed the Office of Strategic Services, the predecessor to the CIA. Around the same time, the Soviet Union began operating the *Komitet Gosudarstvennoy Bezopasnosti* (KGB), or Committee for State Security. After the collapse of the Soviet Union in the early 1990s, the KGB transformed into the *Federal'naya Sluzhba Kontr-razvedky* (FSK), or Federal Counterintelligence Service, which begat the current *Federal'naya Sluzhba Bezopasnosti* (FSB), or Federal Security Service. Perhaps the Russian shell game or rebranding intelligence institutions is part of the strategy.

Russia's use of intelligence for digital espionage and cyber warfare evolved quickly. We now know, from defectors and our own intelligence investigations, that Russia's Glavnoye Razvedyvatelnoye Upravlenie (GRU), which translates to "Chief Intelligence Office," has been responsible for some of the world's most clever and devastating cyberattacks. The GRU is thought to be responsible for the Democratic National Committee breach, the misinformation campaign impacting the 2016 Presidential Election, and NotPetya, the highly sophisticated worm that caused tens of billions of dollars in economic damage. Also known as the Russian Main Directorate of the General Staff of the Armed Forces, the GRU continues to innovate and wage cyber war overtly and by way of proxy.

It is believed that in addition to the plausible deniability the ransomware operations afford Russia's Putin, they serve another purpose. Their access, skills, tools, and data capture are made available to the GRU and, thus, the Russian Federation.

The United States and other Western nations put a much stronger emphasis on HUMINT operations after the terrorist attacks on September 11, 2001. The enemy was no longer a nation-state but a tribal, patently informal adversary operating in areas that technical tools like SIGINT or satellite surveillance could not always penetrate. Military operations in Afghanistan, Iraq, and Syria required HUMINT—human resources on the ground.

From a military perspective, HUMINT consistently provided a depth of understanding that many of the technical tools could not. While the technical tools provide vast amounts of data, HUMINT provides crucial context and human intent, including the inner plans of key adversarial decision-makers. As a result, HUMINT is often used to validate the data and information collected through other sources. Just as critical, the HUMINT operations often detected and neutralized the espionage activities of the enemy. This was a key component of counterintelligence efforts on both sides.

Despite the risks inherent in recruiting, training, fielding, and retaining HUMINT assets and resources, the spy community has long relied on HUMINT to gather information close to their adversary. Spies will often manipulate a source into providing information, perhaps resorting to bribery, blackmail, or any of a huge number of common tools used for more than a century in traditional spycraft. The cyber realm is no different—just like a CIA spy would manipulate a person to get invited to a secret party at a foreign government facility simply to plant a tiny piece of surveillance technology like an audio or video recording device, cyber spies are getting invited to the secret dark web forums. Once their fake persona or "sock puppet" is in, they plant their version of a listening device: a *scraper*, which is effectively a web crawler similar to those used by leading search engines. Many of the sources are simple web content (HTML), so this method is a proven strategy.

The scraper then feeds those conversations to a platform where the information is analyzed. How that information is processed—and whether that information becomes intelligence—differs based on the solution. In recent years the industry seems to have bifurcated into software-as-a-service (SaaS) and tech-enabled services. Both solutions aim to solve similar problems to the use cases described earlier. There isn't one correct way to do this, but there are clear differences in values and outcomes.

Both solutions rely on similar methods to obtain the necessary data. Some vendors collect this data themselves in-house, whereas others buy the data wholesale from companies that have already collected it. Still, others combine the two and use other tactical methods.

The tip of the proverbial spear in intelligence data collection is sourcing. The first step is knowing what needs to be collected and from where. The answers to those questions drive the collection technology used to gather the data. Finding the answers to these questions and gaining access to those properties are often the most difficult steps. We will circle back to source identification and access.

Once the sources have been determined and the access has been secured, technology is leveraged to gather as much information from these sources as possible. Usually this is done in the form of a scraper. There are myriad technical challenges around bot detection, CAPTCHAs, and authentication that need to be overcome in order to scrape these properties. Those challenges are real, they are complicated, and they are ever-changing—an arms race, if you will. (That's right! The bad guys use bot detection and anti-crawler technologies to keep intelligence operatives at bay. The threat actors even implement commercial solutions like Cloudflare to protect their dark web fiefdoms.) Other tools leveraging application programming interfaces (APIs) and harvesters are used to gather information from non-web properties, like chat platforms and social media.

Wholesale data acquisition presents its own challenges. There are a handful of providers that collect and sell intelligence data from the dark web and similar bad operator places. Because their model is a volume game, they collect enough data from enough sources to remain credible in the most efficient way possible. The result is a digital pipe of raw, scraped HTML data, and JavaScript Object Notation (JSON) syntax from basic sources. The more difficult-to-access sources, like sites requiring validation, specialized language skills, referrals or personal relationships, and complex tools to bypass bot detection and CAPTCHAs, are often not covered by these solutions. Unfortunately for the buyer, that is where the "good stuff" resides.

After overcoming the locating sources, access to the sources, and their defenses, another technical challenge is presented: storage and retrieval of that information. This is not a book on data architectures, but I can tell you that many companies fail at this critical component of the technology stack. The scale of what we are attempting to ingest is massive. For example, Google indexes approximately 4 percent of Internet content; the other 96 percent is deep and dark web content. Although we should not be aiming to siphon in all of that data, we should certainly target a meaningful percentage of it. Data science and architecture engineers are adept at anticipating scale and designing the necessary underpinnings to ensure a refactor or rebuild of that architecture is mitigated long term.

Further complexity is introduced when trying to leverage AI models across the data stack. Large language models (LLMs) require significant metadata structures to support the AI operation. It can be a heavy lift to implement the necessary labels, indexes, and metadata on an existing large dataset. A number of companies, like View Systems, are beginning to ease this transition for enterprises and software vendors.

Assuming one has solved for the collection of the relevant data, the next step is to make that data digestible by a human analyst. Most security platforms present data line by line in alert format, but this doesn't jive with how the human brain receives information naturally. Plus, most companies understand the need for this data but do not understand *their* why. As a result, the market is saturated with SaaS cyber intelligence companies that are essentially asking their customers questions they cannot possibly answer and displaying the results in a practically unreadable format.

The SaaS approach is usually a complex web interface front end to the collected dataset. These are usually designed to require that the customer input their own data queries on the platforms. These tools tend to be more tactical in nature and are often used in an investigatory nature rather than as a prevention mechanism. As I alluded to previously, companies often (1) don't know what questions to ask of the data and (2) don't know what to do with the answers they get. Part of this is due to the lack of experience in the commercial/enterprise space with the intelligence process itself. Since the SaaS approach relies on the customer to run the intelligence process themselves, understanding how to develop prioritized intelligence requirements (PIRs) and how to implement those PIRs at a software level is key. Unfortunately, intelligence talent is scarce and expensive. Therefore, many companies who purchase these tools have a difficult time realizing the value of the investment. This leads to companies buying the product only to refuse to renew the software license when the first contract renewal presents itself. The SaaS vendor's primary response to this has been to offer analyst "credits" or "points" with the subscription to augment the SaaS tool with some experienced practitioners. This has worked in some cases but still falls short of running a proper intelligence program.

An effective cyber intelligence program follows the traditional *intelligence cycle* used by traditional intelligence agencies around the world (see Figure 1.1). It consists of

1. Planning and direction
2. Collection
3. Processing
4. Analysis and production
5. Dissemination

These steps are called a "cycle" because they should function as a continuous feedback loop. Most organizations purchasing a product in the cyber intelligence space benefit from the vendor's collection and often simply disseminate that data. They do not know about or intentionally skip the other steps in the process, which is the primary reason these products fail inside the enterprise.

John Holland of IntL8 is an industry expert with years of experience assisting organizations in implementing, fixing, or measuring the value of their intelligence programs. John often writes about the three tenets of a good intelligence program:

1. Cyber intelligence should be a support function.
2. You must understand your stakeholders' needs and whys.
3. It has to be relevant to the consumer of the intelligence.

Why Spy on Bad Guys?

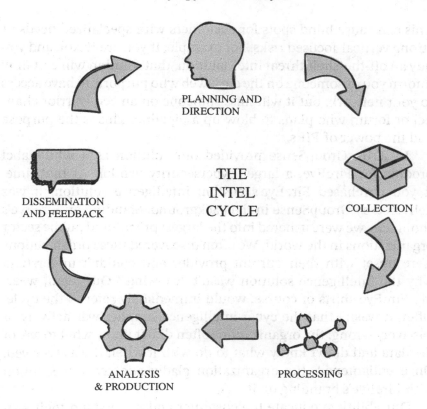

Figure 1.1 Intelligence cycle.

John's firsthand experience repairing these initiatives has shown that skipping the first step in the intelligence cycle can negate or miss the three tenets entirely for an organization.

The first step, planning and direction, is arguably the most important part of the cycle. This step is where the prioritized intel requirements are created. These PIRs should drive the next step, collection. Typical organizational PIRs should drive collection because they involve their company brand assets, infrastructure and software stack, intellectual property, projects, and even their executives or other VIPs. Cyber intelligence vendors are laser-focused on the technical aspects of collection, and those technical indicators drive their collection choices. Cyber intel vendors also try to normalize their collection to support their entire customer base.

This can cause blind spots for customers with specialized needs or strong vertical-focused risks. For example, if you are Exxon and you buy an off-the-shelf threat intel solution, that solution will certainly inform you of someone on the dark web who purports to have access to your network, but it will miss someone on an eco-warrior channel or forum who plans to blow up a pipeline. This is the purpose and the power of PIRs.

In 2016, GroupSense provided our solution as a white-label product for FireEye, a larger cybersecurity vendor. At that time, if you purchased FireEye's custom intelligence solution, it was delivered by GroupSense in the background. Standing on FireEye's shoulders, we were ushered into the largest private and public sector organizations in the world. We often discovered these organizations were upset with their current provider and couldn't understand why the intelligence solution wasn't "working." Our team, wearing FireEye shirts of course, would immediately refer to the cycle. Often it wasn't that the cyber intelligence supplier was actively or passively wrong; the organizations often didn't know what to ask of the data and didn't know what to do with it when it was received. Once enlightened, the organization gladly adopted our solution with FireEye's branding on it.

Our ability to educate the customer and understand their specific needs directly impacted how we onboard clients, as well as the technology and processes we use for collection. We quickly became one of the fastest and most flexible intel providers related to collection. When we got our first big pharmaceutical clients, we began ingesting data from sources that dealt with counterfeit drugs. When we got our first high-tech manufacturing client, we infiltrated markets that dealt with intellectual property trading and theft. We signed a cruise ship company and began collecting data related to maritime threats and information. Because our CTO, Adam Bregenzer, had experience with big data stemming from his time at Venmo, he was able to design a data architecture that became exponentially more valuable as we onboarded new clients and added collections. Every new customer benefited from the PIR-driven collection strategy from the customers that came before them.

Once data collection is tailored to meet the needs of the developed PIRs, the intelligence program must process the data. Processing consists of organizing, normalizing, deduplicating, correlating, and cleaning up the collected data. As mentioned earlier, most ingestion technologies simply scrape the raw code and throw it into an elastic search database. This results in messy results when querying the data, and it lacks any deduplication or prioritization of the data. This is why it is important to ingest the data in an intelligent way and preserve its context. Doing so is technically difficult to achieve and a bit expensive to implement, which is why many solutions don't bother to do it. If accomplished, though, it makes the next steps in the intel cycle go more smoothly.

Many vendors in the cyber intelligence space skip or cheat the analysis and production part of the cycle. Similarly to contextual ingestion, this can be technically difficult and expensive to do well. It is important, nonetheless, as this is the step that *transforms data into intelligence*. Considering that this is not something many of the vendors provide, the product the buyer receives ends up being simply *data or information* rather than true *intelligence*. The vendors, perhaps unintentionally, market their wares as intelligence tools effective at producing . . . intelligence. This leaves the onus on the consumer of the data to produce the intelligence. Unfortunately, most enterprises are not staffed or trained to do this well, if at all. The result is a consumer upset with the value of their investment in the tool, even if in an uninformed way.

The analysis function is best performed by a human trained in the intelligence discipline. The analyst on the receiving end of the data has to reformat that data in a way the customer, whether an individual, a department, or an entire institution, can understand. The analyst has to add a summary of the impact and who or what is affected, contextualize the data, provide some expected outcomes, and recommend remediation action; only then is intelligence produced. At GroupSense, we recognized early on that the total addressable market for data that needed to be turned into intelligence was quite small. Most enterprises did not have the staff with adequate talent, the resources, or the necessary processes to take data from a platform and create intelligence. This is precisely why, in our early days, we began recruiting and training cyber intelligence analysts to "bookend" our platform known as Tracelight. The bookend, as the label suggests, means that our analysts assist the customer in creating the right questions to ask of the data in the platform. The system does the heavy lifting by ingesting data from sources, cleaning and deduplicating it, correlating everything, and adding any additional technical context for the analyst. This creates information from the data, which is then fed to the analyst. The second bookend is the analyst taking this information and creating intelligence for the customer. Only then is an advisory or report published inside the platform. This approach has worked well for the 11+ years we have been building on it. I am encouraged by and proud of the difference we have made for our clients.

The last step, dissemination, is simply making sure the intelligence gets into the right hands quickly and in an easily consumable manner. When possible, integrations with other platforms, such as ticketing systems, dashboards, business intelligence software, and antifraud technology, ease the consumption of the data for the customer.

It is just as important that it does not end up in the wrong hands. The technology and tradecraft, sources, personas, sock puppets, and activities related to the intel process are critically secret. Compromising any of these can create opportunities for counterintelligence or render the whole operation useless. This is why companies like GroupSense hold these functions, indicators, and data so closely. This is also why GroupSense does not buy collection data from third parties. It is crucial that we control the process closely to ensure the data that we turn into intelligence is legitimate. We have been awarded patents on how we accomplish this.

Of course, doing any of this can be largely useless if the intelligence is not relevant or actionable to the consumer.

In Chapter 3, you'll learn how to find and infiltrate sources using personas and sock puppets. It takes careful steps and sometimes years to develop personas that can be tasked effectively in the underground market. This is why many companies, aside from the legal risk, lean on their intelligence provider to take action or validate the intelligence they receive.

If the intelligence suggests that the threat actor has access to internal systems, the intelligence advisory will likely provide context and some dossier on the threat actor making those claims. Does this threat actor normally sell this kind of access? Have other threat actors had successful transactions with this person? How active is this actor on this or other illicit forums? What number of transactions has this actor performed? This information would be followed by a suggestion or action. For example, due to the threat actor's relatively low transaction history, the intelligence advisory may suggest engagement with that actor to get some kind of proof of the stolen access. If the customer approves the engagement, a researcher from our MSIC team will select a persona that makes sense for the engagement, relying on one regularly engaged in this kind of access acquisition or interest in it. The persona would have to be a tenured entity in this particular forum. Other threat actors must say good things or validate this persona as a known bad actor; vouching for them in this environment is critical.

Once the persona is selected, the researcher from MSIC will engage the threat actor. More than likely, the conversation will start on a forum as a reply to the advertising thread. It will likely be in the native language of the threat actor making the advertisement, which is often not English. (Perhaps Russian or Ukrainian; of course, the MSIC researcher who is most fluent in that language would have been assigned.) The conversation typically transcends to a direct chat utilizing another platform, perhaps TOX or Jabber. At this point the persona will indicate interest and will ask the threat actor for some kind of proof. Often the threat actors will provide this proof in the form of a screenshot or a system command-line command. That data, after running through a sandbox and checking EXIF data (metadata inside any images that might hold key information about our alleged attacker), is provided as an update to the original intelligence advisory. Again, if there is a logical action to be taken, it will be provided as part of the advisory.

Another example of actionable cyber intelligence occurred with one of our large international pharmaceutical clients. We provided them table-stakes intelligence around cyberthreats on the dark web, Telegram, and other illicit sources. In cases where threat actors signaled their possession of inside information or access to the company's systems, we provided the finished intelligence to their IT security team. Each intelligence advisory we provide includes recommended next steps or actions to be taken. In many cases, those actions will be taken by our MSIC team rather than the client. Generally, enterprise companies are not willing to take on the risk of interacting with threat actors directly, nor do they have the OPSEC infrastructure or capabilities to do so. In some cases, purchases may be made on behalf of the client, which requires lawyers, contracts, financial agreements, and sometimes an affidavit to ensure compliance. These purchases are typically done through cryptocurrency and often involve a marketplace-supported escrow service.

In the case of the pharmaceutical company, we issued an advisory about a Russian actor who purported to have quantities of a rare and carefully regulated drug produced by the pharmaceutical company. Naturally, the pharmaceutical company was concerned. They were particularly interested in the presence of an ingredient in that drug protected as a trade secret. Curious about how that drug ended up on an underground market, they asked MSIC to engage the threat actor to gain more information. The MSIC team had a few active Russian-speaking personas in the counterfeit drug marketplaces, chose one, and reached out to the actor. After much back and forth, it was determined that it was likely stolen material. Our team arranged, through an intermediary, to have someone purchase this counterfeit item from the actor. In this case, the actor had worked out a deal with a brick-and-mortar pharmacy. Our agent, whom I call "Russian Todd" because he looks like my friend Todd, exchanged cash in person for a brown bag of medicine. Russian Todd then sent the medicine to a lab owned by the pharmaceutical company. Although we didn't get a final report from the client, as it was their private business, we assumed the threat actor was working for a production facility near the pharmacy—an inside job.

Needless to say, GroupSense is likely one of the very few providers in the cyber intelligence and digital risk space currently covering the intelligence cycle entirely and assisting with kinetic outcomes when necessary.

Fairly early in our journey, we were approached by one of our large municipal clients. The client was one of the largest U.S. cities and had a very outspoken mayor. The TI team at the city's cyber command division asked if we could take what we were doing for the city itself and apply the methods to protect the mayor. We thought that theoretically, while maybe some of the sources would be different, reducing a person's digital risk is a very similar use case and should work. Through this experiment, we developed our VIPRecon product that uses a tech-enabled, intel cycle–focused service approach to protecting government officials, VIPs, high-net-worth individuals, and celebrities. Today, GroupSense covers the gamut of digital protection for *people* as well as organizations.

This is how cyber intelligence solutions should work, by developing PIRs based on business or personal requirements that *drive* collection requirements. The data collected gets processed by computers or humans. The remaining information is contextualized and paired with impact assessments and recommended courses of action. Then actions, either offensive or defensive in nature, are taken. That is *intelligence*, friends.

A true cyber intelligence provider is a fundamental part of the customer organization's cyber team and overall cyber program. The provider should work closely with the leaders, cyber and otherwise, and with the boots on the ground to ensure that the necessary actions are taken, risk mitigation strategies are implemented, and results are fed back into the intelligence cycle to improve the overall program—in other words, provide outcomes, not *data*.

In August 2024, Intel471, a provider of cyberthreat intelligence, sponsored a partnership of 28 other industry participants to form the Cyber Threat Intelligence Capability Maturity Model (CTI-CMM; https://cti-cmm.org). The CTI-CMM aims to support cyber intelligence practitioners in the field by providing a framework for cyber intelligence programs. Some of the brightest minds in the industry are contributing to this project. I am encouraged that progress is being made.

If you do one thing after reading this chapter, please familiarize yourself with the intelligence cycle. If you are a business leader, try to understand what elements of the cycle are being missed today and what kind of solution your provider is offering. If it is simply data or information, do you have the staff and intelligence talent to turn that information or data into intelligence? Most importantly, when you have finished crafting the intelligence, can you do anything with it?

Cyber Recon Leader Profile:

Brye Ravattine

Current Role: Director of State, Local, and Education for ShadowDragon

Other Affiliations: Liberty University Athletics Hall of Fame Inductee, Craig Beardsley Award Winner, Presidential Management Fellow finalist

Bryeanne Ravattine

Brye's Bio

Bryeanne "Brye" Ravattine is a cyberthreat intelligence powerhouse passionate about solving tough problems and making the digital world safer. As the Director of State and Local at ShadowDragon, she helps law enforcement and government partners track down criminals and protect their communities using cutting-edge open source intelligence tools. Before diving into cyber, Brye competed at the Olympic Trials and is an NCAA D1 swimmer, where she mastered the art of focus, discipline, and pushing past limits, skills she now brings to every mission in cyber.

When she's not working cases or speaking at conferences, you'll probably find her hanging out with her beloved pups, hiking somewhere beautiful, or catching up on her favorite true crime podcasts. Brye's a big believer in blending strength and empathy, and anyone who's worked with her knows: she's as sharp as she is kind.

Brye's Mission

The problems we face in the world, especially in the digital space, can feel overwhelming and sometimes impossible to solve. But I believe that every action matters. Every small step forward makes it harder for those who seek to harm, and I've dedicated myself to being part of that resistance.

I come from a family rooted in service—military, law enforcement, and a deep sense of duty—and that legacy fuels me daily. My moral compass keeps me grounded, and my drive comes from a simple but powerful belief: If you can help, you should. Whether it's supporting a community under threat or standing up for someone who can't do it alone, I'm here to make a difference—no matter how big or small.

I'm a relentless do-gooder at heart, and I find real fulfillment in lifting others up, fighting injustice, and using my skills to protect the vulnerable. That's my mission, and I'm just getting started.

YouTube URL: https://youtu.be/8TgThakROnE?si=eB0SRQYwPT7voKM9

YouTube, LLC

Chapter 2
FFS DNM

"Kurtis, what did you do to the pillow guy?" he asked.
"Mike Lindell?" I asked.
"Yeah, that guy," he replied.
"I assure you, I did nothing to Mike Lindell," I said.
"Then why is the 'darksquirrel'* upset at you on the GOBRANDON Telegram channel?" he asked.
"My friend, I haven't a clue," I assured him.

I've changed the names of the actor and channel for OPSEC purposes, as the actor that "darksquirrel" represents is well known in the digital communities that question the validity of the 2020 election.

He then sent me a link to the TraceLight advisory portal. TraceLight is the GroupSense platform for collection, monitoring, analysis, and advisory dissemination—notice I didn't say "alerting." This is where our customers go to get details on cyberthreats. As the CEO, I get complimentary monitoring with our executive monitoring service, VIPRecon. After reviewing the advisory, it was clear that my involvement in a meeting in Mesa County, Colorado—one of the counties Lindell claimed was involved in voter fraud—was misconstrued by that community as support for the opposition. I was acquainted with some of the leadership in that community, and they asked me, as a well-known cyber expert, to refer them to someone who could act as an expert witness should this end up in court. I did so and thought that was the end of it.

In a strange twist, I am also well acquainted with another member of that particular channel and consider him a trusted friend, so I messaged him.

"Hey Bob, are you still active on GOBRANDON?"

"Yes, on it daily, why?"

"How well do you know darksquirrel?"

"I know him well enough; did he do something?"

"You may have missed their conversation today, but my name came up," I said. "I need you to tell Mr. Squirrel that I am not part of the deep state, that I was not materially involved in any of the goings on in Mesa County."

"You got it, bro," he said.

Problem solved, right? But it could have gotten out of hand had I not been monitoring this situation.

We have covered the purpose of our monitoring efforts and touched a bit on the technology behind digital monitoring operations. Several questions remain, however, starting with how we choose who we monitor. Once we choose who to monitor, how do we get them to talk to us? Where are they operating? What kind of data or information are they peddling? Let's dig in!

PIR-Zero

As discussed in Chapter 1, "Why Spy on Bad Guys?," collection requirements should be driven by the prioritized intel requirements of whoever consumes the intelligence. That said, it is fair to assume there is a set of baseline collection sources providing benefits to *all* organizations. The philosophy that drives this "table-stakes" collection may be intelligence organization-specific, but for the purposes of this book, we will make some broad assumptions. For example, we will assume that most public and private organizations benefit from knowing about stolen intellectual property, data, documents, trade secrets, project details, employee PII/HII, customer information, contract details, financials, and the like. We can also assume that most organizations benefit from knowing about planned cyberattacks or attack tools that could impact their systems. Finally, it benefits most intelligence consumers to know the likelihood of exploiting known and unknown vulnerabilities on their collective attack surface.

These requirements comprise PIR-Zero. Every organization cares about PIR-Zero; all other PIRs are specific to minimizing the risk to that organization's mission and sit proverbially on top of PIR-Zero. It is important to note that PIR-Zero is not a static PIR; it changes as the threat landscape changes.

PIR-Zero Objective Statement

PIR-Zero provides an evolving, foundational set of intelligence requirements for cyberthreat intelligence programs. It focuses on threat actor activity across any medium. Its primary aim is to guide collection efforts and source acquisition to meet baseline requirements that reduce cyber risk to the intelligence consumer organization (IntCO).

The goal of PIR-Zero is to provide evidence of digital risk artifacts, including but not limited to:

- Threat actor identification
- Indicators of compromise (IOCs)
- Vulnerability exploits relevant to the IntCO
- Attack surface visibility
- Social engineering and phishing intelligence, including IntCO domain fraud
- Geopolitical and regulatory impact on the IntCO
- Zero-day exploit intelligence
- Threats to the IntCO
- Stolen or leaked IntCO credentials
- Stolen or leaked IntCO confidential information
- Fraudulent IntCO mobile applications
- Code repositories
- Cloud storage

In addition, PIR-Zero aims to define best-practice remediation and risk mitigation steps for the IntCO. Priority levels within PIR-Zero are determined on an organization-by-organization basis to ensure relevance and effectiveness. Finally, we can deem PIR-Zero successful when it demonstrably reduces organizational risk. Its overall business impact is reducing IntCO's cyber risk.

As the threat environment evolves, PIR-Zero remains adaptable and dynamic, ensuring it continues to address emerging threats and risks.

PIR-Zero Collection is objective-driven but often includes illicit TOR and I2P sites, select Telegram channels, invite-only WhatsApp groups, Discord channels, domain registration lists, credential databases, metaverse properties, and illicit websites.

Other Common PIRs

Assuming cyberthreat intelligence vendors and companies running a cyber intelligence program adopt PIR-Zero, there are common PIRs that often immediately follow. The most common are provided as data or intelligence from SaaS or solution providers.

Brand Protection

Brand protection involves monitoring and detecting threats that could harm the IntCO's brand through impersonation, cyber fraud, negative campaigns against the IntCO, or damaging online content. Typical collection sources include, but are not limited to, social media, general websites, the dark web, online marketplaces, news and public forums, and online bulletin boards.

VIP Protection

Engaging in VIP protection means identifying, monitoring, and mitigating threats targeting the executives and VIPs of the IntCO, whether those threats are online or kinetic in nature. These threats include doxing, harassment, impersonation, or targeted attacks on the VIP or their family. Typical sources include but are not limited to, social media, news and public forums, blogs, public records, email and communication systems, dark web, and underground forums.

Vertical or industry-specific PIRs are commonly implemented next. There are many ways threat actors can attack a vertical or specific industry. For example, the pharmaceutical industry could be flooded with (or accused of flooding the market with) counterfeit drugs. High-tech manufacturing is always vulnerable to IP theft, and the wider energy industry is often subjected to the activity of eco-warriors. The hospitality industry is vulnerable to loyalty program fraud, as is any other industry (quick-serve establishments, retail, travel, airlines, grocery, etc.) using such a program. Attacks on the banking industry seek to collect account numbers (and sell to or barter them with other threat actors) and engage in money laundering or cryptocurrency crime. PIRs affecting the law enforcement space include sex trafficking, mob or militia activity, and general attempts to defraud the citizenry. State and local governments must be concerned about election interference (a hot-button issue since the 2016 election), disability fraud, income tax fraud, and other forms of identity fraud. Many more potential attack vectors span every industry, institution, and vertical.

- Pharmaceutical: Counterfeit drugs
- High-tech manufacturing: IP theft
- Energy: Eco warrior activity
- State and local government: Election interference, disability fraud, income tax fraud, ID fraud
- Hospitality, quick serve, retail, travel: Loyalty program fraud
- Law enforcement: Sex trade, abuse, mob or militia activity, citizen fraud
- Banking: Account number trade, fraud kits, cryptocurrency crime, money laundering
- And many more...

These programs are useless to IntCO until they can operationalize the intelligence and take action. That action can be a mitigation strategy, risk minimization, or acceptance. It can also involve domain takedown activity, browser-level blocking, security tool instrumentation, law enforcement-driven action, or even legal action.

It is uncommon for the average enterprise to achieve these outcomes in-house simply because only the largest and most well-funded organizations can hire, train, and retain the talent and tools necessary to combat cyberthreat intelligence. Further, most commercial organizations will unlikely accept the risks associated with staff engaging directly in cyber espionage. The legal department, as always, is there to ruin all the fun and will not allow the information security staff to go traipsing around the dark web or engage with cybercriminals in Telegram. As a result, choosing your cyber intelligence partner is a critical component of a successful outcome-driven program.

Now that we have a mission and purpose for intelligence collection, where will we collect it from? How can we get access?

The Internet's vast underground consists of many different marketplaces, forums, chat rooms, and even metaverse locations where illicit activities occur daily. There are plenty of benign transactions happening involving items like used computers, marketing lists, Internet domains, and how-to guides; these are all relatively harmless graft. There are also plenty of legitimate uses for these venues, where you will find sites by ProPublica, DuckDuckGo, Hidden Wiki, and The New York Times. Collectively, these sites may be called the "dark web."

The definition of the dark web and its lexicon have evolved over the years. Initially, it represented alternative networks that sat on top of the standard Internet and Internet protocols that facilitate it, such as i2P and The Onion Router (TOR). Freenet, a college project that created a distributed decentralized storage and retrieval system, was possibly the first version of a dark net. TOR followed Freenet's concepts and built on them, and for many, TOR is synonymous with the dark web. In recent years, the term has been loosely used to describe threat actor activity across a number of other mediums and platforms, including Telegram and Discord. Telegram is a cloud-based messaging platform with end-to-end encryption, chats, channels, and automation features. Discord allows for collaboration, chats, and channels but was initially built for gaming communications. Discord hit its stride during the COVID-19 epidemic, as many groups and organizations turned to collaboration tools for work, socialization, and education. Threat actors adopted these platforms quickly and leveraged and weaponized chat tools like WhatsApp, Jabber, and TOX to conceal their planning, trading, and illicit transactions.

Much of this activity still takes place on TOR. TOR was created by the U.S. government around 2002 with plausibly good intentions. TOR uses "onion routing" to keep browsing and communications activity anonymous. The nonprofit TOR Project took over managing the program around 2004 and launched the TOR browser shortly after to make using the network relatively easy. While TOR remains a resource for journalists, activists, dissidents, and well-meaning techies, it has also become synonymous with underground illicit activity. TOR's privacy-driven design and obscurity make it a natural choice for bad actors who want to remain anonymous and untraceable. TOR is, by its very nature, difficult to index; to access a TOR site, you must know the exact address of that site, and TOR addresses are unlike the web addresses used for a standard Internet site. For example, the official TOR Project's TOR address is http://2gzyxa5ihm7nsggfxnu52rck2vv4rvmdlkiu3zzui5du4xyclen53wid.onion—not easily memorized, or written or typed, for that matter. These attributes make finding and infiltrating forums and sites difficult. As a result, most illicit actors know about the locations of these sites through digital word-of-mouth channels and referrals from other bad actors.

Observing illicit activity on the dark web and other mediums provides organizations with a window and potential warnings. These warnings include pending attacks, stolen data, future cyber adversaries, insider threats, intellectual property theft, and other organization-specific artifacts.

Marketplaces

A major feature of the dark web is its numerous marketplaces selling anything from illegal drugs and weapons to stolen network access and data. These locations vary widely in purpose and community, but the most famous and active marketplaces were Silk Road (1 and 2.0), AlphaBay, Agora, Evolution, Nucleus, Hansa, and Abraxas. Most of these have been shut down or exit-scammed by the administrators. Each time a dark net market was exit-scammed or taken down by law enforcement, new markets would emerge quickly. DarkMarket, Valhalla, Outlaw Market, Evolution, Minerva, Silk Road 3.0, and others emerged to allow the volume of illicit transactions to grow. Some marketplaces specialize in one type of trade or another, illicit drugs, stolen network access, fraud, stolen credit cards, etc. Other marketplaces are free-for-all illegal online (albeit in TOR) stores. As of this writing in late 2024, some of the top active dark web marketplaces included Abacus, STYX, Brian's Club, Russian Market, WeTheNorth, and Torzon.

> An exit scam occurs when the marketplace reaches a certain volume of activity and the marketplace escrow has a meaningful balance; the administrators simply shut down the market and take the escrow cash.

The user experience for most dark net markets is normalized. Sophisticated marketplaces operate and look and feel similar to eBay or Amazon. They offer user profiles with feedback ratings and seller histories. Escrow services and financial products are also available. Users can search, subscribe, follow, and create their own virtual storefronts. The marketplaces have forums for discussion organized by topic and direct messaging capabilities. These are fully functional and sophisticated digital marketplaces. Figure 2.1 shows a typical Russian dark net market.

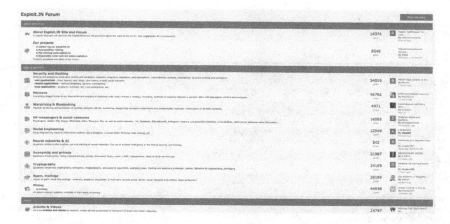

Figure 2.1 A typical dark net market main menu page (Russian language).

In recent years, Telegram, the end-to-end encrypted chat platform, has made headlines for contributing to the illicit online market. Thousands of Telegram channels now operate as their own marketplaces, offering the same goods and services as the dark net marketplaces. Telegram has been referred to as "the dark web in your pocket." Figure 2.2 shows a sample Telegram chat in an illicit Telegram market.

These marketplaces produce an average sales volume of hundreds of millions of dollars per year. Items for sale on the marketplaces are largely illicit goods, drugs, weapons, and stolen corporate information and data. Services offered include deepfakes, DDOS, swatting, spam bombing, hit-for-hire, and other nasty deeds. These sales are typically transacted through blockchain currencies such as Bitcoin (BTC), Monero (XRP), or other cryptocurrency coins and tokens.

A quick note on dark web market "takedowns" by law enforcement. Over the years, law enforcement institutions, both domestic and abroad, have become increasingly effective at infiltrating and disrupting illegal online marketplaces. While their tactics have become more sophisticated, in most cases the methods driving their successes tend to be old-school police work along the lines of

42   CYBER RECON

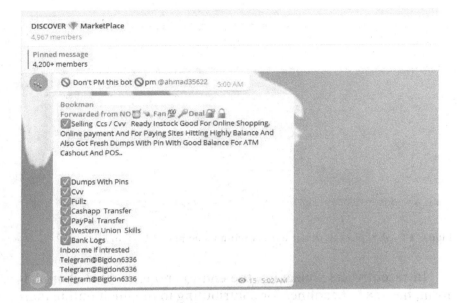

Figure 2.2   Telegram illicit marketplace.

finding one of the participants, threatening them with prison, and subsequently turning them into an asset. Using these tried-and-tested methods, law enforcement is eventually able to get to the administrators, threaten them with prison terms, and get them to turn on their associates. More technically nuanced takedowns have been accomplished, as covered in Andy Greenberg's book *Tracers in the Dark* (Vintage; Reissue edition, 2024) where law enforcement used crypto-tracing tools and warrants to pull disk images of the physical servers. Yet, even these ended with the traditional police providing evidence to turn bad guys into assets. This isn't intended to diminish their work but to give clarity to their technical capabilities. The context becomes more relevant when we explore the ransomware space.

One recent, highly visible, takedown occurred against LockBit-Supp, the leader of the LockBit ransomware operation. In February 2024, while LockBit was leading in the ransomware attack game, the Federal Bureau of Investigation (FBI) and the UK's National Crime Agency disrupted LockBit with Operation Cronos. The bust resulted in the seizure of over 34 servers and 1,000 decryption keys. The data on the servers exposed many of LockBit's affiliates, and the keys were promptly used to decrypt victims' files worldwide.

> Dark web market "takedowns" are not to be confused with the Digital Millennium Copyright Act "takedowns," where a legal request to remove content from the Internet is made to a hosting provider, social media company, or domain registrar.

Within a week, LockBitSupp was back up and running. While the owner admitted to some vulnerabilities on his systems not being patched due to laziness, he arrogantly challenged law enforcement to come at him again. To make things more difficult for LockBitSupp, law enforcement planted the seed in the dark web community that he was, in fact, an informant for the FBI. This was a psychological operations (PsyOps) ploy to make the ransomware affiliate networks hesitant to work with him. Further, they identified him as Dmitry Yuryevich Khoroshev, a 31-year-old Russian national from Voronezh, and placed him under international indictment. Finally, the U.S. government added the LockBit operation to the Treasury Department's Office of Foreign Asset Control's (OFAC) sanctions list, preventing U.S. companies from paying any ransoms to LockBit. (This list consists of enemies of the United States and its allies and includes individuals, organizations, entire nation-states, and apparently, ransomware actors.)

The LockBitSupp disruption played out like many law enforcement efforts against ransomware actors. Law enforcement issues a press release about the disruption, seizes sites, and disrupts the target infrastructure, only to have those actors reemerge—and sometimes rebrand or join other groups—weeks later with fresh resources. The proverbial hydra lives on.

The process of threat actor groups reforming and migrating after disruption causes challenges with compliance, especially with the Office of Foreign Assets Control (OFAC). Since OFAC is a keyword list, a member of one organization who is on the list moving to another organization that is not on the list could cause confusion as to whether the non-listed entity is now in violation. This applies to groups as well; if DarkSide ransomware is listed on the OFAC list (it is), does the BlackMatter ransomware group become collateral damage because they share many of the same software and members? We will discuss this more deeply in Chapter 4, "Whodat?," which focuses on the ransomware economy.

Ransomware gangs are part of the larger underground economy where files, credentials, and systems or network access are sold in markets. Each participant plays a specific role in these illicit underground markets that make the cybercrime economy work.

While online criminals want to maximize their total addressable market, gaining access to some of these illicit markets can be tricky. This is especially true if you are concerned about operational security (OPSEC). Most markets will allow anyone to make an account on the marketplace, but you cannot post items for sale or transact until you have established a certain level of activity. Some markets require a joining fee, typically paid in Bitcoin (BTC) or another cryptocurrency. The most valuable markets—where the "good stuff" is sold—require the individual applying to be vetted, have a reference, and even perhaps evidence of an illicit transaction before they can create a profile.

Take, for example, the initial access broker (IAB) markets, where threat actors offer stolen network or system access information for sale. The IAB market is smart about their pricing model, and often, IABs do as much or more intelligence on their victim than ransomware operators do. They know when they have a whale, and they price accordingly.

However, the IAB market is far from consistent. You can be sure, though, that when a new sneaky exploit is discovered, especially for a remote access software or system, there will be a bonanza on the market. The initial access community wedges its foot in the digital door and starts deploying its attack tools. They will often script new tools for this very purpose, scanning for new vulnerabilities across the entire Internet. Once they gain access, the ease at which they traverse the target network and escalate access is mind-numbing, especially considering what has been invested to detect and mitigate such activity.

There are other kinds of access beyond persistent system, admin, or network access. Take infostealer logs, for example. Infostealers are malware designed purely to harvest and transmit sensitive information from a given system. These nasty agents target various kinds of data, especially passwords, other credentials, banking account numbers, PII, HII, cryptocurrency wallets, session cookies, clipboard data, and confidential documents.

Infostealers typically affect systems through phishing campaigns, malicious websites or ads, or weaponized software. They are cleverly designed to avoid detection and have a very low system profile. They are carefully designed to avoid detection by endpoint detection and antivirus software using techniques like code obfuscation. Some infostealers never write to disk and run completely in memory, making them that much more difficult to detect. See Figure 2.3 for a sample of redline infostealer logs.

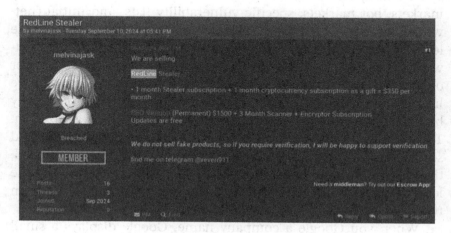

Figure 2.3 Redline infostealer logs.

Once they harvest the data, the infostealers connect back to their command and control (C2) servers for instruction. They then transmit their stolen data through FTP, email, or even through Telegram or Discord. After the malware has exfiltrated the data from a host, it organizes this data into logs, which are then sent back to the attackers via the C2 servers. Some examples of infostealers are RedLine, Raccoon Stealer, and Vidar.

Infostealers provide a number of opportunities for the threat actors to monetize their efforts. Of course, the stolen data is valuable in the dark net markets. Credentials can be used to gain persistent access for IABs, session cookies can be used for further infiltration, and so on. It is also common for attackers to then sell the *logs*, and indeed infostealer logs are a hot commodity in the dark net markets. Selling the logs allows the stealer botnet owner to create a kind of passive income, as they do not have to leverage the stolen data themselves but can sell the data and information to another attacker, perhaps even an IAB.

The underground economy for stolen access into the networks of public and private organizations relies on layers of participants and products, just like any standard economy. They include developers selling the newest remote access tools (RATs), infostealer log markets, bot markets, specific vulnerability lists, and initial (network) access brokers. Most initial access brokers will offer some level of persistent access to a particular victim organization's network. Of course, the IAB wants to advertise to the largest number of possible buyers, yet is aware that security research companies are lurking on the marketplaces, so they cannot identify the company by name. Instead, they advertise metadata about the organization. Typically, this consists of the company's industry, continental and sometimes country of origin or where their headquarters is located, the number of employees, sometimes the annual revenue, and the level of access for sale. The IAB usually gets this information from two sources: Google and ZoomInfo.

When you Google a company name, Google displays a small information box to the right of your search. It is unclear where

Google gets that information, and it is often incorrect. ZoomInfo, on the other hand, is a sales intelligence tool that sells access to prospective company information such as organizational charts, budget information, products adopted, and more. My sales team uses it on a daily basis, and as it turns out, so do bad guys. In fact, both IABs and ransomware actors often reference its use, especially when justifying their ransom demand. Unfortunately for the access broker, when you combine two or three of these metadata elements, it is easy to backward-engineer which company is affected. This is a fundamental part of the GroupSense Open Findings process. Figure 2.4 shows an IAB advertisement.

Threat actors post hundreds of these kinds of advertisements per day. Most are sold, and some are patched before any real damage is done, but the value of monitoring these forums is clear. If you or your business partner's name shows up, it is an opportunity to fix it before any actual harm is done. Yet, you do not know the details of how the access was acquired. The options are as follows: A victim can either buy access or convince the seller to share information about access without paying. Obviously, the latter is preferred but more difficult to pull off—more on that later.

When the seller eventually finds their buyer, bad things happen. Typically IABs are selling to ransomware operators or nation-states, neither of which forecasts a positive outcome for an enterprise. Ransomware operators often calculate the "cost of goods" in their ransom price, and that cost of goods includes what they paid the

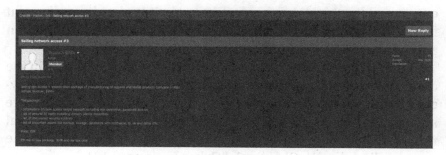

Figure 2.4   A typical IAB advertisement.

IAB for access. On top of this, they attempt to maintain a desired margin. Intelligence on some of the more sophisticated ransomware groups has shown that group members are assigned a quota or a margin target per victim and are compensated based on their ability to hit that margin, complete with accelerators when they can hit higher margins. Does this model sound familiar? Sounds like a business to me!

GroupSense has experienced the "cost of goods scenario" on multiple occasions, but one in particular comes to mind. We were retained by a charity whose files were locked by a ransomware gang. After seeing their financial documents, the ransomware actors felt comfortable asking for $2 million for the ransom. Paul (a former undercover detective), a trusted team member, led the negotiation on their behalf. Paul appealed to the ransomware actors, saying, "Look, this is a charity. Nearly every dollar in their account was donated to help people of lesser means fight cancer."

TA: Okay. What do you think is a fair price, then?
Paul: Zero. Zero dollars is a fair price!
TA: We can't do that; this access cost us money.
Paul: Okay, what is your cost?
TA: $5,000.
Paul: Fine. 5K it is.

The ransomware operators presumably paid an IAB $5,000 for the network access and simply needed to cover their costs. The client was obliged to take the deal because it was quite a discount from the original $2 million ask. They were spared annihilation and were back to treating cancer patients in no time.

Similarly to IABs, there are infostealers that are marketed in the dark web markets rather openly and those that are for trusted buyers. Creating a persona network that is welcomed into the private and trusted buyer's circle is key to offering a comprehensive digital risk program. We will dig into the science and process behind the persona discipline in Chapter 3, "Cyber Espionage 101."

COVID-19 Fraud

During the pandemic, these cybercrime markets became a haven for insider threats and cyber and financial fraud, targeting government subsidy programs. COVID subsidy programs were announced and put in place to help businesses financially challenged by the pandemic. Programs like the Paycheck Protection Plan (PPP) and the Economic Injury Disaster Loan (EIDL) included large payroll loans to help companies remain in operation and make payroll when revenues were down.

The cybercrime markets were the ideal place to announce and sell "fraud kits" for different programs and participating financial institutions. Our investigation for a particular government customer uncovered numerous fraud activities, including spearphishing kits, loan-directed fraud, stolen loan data for sale, counterfeit treasury checks as a service, business information for use in fraud kits, and government systems login information. Figure 2.5 shows a threat actor offering to use stolen or leaked information to generate false documents. These documents are subsequently used to file for COVID benefits and loans.

During the pandemic, it was estimated (www.gao.gov/products/gao-24-105833) that nearly 15 percent of the total subsidy amounts

Figure 2.5 Threat actor offering to use stolen or leaked info to generate false documents.

were successfully stolen through these fraud efforts, amounting to nearly $35 billion in losses. These losses culminated in the creation of new antifraud government agencies like the COVID-19 Fraud Enforcement Task Force (CFETF) and optimization in the Government Accountability Office antifraud efforts.

Ultimately, much of this could have been mitigated with proper visibility into the fraud networks populating the cybercrime markets. Unfortunately, even though the agencies who had ultimate responsibility knew this, they did not act quickly enough to curb the impact, costing U.S. taxpayers billions of dollars.

Just as there are dedicated markets for cyber fraud, there are dedicated marketplaces for multiple specific cybercriminal activities. The credit card markets are some of the earliest markets to emerge. Dedicated entirely to stolen account information, with a focus on credit cards, these markets are awash with personally identifiable information (PII) and stolen credit card dumps and packages. There are specializations within these markets as well. "Fullz" (full information) markets are markets that include all the necessary information to clone a card physically. This includes information contained within the magnetic strip and the CVV numbers. Some markets specialize in particular kinds of gift cards, or software-as-a-service (SaaS) market cards, like Amazon.com. Figure 2.7 shows an example of a typical carder market. Figure 2.6 shows an example of a Russian market carder page.

Perhaps the most damaging markets are the credential markets, where threat actors sell stolen or leaked corporate credentials in bulk. The comprehensive and respected 2024 Verizon Data Breach Investigations Report (DBIR) found that 24 percent of the successful breaches they investigated were caused by the threat actor using legitimate corporate credentials. Most of the time, these are purchased in a credential market. These markets exist across platforms, including the dark web, Telegram, WhatsApp, and others. Many of the credentials harvested and sold there are the result of infostealers or third-party breaches. In third-party breaches, employees use their corporate credentials on a third-party site that is unrelated to their employer or their job. They often reuse

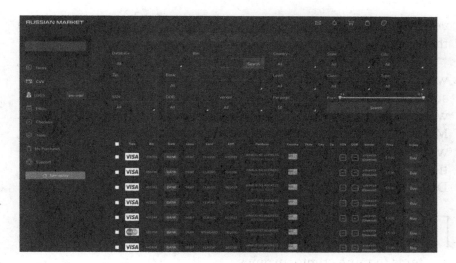

Figure 2.6 Russian market carder page.

passwords or use similar credentials to those they use at their employer. These breaches pose significant problems for the security teams, as many of our defense technologies are designed to look for bad behavior. Logging in with legitimate credentials is not bad behavior and thus is not picked up by those systems. The result is long threat actor (TA) "dwell times" inside the organization, during which the TAs gather critical information for future, larger exploits and business email compromise attacks. Part of the digital risk stack is monitoring and gathering these credentials to provide account takeover (ATO) protection for the client. This is achieved by notifying the client that a particular credential is available "in the wild" and the resulting level of exposure while resetting that credential in the organization and notifying the employee of any policy violations.

Malware markets sell various types of malware targeted to meet specific cybercriminal goals. These are often also referred to as malware-as-a-service (MaaS) markets and usually traffic Trojans, rootkits, spyware, and remote access toolkits heavily.

Similarly, zero-day and exploit markets focus on selling (typically high-priced) vulnerabilities unknown to the affected software vendors. They also sell various exploit kits with packages to exploit these vulnerabilities.

There are markets that sell services simply for disruption, whether they be distributed denial of service-as-a-service or booter/stressor services. These services take certain systems, networks, websites, or users offline, typically by flooding them with traffic. Many of those DDoS services are powered by the botnet markets, which sell access to a large number of infected systems for a particular purpose. That purpose could be data theft, ad click farms, DDoS traffic, or cryptojacking.

> Cryptojacking is using the processors of the infected systems to mine cryptocurrency.

Many sites will sell kits for use in other cybercriminal activities. There are sites that sell phishing-as-a-service (PhaaS) services that come with readymade templates and phishing pages and email templates—even services to do phishing email distribution. Some of these kits include pages designed specifically for credential-harvesting activities.

Counterfeit markets sell anything from fake ID cards and passports to credentials for social benefit programs. These sites also market fake diplomas, certificates, and licenses to assist in kinetic fraud activity. These markets also often sell services for check fraud and card-cloning services or bank drop services.

Money Laundering

All of these markets exist to disrupt or steal in some way. Upon receiving the cash related to the cybercrime effort, the cybercriminal will typically need to launder it. Great news, my cybercriminal friends! There is a market for that.

Cryptocurrency and money laundering markets provide access to crypto mixers and tumblers. These systems and tools obfuscate the source and destination of large amounts of crypto capital, making it difficult for crypto investigators to trace the money. They also will sell services that assist with the cashing-out process, transferring the illegitimate funds to some legitimate asset or currency.

Some nefarious activity indeed occurs on these markets and messaging platforms, and there is an art form and a discipline for knowing where the relevant activity is occurring and being there to collect the intelligence information about it.

When You Shine a Light, the Roaches Will Run

In 2022, one of our analysts gave an update to our broader MSIC team that threat actors were discussing meeting places in the metaverse. In this case, a well-known actor had secured a private "dorm" in the metasphere and was using it to convene with fellow actors to transact illicit business. Of course, this evolution presents a series of new challenges to the cyber intelligence and espionage community. Whereas before we could simply hide behind forum avatars or chat personas, the metaverse was even more HUMINT-centric—not to mention the challenges of capturing conversations for analysis. Fortunately, we had some cards in the deck that allowed us to pivot quickly.

Since the Daesh terrorist attacks in Paris, international law enforcement has long suspected the use of online gaming and gaming-adjacent communication tools in not only the recruitment and grooming of extremists but also the planning of actual terrorist attacks. Figure 2.7 shows an analyst using VR goggles to perform espionage in the metaverse.

Figure 2.7 Analyst using VR goggles to perform espionage in the metaverse.

As artificial intelligence and virtual spaces continue to evolve, this will quickly become the new battleground for cyber and virtual world intelligence. Teams in the cyber spy space will be innovating to keep up, perhaps reverting to a more traditional HUMINT operation in the process.

Still, many of the digital risks to individuals and organizations occur in the most benign places. These places are often overlooked by the intel community but seldom by the threat actors. We experienced this in the early days of building our intelligence operation. A large manufacturing customer had been receiving our service for nearly a year. Around this time, there had been an emergence of "paste sites." Paste sites were effectively free digital ephemeral notepads where anyone could post anything and point other Internet users to it. We had begun a scraping operation of these paste sites because the threat actors would sometimes use them to paste evidence, menus, or communications about exploits there. Since they were ephemeral, they would time out and disappear, so getting a point-in-time copy of this data was invaluable. In the case of the manufacturing client, we discovered that it was not threat actors presenting the digital risk; it was their employees. One of their developers was trying to solve a particular problem. He was stumped, so he did what any normal technical person would do: He asked other smart technical people for help. Since the problem revolved around confidential code, he pasted some of the code to PasteBin (one of the more popular paste sites) in order to point some development buddies at other companies to the code. Unfortunately for the manufacturer, the snippet of code posted contained Amazon Web Service (AWS) keys, allowing anyone to spin up new Amazon services on behalf of the manufacturer. Our services caught this innocent slip-up before it was exploited. In the meeting with the (*very* grateful) manufacturing client later that month, we quipped about their near investment in a DDoS botnet.

The same is true for other cloud services. In fact, SaaS software and tools have become the new "shadow IT." The concept of shadow IT emerged in the late 1990s, and it represented scenarios in which management denied a staff member's request to use, buy, or build a particular system or feature for their specific use. The undeterred staffer would simply go to Best Buy or Micro Center and buy the necessary software or systems, deploying them without the knowledge of IT. Unfortunately, this causes a series of serious problems for IT and corporate management, as they can only enforce policy on or strategically secure systems that they are aware of. Often, this led to security vulnerabilities.

Sometimes, shadow IT can surface with more nefarious intent. When I was a security subject matter expert at Southwestern Bell Corporation (SBC), one of my customers was an underfunded hospital in a poor neighborhood in Chicago. Due to their limited resources, I offered pro bono services to the hospital in my free time, something I still do for healthcare institutions and small businesses. In one case, I ran a vulnerability scan against their newly deployed external firewall, only to discover a server no one knew about. Some poking around uncovered the server was being used to provide pornographic material and illegal music downloads. The physical device resided under a staffer's desk and was patched through to the perimeter switch using the Ethernet infrastructure. That was a rough day for my colleagues at the hospital, Frank and James. However, the scanning prevented a legal issue and possible vulnerabilities for the hospital network. Today, it is common for staff to spin up unsanctioned SaaS tools to accomplish something work-related, thereby putting confidential corporate information on those systems without the knowledge of the information security teams. This is the new shadow IT.

There have been myriad large data leaks from unknown or misconfigured open Amazon S3 (data storage) containers, exposing millions of consumer records. The same scenario occurs with other cloud collaboration platforms such as GitHub, Trello, and Twilio.

The point of running a cyber intelligence operation or digital risk protection program is to discover this misappropriated data before the bad guys do and clean it up or mitigate the risk. As a result, it is necessary to operate not only in the dark net and dark web properties but also in the chat rooms, virtual spaces, metaverse, collaboration SaaS tools, and the open web.

A trusted colleague recently asked me if there was software that could tell him whether a particular file appeared on the web or web property. I told him, "Yes—Google!" Cyber spy practitioners need to be efficient at infiltrating the Internet underground and proficient in the tools offered by search engine companies, like "Google dorking."

> Google dorking is a syntax set that allows someone to carefully craft Internet searches.

A whole submarket of OSINT-focused tools has arrived on the scene. Tools like ShadowDragon are favorites of the OSINT investigators and law enforcement. There are dozens of companies focused on specific OSINT data collection. In ShadowDragon's case, it is focused on social media and communication platforms. Others focus on domain intelligence, phishing intelligence, vulnerability intelligence, attack surface intelligence, and even companies that give you intelligence on what *not* to monitor, like GreyNoise. Of course, our opponents also use OSINT data. This is why I have dedicated an entire chapter to OPSEC—Chapter 5, "OPSEC or Die."

As I write this, the digital risk landscape is evolving—by the time you read this book, new markets, illicit forums, chat platforms, and tools will be available. None of this changes the discipline of the cyber espionage professional or the digital risk protection market. The depth and reach of their personas create the aperture from which intelligence is derived. As a result, practitioners will have to develop clever tools to gain access and visibility to these dark places.

> *If you do only one thing* after reading this chapter, it should be to look at your personal digital risk. Tools are available to evaluate your exposure and recommend or take action to reduce the likelihood of being personally compromised or having your identity stolen.

Cyber Recon Leader Profile:

Jon DiMaggio

Current Role: Chief Security Strategist, Analyst1

Other Affiliations: Author, *The Art of Cyber Warfare*; Author, *The Ransomware Diaries*; Winner of SANS Difference Maker Award; Book of the Year 2022 and 2023; Featured on *60 Minutes*

Jon's Bio

Jon DiMaggio is a highly experienced cybersecurity researcher with over 16 years in the field, specializing in ransomware and nation-state cyberthreats. Jon focuses on investigating and disrupting cybercriminal operations. His expertise includes both open source and covert intelligence–gathering techniques, which have helped him infiltrate major ransomware groups like LockBit, providing valuable insights to law enforcement agencies.

Jon's Mission

I live in the shadows of dark web, standing as a vigilant guardian, driven by an unwavering commitment to protect the innocent from digital threats. Like a modern-day vigilante, I use my skills and knowledge to track down cybercriminals and bring them to justice.

My mission is to relentlessly hunt cybercriminals, leveraging both technical expertise and human intelligence to unmask those who would harm others. I have a very particular set of skills, skills I have acquired over a very long career that make me a nightmare for cybercriminals.

Just as Batman uses his resources and determination to protect Gotham, I dedicate myself to safeguarding the digital world from those who exploit it for malicious purposes.

My mission is to

- Maintain unwavering ethical standards while operating in morally complex situations
- Use my skills to protect the vulnerable and expose those who prey upon them
- Find, breach, and expose those who commit crimes from behind a keyboard
- Strike fear into the hearts of cybercriminals by demonstrating that no digital shadow is deep enough to hide their misdeeds

- Build alliances with others who share this mission, knowing that the greatest victories come through collaboration
- Never compromise my principles in pursuit of justice, even when faced with difficult choices

Like the symbol of the bat striking fear into criminals, my presence in the cyber underground will serve as a constant reminder that justice reaches even the darkest corners of the digital world. I am not just a security researcher; I am the guardian the cyber world needs, the silent protector of digital justice.

YouTube URL: www.youtube.com/watch?v=rpNuGaxmUwA

YouTube, LLC

Chapter 3
Cyber Espionage 101

Bro, we know there are cyber researchers in this forum. I am creating a new private group; sending you channel invite via TOX...
— *Unknown author / Rando Threat Actor*

Once again, one of our carefully curated sock puppets got an invite to a private chat designed to avoid us. Nikol, one of our top researchers, carefully crafted this sock puppet over years, building a high level of trust among the marketplace leadership. If the intelligence researchers are doing their job well, these kinds of invites happen often.

In Chapter 2, "FFS DNM," we discussed illicit markets, open web, chat channels, and other places a good cyber intelligence program should be paying attention to. Getting access to those online properties and chatrooms often requires creating a false persona—a "sock puppet"—in order to infiltrate . . . an undercover agent, if you will.

Undercover agents and personas have been stalwart tools of espionage, law enforcement, and nations for centuries. The concept of developing a false identity in an effort to gain access or information while simultaneously limiting access to the perpetrating entity is the tip of the spear for intelligence gathering and HUMINT operations, both in the real world and in the cyber world.

The term *sock puppet* probably surfaced in the mid-to-late 1990s in Internet chatrooms and USENET bulletin boards. It's a reference to actual puppetry, where socks are placed over the hands of the puppeteer, representing an apparently separate, independent personality. The sock puppets often represented a persona that furthered the cause of a particular avatar in the chatroom or board, but in reality was controlled by that avatar. By the mid-2000s, *sock puppet* had entered the Internet vernacular and was being used in various Internet forums and bulletin boards to drive narratives and gather information.

Internet actors on all sides have made use of the concept of sock puppets over the years. Persona development and use branched out to a number of regular use cases. The primary uses have evolved into a few specific use cases:

Anonymity/Privacy   In a paradigm where no one can be trusted, hiding your real identity is crucial. Creating a false identity and persona allows dark web and chat users to remain in the background. Assuming they follow proper OPSEC, they will remain anonymous to the other participants.

Cyber Reconnaissance   This is GroupSense's use case, and we use these personas to lurk and monitor in the forums. These "fly on the wall" spies should appear to be regular, insignificant users of the platform or forum and thus draw little attention. As stated in the first chapter, the actual monitoring is often done in an automated fashion, slurping up the conversations and throwing them into a large data repository, where complex platforms analyze the conversations and correlate them with other data points, often creating profiles and behavioral analyses of the other forum participants.

Infiltration/Trust Building   This is a fundamental but critical reconnaissance use case. In this chapter, we will give examples of how building trust and relationships with threat actors can yield invaluable information and intelligence. It is through trust building and establishing a reputation that an undercover persona will gain access to the most illicit Internet underground properties.

Undercover Ops This is similar to the reconnaissance use case but is used by law enforcement. Law enforcement has been using fake personas for more than a decade to do investigations on the dark web but also to catch would-be child abusers and pedophiles.

Misinformation Fake accounts, personas, and repurposed orphaned accounts are the backbone of any misinformation campaign. Whether championed by a nation-state or a political faction, misinformation can be one of sock puppets' most socially impactful uses.

OPSEC The follow/connect fabric of social media platforms attempts to reveal the identity of someone who would like to know more about you. Using sock puppets or fake personas allows someone to obscure their identity in order to see social activity.

Our early attempts were sophomoric at best, but they did the trick. In 2013, our founding team directly controlled the puppets and primarily leveraged activity in the hacking forums—and clever use of Internet slang—to get us invited to the illicit parties. In 2018 we acquired BitCrime, a company engaged in building relationships in the underground, before we wrote our first line of code. Not only did the acquisition of BitCrime accelerate our espionage efforts, but it also gave us critical language capabilities. This allowed us to tactically interact with various actors in their native languages and use appropriate dark net parlance.

Sock puppet and persona development became more mainstream with the maturation of OSINT as a legitimate cybersecurity practice. As social media became a safe haven for illegal and illicit behavior, not unlike the dark net forums, it required a persona or account to safely and covertly access.

We were early adopters of social media sock puppetry. GroupSense quickly developed an army of these personas to assist with the detection of election misinformation and disinformation and to mitigate these activities for state and local government customers. We built networks of undercover operatives to assist in anti–sex trafficking activities. Most importantly, our team developed personas that were able to assist in the identification and arrest of foreign cybercriminals such as ransomware actors, initial access brokers, and counterfeit drug operations. Our sock puppets "lived" in dozens of countries and spoke the requisite languages and contemporary slang natively. We insist on native language skills because translation software can be unreliable when it comes to the natural flow and feel of a language, and therefore, we cannot trust this kind of software.

One can find numerous guides on how to build a sock puppet online, and thanks to new AI tools, it is easier than ever to build one. Our experience has derived some basic rules, tools, and processes that have worked well for us:

- **The persona must have depth,** and the more depth, the better. What we mean by depth is the persona being identifiable outside the immediate platform in some other way—a verifiable email address, perhaps a social media account, or simply active on multiple dark web forums under a similar moniker.
- **The persona must have a purpose** and be online for a specific reason. They are focused on a particular part of the dark web trade, such as buying access from IABs or seeking breach data.
- **The persona must be consistent.** For each persona you develop, craft a narrative or backstory for that persona—and stick to it! If the persona is from Zimbabwe, the persona is always from Zimbabwe. They speak Ndebele and *some* English (more on this trick later). You will also need to define the persona's age, gender, sexual orientation, race, education level, etc. It is absolutely critical not to get your personas mixed up. It helps to track them in a Google spreadsheet, CRM, or similar tool.
- **The persona should not be attributable to the host.** Serious OPSEC considerations and precautions must be taken when wielding the persona. I find it is best to have an OPSEC

"pre-flight" checklist when manning a persona. It might look like this:

- Virtual environment or research machine (not your main workstation)
- Persona documentation (usually a page with details on the persona followed by pages of activity notes [recent activity, who we have been working with, etc.])
- Virtual machine (VM) or workstation set to the proper time zone
- VM or workstation set to proper hostname
- VM or workstation—modified UserAgent (what the machine tells systems it connects to)
- Separate network (not your home Wi-Fi)
- VPN or proxy
- TOR
- Crypto wallets
- Language support

A note on language support. Many of us will not have a team like BitCrime at our immediate disposal to support various languages natively. As I expressed earlier, it is ill-advised to rely on translator software. If our persona is a native English speaker, there is an immediate credibility loss and risk associated with it in the underground. A colleague once let me in on a trick he uses when navigating language barrier challenges.

I attended a book release party for *The Ransomware Hunting Team*, by Renee Dudley and Dan Golden of ProPublica. Renee featured me in the book, and I wanted to thank her in person for the opportunity. Plus, they were hosting the party at the now-famous Comet Ping Pong Pizza. Comet was made famous through conspiracy theories relating to secret Democratic rituals in the nonexistent basement, infamously known as *Pizzagate*. I had never—well, not since the last ritual—been interested and wanted to check it out. My plus-one was another researcher who has made a name in the cyber espionage business. After the book reading, we were enjoying our beverages in the beer garden out back and discussing our cyber underground exploits. In the course of the discussion, we realized our covert personas had interacted on a particular Telegram channel.

Wine having removed a filter or two, I blurted out, "Hey, but that persona speaks Romanian! Do you speak Romanian?"

"No, sir, I do not," he replied.

"Why choose Romanian as the language then?" I asked.

As it turned out, my friend had a clever trick. There are a handful of languages that threat actors are less suspicious of but do not necessarily speak fluently. The trick is to make one of these languages the persona's primary language and then claim to speak *some* English. As a result, you can speak that language through a translator or just use the primary language of the person you are speaking with, reversing it to English through a translator. Doing so might look like this:

Primary Language: Romanian
Translation: English > Romanian, then bad guy translates Romanian > English
or
Translation: (assuming the bad guy speaks Russian) Russian > English, then bad guy translates translated English > Russian

This ploy is defensible. Romanian is a favorite because it was once part of the Soviet Union, and there are plenty of bad actors operating there. But Romanian is not a Slavic language or Cyrillic alphabet; it is Latin, more akin to Spanish or French than Russian or Ukrainian. Further, the last couple of generations of Romanians may not speak Russian at all, so the bad actors assume the persona is credible even though they don't speak their language. The threat actors find themselves in the position of needing to use translator software or fall on communicating in messy English—both defensible and brilliant strategies to get around the language barrier. I believe my colleague also often used German or Swiss-German.

Cu plăcere. (Google translation of "You're welcome" in Romanian.)

There are numerous tools available to assist in setting up your persona. As I mentioned earlier, you will want to create a comprehensive persona document for each persona, and if you have multiple, perhaps a dashboard in Google Sheets linking to all the documents to manage them all. Try to capture all the details about your persona in the sheet, then add a narrative reflecting those details. The remainder of the document should be detailed notes on activity and interactions. I manage my personas' user IDs, avatars, handles, and requisite passwords in a password manager, which is also a good place to also store any passkeys and codes for items like cryptocurrency wallets. BitWarden is a good example of an open source password management tool that can be used for this purpose. I frequently use FakeNameGenerator and "This Person Does Not Exist" to create names and photos for the persona; you should store those in the directory with the Google Sheet and Docs. For many social media platforms and some activities, you will also need a burner phone populated with SIM cards that can be easily obtained online. You may need a burner credit card, as well—Privacy.com offers this, and it seems to work reliably.

You can also rely on services like Authentic8 Silo to achieve much of this obfuscation in a single affordable tool, including proxy/VPN, TOR, burner phone numbers, language support, UserAgent spoofing, etc.

Of course, you will need burner or unattributable email addresses. We use a variety of services for these kinds of email addresses, such as Gmail ProtonMail, Mail.ru, cock.ru, and tuta.com. Once you have an email address, you will want to create some form of proof that the persona is a real person. This can be done by participating in forums or having some social media presence. If you are creating this sock puppet/persona *for* use in social media intelligence, you will absolutely have to create social media accounts and history. Luckily, this process is made easier with AI, which can create synthetic content on the fly. When creating social media accounts, try not to reuse photos from the Internet; a reverse image search will quickly give you away.

Start this process early, as the threat actors you're trying to gain the trust of will take into account the age of your persona properties. It is good practice to let these accounts and their connected social media and other presences age before engaging in any direct contact with your target. During this time, you should continue to create content and general activity for those properties. Once you have your personas created with content and aged them, refer to your checklist. Our PIR-Zero would drive a collection requirement for all of the marketplaces, chatrooms, social media platforms, and forums.

None of this is accomplished easily or quickly unless one has developed personas and sock puppets in and around the dark web for a decade; many of these personas require significant age, and unfortunately, your time machine is broken. In this case, the intelligence team should have enough relationships to pass the background check or perhaps vet themselves with another owned persona. In cases where some evidence of prior illicit activity is required, an intelligence practitioner with multiple personas can transact with themselves. This is a common practice that includes public discourse between the personas in the native language chosen for the personas. Sometimes, an intel practitioner may manufacture a conflict or drama between sock puppets to draw attention to certain faux illicit activities. That scenario might look something like the following exchange, which has been translated from Russian.

SP1: @SP2, the credentials I bought from you yesterday are shit. Money back or problem.
SP2: Take it easy—remind me which cred list.
SP1: "HII-Dump2," these are mostly reused shit.
SP2: I checked those, they're good.
SP1: Money back or problem.
SP2: Send me the repeat list @TOX DM.
SP1: ... Sent.
SP2: These aren't reuse, but here I send latest rip from SP3, no charge.
SP1: We are good.

A back-and-forth like this on the forum accomplishes a number of objectives. First, it raises the brand of the particular personas in the marketplace. Second, many of the illicit or underground forums require comments and activity for the account to stay active. While some of this can be accomplished with automated software, this conversation is likely going to get some attention, so humans who speak the native language—again, not using translator software—are a sure way to ensure quality and avoid suspicion. In general, automated conversations via AI and translator software are a bad idea, as they can be riddled with bugs and mistakes, and the threat actors pick up on their use quickly. It is a sure way to get kicked or even banned from a dark net property.

You can begin collection once you've established a persistent presence inside the desired source. This can be done in a number of ways: manually, with a browser plug-in program that screen-scrapes; automatically, with a proper scraper or harvester software; and in some cases, forum administrators have even offered API access for basic scraping. (Not that anyone would take them up on that!)

While the original purpose of these sock puppets is wholesale collection of threat actor conversations in the forum sources driven by the customer PIRs, they serve other important purposes. One purpose is the aforementioned tenure and vetting capabilities, but they also add value as true HUMINT espionage assets. GroupSense has always had a process in which for any given critical source, we maintain multiple sock puppets, perhaps as many as three or four. We do this for redundancy in case a suspect persona is booted for scraping. This does happen. When using multiple personas, we'll split them between collectors and high-value espionage personas. The espionage personas build long-term relationships and carry out strategic theatrics to maintain their status. The other common use case is the private menu and interacting with initial access brokers.

Initial Access Broker (IAB) Markets

As a cyber espionage expert, if you happen to have befriended the right IABs, you may be offered something that isn't on the public menu. Where the typical advertisement on the forums is lightly obfuscated, these offers are not. Our team's personas are routinely offered private menus of companies' network access for sale—by name. Often it comes through like an ad from Amazon, "If you like Company X, then check out this list of similar companies we have breached." There are a number of IABs who routinely offer these private menus; some are general, whereas others are more specialized. For example, we have some actors who specialize in a particular vulnerability or type of access. In these cases, they assure us the offer is only being made to a small inner circle of buyers. If we express interest in a particular company but do not acquire the access immediately, the IAB will let us know when it has been sold to another buyer. There have been cases where we have acquired the access on behalf of a client, but we see the access offered publicly (via metadata reverse engineering) on a forum. In these cases, we are issued an apology and perhaps a refund or a credit. I referenced this in Chapter 2. Very good customer service on the part of the threat actors!

Trusted personas are also fundamental to acquiring infostealer logs. It is obvious how valuable buying infostealer logs would be to any organization. Of course, the infostealer owners don't just sell those logs to anyone. Considering the primary value to the broader threat actor market, they will gain access to private information on the systems and networks the logs are representing, and it is in their best interest to sell to other bad actors. If the infostealer admin consistently sold those logs to enterprises or security researchers, the compromised systems and networks would be repaired, cybersecurity holes plugged, and the infostealer admin would gain a reputation for selling bad logs, curtailing their ability to continue operating in that space.

This presents a challenge for enterprises that want to get their digital arms around their security posture. Enter the cyber espionage practitioner. Once again, one cannot simply create an account in these forums or markets and begin chatting with the purveyors. The bad actors use a carefully guarded reputation system to determine the risk level of transacting with a particular avatar in the markets. A carefully curated persona or sock puppet will have the necessary tenure and dark net street cred to engage in a negotiation for the purchase of various log and log sets with the seller, and this reputation builds on itself if this persona has a history of this kind of activity. A well-run cyber espionage operation will have a handful of personas for this purpose, with varied levels of persistence and activity history.

Law Enforcement Use of Sock Puppets

Law enforcement has made significant use of sock puppets to catch and prosecute child predators, petty Internet criminals, ransomware actors, and international organized crime.

Early law enforcement use of sock puppets was featured on the primetime TV circuit with shows like *To Catch a Predator*. An NBC *Dateline* show featured host Chris Hansen, alongside law enforcement, pretending to be a child online and luring would-be adult predators to meet, where they were subsequently arrested. Hansen continued this mission long after *Predator* was off the air, founding a streaming service called TruBlu, where he carried out a similar playbook on the web series *The Takedown*. He received eight Emmy awards for this work.

Regional municipal police continue this practice throughout the world. I read a headline in the town where I live just last week where the county sheriff's office arrested someone under the same formula.

Law enforcement's tactical use of personas played a key role in one of the most famous Internet busts ever, the Silk Road takedown in 2013. The FBI and its partner agencies used sock puppets to make illicit purchases, gain trust, and eventually uncover the intelligence that led to the arrest of the Silk Road's founder, Ross Ulbricht. Likewise, Operation Pacifier used sock puppets to infiltrate Playpen, a child exploitation site. The sock puppets gained the trust of Playpen's users and culminated in many arrests, saving countless lives.

GroupSense made its mark on child trafficking in our early days when we developed and taught a course for what is now known as the Mercyhurst School of Intelligence, Computing, and Global Politics. Mercyhurst is well known for turning out high-quality intelligence professionals, many of whom end up working in the federal intelligence community (IC). In our nascent days, we partnered with the school and a nonprofit that would use intelligence tools and some of our collected data to identify and save child trafficking victims.

These strategies and complexities have also cross-pollinated into law enforcement investigations. Of course, using personas and sock puppets in law enforcement investigations is mired in legal challenges. Among these are entrapment concerns and Fourth Amendment issues. Entrapment is defined as when the government induces someone to commit a criminal act who was not predetermined to commit the act in the first place. In sex trafficking cases, it is often clear that the person was attending the chat or the forum with the intention of committing the crime. Other matters are more murky. Even still, the Fourth Amendment's purpose of protecting U.S. citizens from unreasonable searches has a clause that affords the citizen a "reasonable right to privacy." In the case of sock puppet spying, the question of whether or not the threat actors had a reasonable expectation of privacy arises. If so, a warrant—similar to a wiretap—would be required to make that material admissible in a courtroom. These concerns have fostered a set of standard operating procedures for law enforcement around the use of sock puppets, dictating how they should be developed and used, recorded, and managed. These processes are aimed at ethics, protecting the civil rights of the forum members, and strictly maintaining the chain of custody should the investigation land in a courtroom. I further address this in Chapter 6, "How Not to Go to Jail, Hell, or Worse."

There have been a number of cases where law enforcement's use of sock puppets has gone awry, including Operation Pacifier and *To Catch a Predator*. In Operation Pacifier, the FBI deployed a method referred to as a network investigation technique (NIT), in which the agency used false personas to operate the network in which the illegal activity took place. In this case, the NIT was the child exploitation site Playpen itself. During Operation Pacifier, the FBI operated Playpen for almost two weeks, allowing thousands of users to access its illicit content. This became a legal issue when it came to prosecution. In one unfortunate case in *To Catch a Predator*, a target of the investigation died by suicide when learning of the operation targeting him. His family pressed charges against the organizations involved.

Of course, these ethics extend to those of us in the cyber espionage space. Any organization actively facilitating a sock puppet operation should develop clear operating procedures and ethics rules. Also, a "north star" must be developed to keep the use of the sock puppets on track. This means that the use of these personas must be driven by a clear mission with clear desired outcomes. Sock puppets are tools for a specific business operation, not toys. Cyber espionage is not a game. For example, while entrapment is primarily related to law enforcement activity, a variation of entrapment can occur in the private sector. If, hypothetically, the mission of the organization operating the sock puppets is to uncover any stolen or leaked data related to a particular customer, it would be unwise for the sock puppet to ask other forum actors questions like "Do you have any data from company Y?" This is because at the moment the question is asked, the forum actor may not have that data. Yet, the mere act of asking for it could incentivize the actor to seek it out, potentially illegally. Some considerations for operating procedures for the commercial use of sock puppets include the following:

Clear Legal Guidelines   The operators must be trained in the legal boundaries for operating clandestine personas. This will vary from country to country and, since the Internet is not bound by regional boundaries, can be one of the more challenging elements.

Risk of Entrapment or Facilitating a Crime   As with the previous example, the operators must understand where the line is for collecting information from their targets. Clear examples must be given of what is right and wrong. This is especially important when dealing with public sector clients.

Ethical Responsibility   The concepts under this directive should be derived from the core values of the organization. The north star of the mission will play a role here in keeping the practitioners on the right track. If possible, an ethics review team should be assembled to spot-check engagement activity and provide tactical feedback for the overall team.

Terms of Service Adherence   This is a tough one to navigate. Each one of the properties that are being infiltrated and acted upon will have their own terms of service. If the data, information, or conversations collected from any given property are intended to be used for legal prosecution purposes, the adherence to the property's terms of service will be extremely relevant. In the real world, these are often overlooked or conveniently ignored by many practitioners, especially when it comes to social media collection. Furthermore, many of the forums will have terms against automated collection or scraping. (Not to mention sophisticated tools to prevent it.) While in general practice, skirting the terms of service of a given source is often benign, it becomes tangible in a courtroom.

AllForUSA, the SHARKS Report, and the Bill of Rights

Our data collection surrounding illegal dark net activities, enabled by carefully crafted personas, also played a role in global politics and disinformation campaigns. The *Washington Post*'s piece called

"The strange birth, death, and rebirth of a Russian troll account called 'AllForUSA'" (August 10, 2018) captured our research and discovery of a multimillion persona network composed of orphaned accounts that were used to spread disinformation and misinformation online.

Orphaned accounts are defined as accounts with access to specific networks or systems but no longer controlled by an active owner. This happens when an employee leaves an organization, and the account is not fully or accurately de-provisioned. It also happens when someone passes away but their accounts are not shut down. The value of the use of orphaned accounts is their history; the account has the age and activity needed for true legitimacy, and it still appears as a real person.

The AllForUSA research culminated in a report called "The SHARKS Report," published by GroupSense in 2018. Our team's curiosity was piqued after reading the indictment illustrating the Russian misinformation campaigns aimed at manipulating the U.S. 2016 elections put forward by Special Counsel Robert S. Mueller III. The SHARKS Report continued to pull on the thread highlighted in the *Washington Post* article. Ultimately, our investigation unearthed a network of roughly 4.7 million orphaned accounts that were repurposed by threat actors to create false Internet content. The content spanned from social media activity to thousands of computer-generated comments on the Federal Communications Commission's website attempting to sway the agency's ruling on net neutrality.

In the cybersecurity space, it is widely known that false personas and sock puppets have been used to proliferate misinformation and disinformation online. Often, these puppets can be attributed to nation-state activity with political motivations. The nation-state uses puppets or false accounts to influence a particular political process or to shape a particular public perception of a specific issue. Through our research during the SHARKS investigation, GroupSense was able to loosely tie the orphaned account army to the Russian Internet Research Agency (IRA), which, of course, was operating the AllForUSA Yahoo account.

In addition to the IRA's activity undermining the 2016 elections, we have seen a number of other sophisticated campaigns utilizing sock puppets for misinformation and disinformation. These include the COVID-19 misinformation campaigns attributed to multiple nation-states, including Russia and China. While the American public is most familiar with the campaigns targeting our institutions, these operations have targeted other elections and institutions around the world, including in Ukraine, Syria, Moldova, Saudi Arabia, and China. Their strategies have run the gamut from false flag activities and distraction or smoke screens to false narratives and harassment of dissidents and political opponents. This militarization of sock puppets is shaping the future of information warfare and adding to the complexity of navigating the online experience for everyone.

The concept of core values and a North Star are respectable approaches to keeping the collective organization on track when it comes to cyber espionage and research. Just the same, these things can be used to justify risky behavior. I have had the fortune to work with some of the best and mission-driven cyber espionage practitioners in the world for more than a decade. I can confidently say that a sense of purpose burns inside each of these people. They wake up each day with the singular goal of making the world a better, safer place for the rest of us. As you can imagine, a team of espionage professionals spend much of their time in and on some of the darkest parts of the digital world, and it can be difficult for them to become aware of evil things and not take immediate action. Working in service of their core mission, they will see myriad wrongs in the margins on a daily basis. The organization has to create clear guidelines on how to handle this. I can confidently state that telling the team to ignore these things is not a good option; they will not be able to do so and must have an outlet for or a handoff to those with whose mission it aligns. In our case, throughout the years, we have partnered with a number of law enforcement agencies and nonprofit organizations to pass the baton on non-core mission evils we come across. These partnerships have resulted in some of the most fulfilling and proud actions in which the company has been involved. From dismantling child exploitation networks to sending a SWAT team to kick in the door of a sex trafficking operation, GroupSense has secretly made an impact on many lives.

These partnerships and the outcomes they produce hopefully mitigate the tempting vigilante actions of the practitioners. The organization also has to honor and stand by its core values. In some cases, this may mean forgoing revenue to do the right thing.

In one case, we were offered a contract to provide our VIP monitoring service for a particular celebrity team. The lucrative contract would have GroupSense focus on the social media activity around the celebrities on the team and provide advisory and mitigating steps in our portal to the parent organization. As with all of our customer engagements, we sat down with the client to develop the PIRs related to the mission. It was quickly apparent that the mission was not to protect the celebrities but to restrict their First Amendment rights. The performance targeted team had recently been contracted to perform for a polarizing figure and had expressed their distaste for the engagement. The parent organization wanted GroupSense to monitor and alert on their online activity. We subsequently canceled the engagement.

Examples of adherence to core values at the executive level, especially when choosing the right thing over revenue, send a clear message to the broader team about who the organization is and what it stands for.

Since I am pontificating on the team aspects of running a digital espionage business, I would be remiss if I did not discuss mental health. As stated earlier, the teams involved in this business constantly observe evil acts and communicate directly with evil actors. While this might seem like fun in practice, over time, such activities can tax the human psyche and culminate in tangible negative outcomes for the practitioners and their families. Therefore, it is incumbent upon the organization to create a safe space for communicating these challenges and, if financially feasible, some subsidized mental health programs for the team. Further, a flexible work schedule and time-off policy for the analysts and research teams will yield positive benefits for both the individuals and the company. GroupSense has implemented much of this, but often, our team members—mission-driven as they are—do not take time off. Sometimes, our team leads have had to resort to mandating time off. Taking care of our people and enabling them to nurture their own humanity plays into my core values—as well as those of the company: Do the right thing.

The proliferation of sock puppet use and cyber espionage across all areas of the deep and dark web, social media, chat platforms, and the metaverse have given birth to a set of tools and practices in an effort to mitigate their use. A Google search for *sock puppets* will yield a series of guides for their creation, management, and detection. However, never forget that the target threat actors are aware of this paradigm and have developed tools to defend themselves from cyber espionage.

Manual Collection

There are cases where we need to infiltrate a new source and gather the data from that source immediately. We developed a browser plug-in for these cases that connects back to our Tracelight platform.

An analyst may interact with another threat actor through a sock puppet account when the threat actor sends a direct message to the sock puppet, directing them to another dark web property or forum. If the platform is not automatically collecting that forum, the analyst can collect the forum data while doing the initial forum research using the browser plug-in. The plug-in does almost everything the platform scraper would do. As the analyst browses the site, the plug-in can capture all of the web code and screenshots, sending the data back to the platform for analysis. After familiarizing themselves with the new dark web property, the analyst can decide whether that property should be in the Tracelight automated collection. The browser plug-in data can then be used to create the configuration file for the scraper for that site.

The other use of the plug-in is tactical. Analysts responding to requests for intelligence (RFIs) engage in tactical investigations for their clients. The plug-in allows them to capture data from sites related to the investigation that may not be appropriate for automated collection. Again, the data is then stored on the platform for later analysis and can be referenced from the resulting RFI report.

GroupSense built our own custom plug-in, but there are a number of open source and for-fee tools that can accomplish these use cases. Authentic8 Silo has some of these features as well.

Wholesale Collection

A number of companies offer wholesale access to the dark web and chat channels via an enterprise API. In fact, some of the commercial threat intel and digital risk platforms simply subscribe to these feeds rather than build their own collection infrastructure. Large enterprises with mature intelligence programs may also use these wholesale dark web feeds in their security operations center. The benefit is full access to the dataset for any number of use cases involving investigations or correlation with attack indicators of compromise (IOCs). However, this can be prohibitively expensive for most companies due to the cost of the wholesale API and the infrastructure and software required to digest and analyze it.

The wholesalers give a comprehensive view into the basic dark web properties but often are slow or miss the specialized forums, especially those that are difficult to infiltrate.

Recently, a handful of focused Telegram wholesalers surfaced. As more platforms are created, more focused collections will likely be created.

There are many benefits to outsourcing the collection and collection management and the advanced intelligence operations to a threat intelligence vendor or a digital risk solutions provider unless your enterprise has the resources to run a full intelligence program and can accept the risks around threat actor engagement.

Wrapping Up

Artificial intelligence has made leaps in the last couple of years and contributes to the efficacy of cyber offense and cyber defense strategies. It is only a matter of time before AI is instrumentally impacting cyber espionage and the use of sock puppets. As of this writing, the use of AI is nascent in cyber espionage. The art of operating a sock puppet remains the tip of the spear for intelligence collection, requiring traditional HUMINT skills and a human being . . . for now.

If you do one thing after reading this chapter, it should be to familiarize yourself with the use of sock puppets at the enterprise level. Attempt to understand their uses in social engineering, corporate espionage, and brand defamation and damage. Consider using brand monitoring and digital risk platforms to mitigate those risks and educate your teams about misinformation and disinformation practices.

Cyber Recon Leader Profile:

Steve Ocepek

Current Role: Managing Director, Kroll

Other Affiliations: Volunteer, Akron STEM, Western Reserve House; musician and drummer

Steve's Bio

Steve Ocepek is a seasoned cybersecurity expert with a knack for blending technical prowess with an entrepreneurial spirit. With five patents under his belt, Steve co-founded WholePoint Corp. in 2001, pioneering network access control (NAC) technologies. His journey led him to Trustwave's SpiderLabs, where he expanded their capabilities by founding the SpiderLabs Research division, focusing on threat intelligence and malware analysis.

Steve's expertise has made him a sought-after speaker at major conferences like RSA and Black Hat. At Black Hat USA 2012, he served as the Senior Security Research Manager for Trustwave's SpiderLabs division, leading advanced security teams in penetration testing and incident response.

Beyond the corporate realm, Steve is passionate about education. He volunteers at Akron STEM High School, where he helps teach cybersecurity as a sport, engaging students by framing hacking exercises as competitive challenges.

Steve's Mission

Sitting down with people and listening has brought about more powerful change than hours of coding, writing, or making slides. I used to think about the world's problems as a series of obstacles that were all solvable by technology. Today I believe technology is the least of our issues: ensuring wholeness and preparedness in the person, and simplicity in the process. I've had some hospital time, thinking about the vast knowledge we all acquire, how fragile that is, how much it needs to be shared to benefit our fellow travelers. From experience, knowledge wants not only to be free, but to be taught and held dear. To know this is true, teach a new trick or skill to a good friend and watch them light up. These are precious times together.

There's a path like this in security. Computing at its core is fascinating if we teach it right, and there are more hacking-focused courses and materials than ever before. Why is it still so hard? They need a bridge. They need you and me to invite them in, sit down with them, tell them, "It was hard for me, too," and "This is how I got started."

YouTube, LLC

YouTube URL: www.youtube.com/watch?v=H61OMe-UtX4

Chapter 4
Whodat?

"Do you want us to call him and tell him to delete it?" I asked.

"Wait, what? Are you serious?" My friend and former colleague, astonished and bewildered, continued, "You can just call them up?"

"Yes. Well... one of them. The boss."

A week prior, a friend phoned me in a panic. His SaaS software company received an email from a stranger claiming to have access to their customer's data. The extortionists said that for a "consulting fee," they would tell my colleague how they came upon the data and would delete it. The email included a sample of the data, which seemed to reflect a credible threat. I asked if they knew from where that data may have been taken. They had ideas, but nothing conclusive. I offered to run one of our attack surface tools, FirstRecon, against the company to see if we could locate the hole. FirstRecon uses advanced OSINT techniques to discover an organization's digital footprint, a complete picture of its online assets and intellectual property. An hour later, we were on the phone with a smoking gun. There was a developer test network on Amazon Advanced Web Services (AWS). An S3 bucket was open to the public; in most cases it wouldn't have been that big of a deal, as the test data is not supposed to contain real customer data. In this case, someone neglected to read the policy documentation and used *actual* customer data in the developer test network. Using the data from the FirstRecon report, they identified the culprit and subsequently closed the hole.

> "What do we do about the extortion email?" my friend asked.
> "Do you want us to call him and tell him to delete it?" I asked in return.

The small world we operate in seemingly gets smaller rather than the other way around. The "boss" of the extortionists was from Belarus; let's call him Fred. Until most recently, Fred was a student at a U.S. university and made a name for himself in the security research community due to some strong content on cyber attribution on his personal blog. He was wrapping up his university studies and contacted us about doing some contract work. Excited to collaborate with Fred, we inked a contract and put him on a cyber counterintelligence mission.

A few months into our business relationship, he told us that he needed to find a full-time position that would sponsor his U.S. work visa. Despite his clear talent, our board and advisers had some concerns about accommodating Fred, including the cost. We politely declined, and our paths diverged. Fred ultimately returned to Belarus.

Shortly after the start of Russia's invasion of Ukraine in February 2022, we received a Telegram message from Fred. He asked if we could give him access to Telegram channels related to the war effort. He needed to communicate with some border guards about friends getting into Belarus. Based on our prior working relationship, we obliged.

Fred was the "boss" of the extortionists.

I reached out to him and asked, "Fred, can you do me a favor, bud? Your talented team reached out to this company via email about some data. I need you to let this one go."

"No problem," he said. Needless to say, Fred deleted the data, and the company got out of digital jail for free that day.

It is easy to dehumanize our cyber adversaries. They are far away and have very little in common with us. But 100 percent of the time, they are *human beings*. They come from somewhere. They have families, friends, and goals. This is the sole basis on which we can reason with them and negotiate. As practitioners, we have to understand and empathize. Their world perspective, values, and history are much different from ours. In order to engage them effectively, we have to get in their heads and walk in their shoes.

The lens through which many Americans see cyberthreat actors is distorted by television and pop culture. The term "hackers," when used in derogatory parlance, embodies an image of a young kid in the family home, perhaps in the basement, sitting behind a screen and drinking Red Bull. Maybe we visualize them wearing a hoodie (hood on, of course—*why?*). We assume this person is bored, mischievous, and talented with technology. Some of these tropes can be true but often miss the proverbial mark.

Instead, we are most often dealing with a business operation in which the perpetrator reports to an office—perhaps wearing an untucked (designer) dress shirt, a knock-off timepiece, and a pair of fashionable basketball shoes. They sit at a desk or a table next to a dozen other similarly dressed individuals, all focused on multiple screens. They might have a whiteboard with a thermometer drawn on it, reflecting the income they have brought in as a team that week, with a prize written near the top of the thermometer. If the thermometer is colored all the way in, they win. They arrived by train at the "office" that day, but plan to get there in a new car next week. They took this "job" because their friend told them how easy it was to make money. Despite their limited experience with "hacking," they were given a guidebook, attended a training course, and supplied with a series of software tools and playbooks. The "job" is fun and rewarding. Their victims—ahem—customers are not only far away but can survive the impact. Plus they *deserve* what happens to them (more on this later).

This is not news. Professional criminal profiler Mark T. Hofman presents this concept brilliantly in his widely viewed 2021 TEDx talk "Profiling Hackers: The Psychology of Cybercrime," in which the picture of the cliche' hoodie-wearing hacker at keyboard illustration morphs into a picture of a professional call center.

(For a transcript of Mark's talk, visit www.ted.com/talks/mark_t_hoffmann_profiling_hackers_the_psychology_of_cybercrime/transcript.)

The societal elixir whetting the palate for not only illicit activity like cybercrime but *organized* illicit cybercriminal activity has been on happy hour in a number of nation-states for years. The United Nations Office on Drugs and Crime (UNODC) claims there are a few key factors that drive organized criminal activity. These factors indicate a broader societal situation driven by economic, education, and governance gaps in a given state. The UNODC's research claims that failing or weak states can foster an environment in which organized crime can flourish. Weak does not necessarily mean weak militarily, but rather weak institutionally, possibly due to high levels of corruption. Many of the states from which organized cybercrime emanates fit this definition squarely. Further, certain states either sponsor or provide immunity to their domestic cybercriminal contingents. Russia is well known for permitting cybercriminal gangs to act with impunity so long as their targets are not Russian or Russian-friendly. Belarus, Moldova, Romania, Serbia, and parts of Ukraine are similar.

While Russia claims plausible deniability with regard to cybercriminal attacks on Western countries, other countries like Iran, China, and North Korea have been training cyber armies for decades. These perpetrators are not wearing fashionable shoes or timepieces. They don't get a prize when they succeed. They are uniformed, firearm-wielding, enlisted military servants of their country. Their mission may differ, but the impact on the U.S. economy and national security is measurable. Adding to the severity of the threat, these attackers have the full support of their nation-state and its resources behind them. China's cyber mission is known to be multifaceted and includes cyber espionage in an effort to gain intellectual property and military-related secrets, laying the groundwork for cyber war against our critical infrastructure. North Korea's efforts are largely financial in nature, while Iran's are idealistic.

Regardless of motivation, the West and especially the United States are prime targets for myriad well-resourced cyber groups that have no regard for our well-being. Paradoxically, this is precisely why we, as cyber espionage experts, need to be empathetic toward *them*. To do this, we must shift our lens to see the world from their perspective. In this chapter, I will focus on cybercriminals specifically, taking into consideration the simple directive of the military adversary.

We live in an echo chamber. In the U.S., our day-to-day activities, lifestyle, and cadence are normal to us. The U.S., unlike many other countries, has been relatively stable for a century. This has fostered feelings of collective safety and abundance. The American Dream, while not pursued by every citizen to success, is, at a minimum, assumed possible. While imperfect, our institutions are largely transparent and accessible to the average person. If you are reading this book, you likely have at least a high school diploma, perhaps some college or a higher education degree. You have a car, a roof over your head, and career plans. You may even have a 401k, IRA, and some cash in the bank. You are safe. Many of us take these things for granted. It is not the case in much of the world to have any or all of these things. As a result, citizens of other countries may have a very different perspective on day-to-day life, right and wrong, and the world itself. This is the worldview that we must understand to put ourselves in the heads and walk in the shoes of foreign cybercriminals in order to better protect ourselves.

Before digging into undercover operations and the science of criminal profiling, let's agree on the obvious state of things. We in the West are partially responsible for the situation we are in. We continue deprioritizing personal cybersecurity, oversimplifying world politics, exalting extravagance, and flaunting wealth. Exposure to Western culture via television, movies, and music in Russia and Eastern Europe codifies the impression that the average U.S. citizen has more than they need. The result is generations of people who are indifferent to the economic impact of cybercrime on the United States and to its citizens. Further, we have developed and recklessly set loose or lost control of a cache of sophisticated cyber weapons that not only paint the U.S. as a cyber aggressor but that have aided in arming our opponents.

Early attackers were largely motivated by ego and curiosity, but threat actor motivations have shifted over time, culminating in today's chaotic cyberattack landscape. The paradigm shift to financially motivated crimes accelerated along with dark web technology and cryptocurrency infrastructures. Sure, there were financially motivated crimes going back decades, but the difficulty in obfuscation and payment made them unscalable. For example, early versions of ransomware involved shipping floppy disks to the victims. When the curious recipient inserted the drives, an autorun would execute the malware, locking their machine. The demand was for some amount of money via a money order sent to Panama or a similar place. As connectivity, privacy technologies, and blockchain technology developed, the move to financial-driven cybercrime followed. Ubiquitous and gratuitous connectivity made it inexpensive and efficient to spread malware. Dark web technologies like TOR made it possible to attack with impunity and invisibility. Blockchain and cryptocurrency have made it possible to transfer seemingly limitless amounts of money across international borders with ease. As with most technology, our laws, law enforcement activities, and defense lagged behind cybercriminals in terms of sophistication and attack volume. Further, mirroring kinetic criminal patterns, the aforementioned unstable environments fostered the organization of the criminal effort.

So here we are, facing literal armies of sophisticated cyber adversaries hiding behind privacy technologies (which we developed) and stealing millions of dollars' worth of cryptocurrency daily. Dazed and confused, victims look to law enforcement and the government for support, but virtually none is offered or available. The onus, then, is on the cybersecurity practitioners—us. As we discussed in previous chapters, understanding with whom we are dealing is fundamental to developing a defensive (and offensive) strategy. Strategic infiltration of the adversary continues to enable the most effective undercover operations. Spies, law enforcement agencies, and a new cadre of commercial cyber sleuths cleverly *become* their adversaries.

Years ago, when I was pulled into what would become a specialized niche in the incident response space, ransomware response, I realized I had a gift for understanding my opponent. Of course, I did not yet have the background or the in-depth knowledge of the attacker ecosystem, but I did feel like I knew them. In my first cases, I found myself discussing with the threat actors the effort that they put into the attack. We discussed the value of the data they exfiltrated and the cost of the disruption. To me, they saw that they had made an investment, and they wanted a return on that investment. In an effort to build rapport and trust, I acknowledged their skill and effort. I assured them that we—myself and the victim organization I was representing—did not take their skills or effort for granted. Over days, I could build a casual relationship with the attackers and reason with them. My first cases saw ransoms reduced from seven figures to low six or high five-figure settlements.

Over time, the opponents became more organized, systematic, and cold. They realized they were up against professional negotiators and, in this next iteration of ransomware, began to form cyber gangs. They became more quantitative in nature and used business speak in their messages, some of which almost comically parroted legal documents ("WHEREIN" or "THEREFORE"). In those cases, I used the same language and logic to make my argument. I referred to legal agreements and financial statements and explained the concept of margin and profit and loss (P&L) to successfully and reliably drive ransom payments down. When the ransomware gang would ask for a ridiculous starting number, assuming that the opposition would immediately resort to cliche positional bargaining to drive the settlement to a higher mutually agreed middle number, I pushed back. I questioned their rationale for the sticker price, one time asking, "How did you come up with $25 million?" When they came back and stated they understood my client's financial capabilities, I also challenged that.

When one ransomware attacker claimed to have insight into the financial documents of their victim—my client—I called their bluff, saying, "With due respect, perhaps you have your files mixed up. If you had looked at our financials, you would never have asked for such an unreasonable number."

These tools continue to work with many groups to this day, but in other cases, the actors make so much money they can afford to "let them burn." This fosters an environment where the actors can set quotas and thresholds and toe a hard line. Further, some groups have announced on their blogs that if they find out they are dealing with professional negotiators, they will delete the decryption keys and immediately dump any exfiltrated data. This forces the responders to remain clandestine, pretending to be a member of the victim's staff and varying or obfuscating negotiation tools and tactics. Still, I have, on occasion, been identified by a ransomware group while negotiating, particularly the "repeat customers." It is not uncommon for members of my negotiation team to be dealing with the same cybercriminals across multiple victims. As you can imagine, this makes it difficult to use particular playbooks or psychological tools. This occurred in a case that was being litigated while I was writing this book; the threat actor group Akira stated in a message, "We know who you are, and we know your tricks." I ignored the comment and continued as if they said nothing of the sort, successfully concluding the negotiation.

Why and how have I executed these successful negotiations with confidence is because I remember that in the end we are still dealing with human beings. Human beings, organized or not, have predictable behaviors. I am not claiming to be some kind of psychological ninja. We all have the tools to do what I do and we have been practicing and honing those skills since we left our mothers' womb. Some of us are better at this than others, while others have attempted to build science and rigor around identifying and classifying bad actors in an effort to predict future behaviors.

Without question, there is a benefit to better understanding these actors and why they do what they do. Profiling has been a fundamental part of criminal prediction and investigation for nearly a century, but like much of the rest of law enforcement, it has not kept up with the times. The first versions of profiling date back as far as 1888, when a police surgeon developed a basic profile of Jack the Ripper. The FBI's establishment of the Behavioral Science Unit in 1972 paved the way for modern criminal profiling. The Bureau implemented a system of psychological and behavioral analysis to determine the past and future behaviors of murderers and other baddies. However, academic research on criminal profiling didn't really take off until the 1990s and 2000s. Research at that time incorporated information like geographic profiling and statistical data into the profiling process. Contemporary approaches began to use technology, including early versions of machine learning and AI, to perform modeling and predictive analysis in the late 2000s, efforts that continue today.

Regardless of technological advancement, criminal profiling is based on some fundamentally agreed principles. These principles are that evidence at crime scenes, such as how a particular crime is carried out, can provide insight into the psychological traits of the criminal who committed the crime. When you combine this with the "consistency hypothesis" that criminals have repeated patterns of behavior in both the crimes they commit and in their regular lives, you can then predict their behavior. The behavior pattern could be used to predict behavior but could also be used to identify the criminal at large. Several different approaches to profiling were developed through years of experimentation and academic research:

Deductive Profiling This is based on basic crime scene investigative evidence. What happened at the crime scene? What evidence was left behind? What can we deduce from that evidence?

Inductive Profiling This technique uses analytical data from previous crimes to determine what may have occurred at the current crime scene.

Geographic Profiling This is sometimes combined with the previous methods, and uses spatial data to determine the criminals' behavior.

Clinical Profiling This involves using psychological evaluations of criminal suspects to identify the offender(s).

While relatively little scientific work has been done that focuses on cybercriminal profiling, the work that has been documented largely revolves around a few key profiling elements. *Victimology* is gaining an understanding of the criminal's behavior and lifestyle. Criminology focuses on the *modus operandi* (M.O.) of the criminal. Profiling *analysis* in criminology looks for patterns or signatures in the crime itself, and *typologies* determine the actor's psychological profile and whether they acted alone or in a group.

The 2008 publication *Profiling Hackers: The Science of Criminal Profiling as Applied to the World of Hacking*, written by Raoul Chiesa, an alleged former black hat hacker, attempts to put scientific rigor behind cybercriminal profiling. Together with authors Stefania Ducci of Counter Human Trafficking and Emerging Crimes Unit at the United Nations Interregional Crime and Justice Research Institute (UNICRI) and Silvio Ciappi of The University of Pisa, Chiesa not only digs into the history and science of profiling but also conducts extensive interviews with alleged hackers in an attempt to apply these techniques. This book is a culmination of the efforts of the Hacker Profiling Project (HPP), a project whose mission matches its name. Among its objectives, the HPP planned to open source its tools and findings for use in cybersecurity log analysis and other investigative initiatives.

While now technologically dated, the book provides interesting analysis and insight into hackers' minds. I applaud its spirit, but the cybercriminal landscape has shifted in the 15 years since its publication.

Through its investigation of the hacker personality, the book attempts to categorize or label hackers. The categories are as follows:

- Wannabe lamer
- Script kiddie
- The "37337 *(did they mean 31337?)* K-rAd iRC #hack 0-day exploitz" guy
- Cracker
- Ethical hacker
- Quiet, paranoid, and skilled hacker

- Cyber-warrior
- Industrial spy
- Government agent

Without getting into the attributes that make these categories, or disputing the categories themselves, I propose that these are actually subcategories of the opponents we face today. I am not an academic researcher, social scientist, or psychologist, so I cannot debate or reframe their assessments with authority. Regardless, I believe that if those categories are remotely accurate, they roll up into a much smaller subset of actors today. Those are:

- Professional penetration testers
- Hacktivists
- Freelancers
- Organized criminals
- Nation-state actors

Freelancers are the most variable group. They may be exacting revenge, monetizing their hacking (seeking bug bounties or monetizing illicit activity), or simply hackers in the traditional curious sense.

Another challenge with "profiling hackers" is that much of the information on hackers was collected through surveys. This poses two challenges for the application of the findings: First, is the kind of cybercriminal who will willingly fill out a survey representative of the greater population? And second, in practice, we are not able to send our adversaries a survey to get our arms around their psychology and motivation. We have log files and cyber intelligence and have to back into the science from the evidence.

Another limitation of the surveys is global participation. The book states it represents a "truly global view," which may have been true in 2008. Today, however, the bulk of cybercriminal attacks emanate from unfriendly countries such as Russia, China, and Iran. The participation in the HPP surveys listed one participant from Russia and none from China or Iran. As a point of reference, there were 80 from the United States.

While it is difficult to determine whether the project was a success, the information the project and the book provided is useful, if not entertaining. I enjoyed reading the interviews and survey responses from the alleged black hat hackers. Unfortunately, as of the writing of this book, the UNICRI page for the Hacker Profiling Project is unavailable.

Other research has been done but has used many of the same methods and thus has similar limitations. These include academic papers like "Psychological profiling of hackers via machine learning toward sustainable cybersecurity," by Mema Hani, Osama Sohaib, Khalid Khan, Asma Aleidi, and Noman Islam (College of Computing and Information Sciences, Karachi Institute of Economics and Technology, School of Business, American University of Ras Al Khaimah, Department of Computer Science, University of Technology Sydney, College of Humanities and Social Sciences, Libraries and Information Department, Princess Nourah Bint Abdulrahman University, respectively) and cybersecurity research papers like "Profiling Hackers," by Larisa Long for the SANS Institute. I am encouraged that we continue to push the boundaries of this discipline. Perhaps we can now push it into the dark web; stay tuned for that development.

> Read the papers mentioned here on the web: Use www.frontiersin.org/journals/computer-science/articles/10.3389/fcomp.2024.1381351/full for "psychological profiling" and www.sans.org/white-papers/33864 for "profiling hackers."

As I stated earlier, we cannot issue surveys to our attackers easily, so research of this nature remains difficult because *attribution* is difficult. While I applaud attempts to quantify the research into objective and concrete tools that would allow a practitioner to identify a particular pattern in a log file and predict behavior, this doesn't sound new. It sounds a lot like tactics, techniques, and procedures (TTPs).

Profiling actors utilizing cyberattack evidence and TTPs diverges from traditional criminal profiling for a number of reasons. Identifying a human being and understanding their psychology through TTPs looks more quantitative and systematic than reality. I believe this is where the cyber landscape is particularly different from our kinetic approaches. For example, in the case of a kinetic homicide, the perpetrator has a limited number of tools and methods available to them, it is difficult to obfuscate their participation in the crime, and they have a limited set of motives. In the cyber world, the attacker has anonymity, a much larger toolset, and their motives are difficult to differentiate. The concept of cyberattack tools and frameworks presents another problem in that they are programmatic in their use. When we begin to analyze threat actors via log files and TTP evidence, there is a commoditization effect, further obscuring the threat actor or threat actor group. For example, a number of years ago, a researcher could relatively easily identify a particular ransomware group based on their locker malware. At that time, many groups used proprietary versions of these. Now, groups like Black Basta (a spin-off of Conti) use a number of lockers and change up the lockers frequently. As the groups disband and reform, they take a particular codebase with them, then slightly modify and redeploy it. Further, some groups (Lockbit, Conti) have had their codebase leaked. These codebases were then effectively open sourced to the ransomware community. All of these factors contribute to the difficulty of identifying actor groups or specific actors in order to profile them.

The origin of the TTP concept originates from—surprise!—the military. The U.S. Army is said to have popularized the acronym, yet long before the letters were assigned, military practitioners were taking inventory of how their opponents behaved in an effort to predict future behavior. These observations were documented and also used to inform the military budget allocations and defense strategy, among other things—in other words (or fewer of them) intelligence.

Identifying individual threat actors in an effort to predict future behavior using TTPs is challenging. This is because threat actors use many of the same tools and TTPs in their attacks, making it difficult to differentiate between given actors. Connecting behavioral science to TTP activity could provide the answer.

Formal scientific methods aside, it appears that those of us in the cyber intelligence space have been performing cybercriminal profiling for decades, somewhat successfully, too. Take a look at any cyber intelligence report from Mandiant, Intel471, or GroupSense, and you will be flooded with context about various actors and actor groups. These reports will then deduce from these attributes, tools, motivations, and past behaviors how the threat actor may continue to act and, therefore, how grave the threat may be.

This is also evident in many of the common security frameworks. The MITRE ATT&CK framework structures TTP approaches very well. The framework aims to improve the cyber posture of a given organization by providing both a common nomenclature for TTPs and a structured method of mapping the TTPs to a given environment. ATT&CK was developed using real-world attacker tools and behaviors and referencing those behaviors against vulnerable systems. From Windows to an array of common operating systems and industrial control systems (ICSs), MITRE ATT&CK is evolving to be a credible standard for applying TTP intelligence.

> For more information, visit MITRE at https://attack.mitre.org.

The 2023 CISA guide, "Best Practices for MITRE ATT&CK Mapping" (see www.cisa.gov/sites/default/files/2023-01/Best%20Practices%20for%20MITRE%20ATTCK%20Mapping.pdf), gets straight to the point. In the section "Mapping MITRE ATT&CK into Finished Reports," the mapping steps are as follows:

1. Find the behavior.
2. Research the behavior.
3. Translate the behavior to a tactic.

4. Identify the technique that applies to the behavior.
5. Identify the sub-techniques.
6. Compare results to those of other analysts.

Before digging into how to improve threat actor profiling, let's quickly cover what makes good analysis. This is necessary because of the difficulty in accurate attribution in digital forensic—based evidence. In Jon DiMaggio's book *The Art of Cyberwarfare*, he explains the pitfalls of poor analysis discipline and structure, particularly regarding attribution. After making a strong case about why misattribution is dangerous, he drives home the need for structure. In this case, he utilizes an "attribution quadrant" tool for which the percentage of confidence in the attribution increases as he checks off quantitative items within it. Later in this chapter, the need for peer review and the risk of cognitive bias are discussed. These are solid points and common mistakes made by even the most seasoned threat intel practitioners—thus, the need for frameworks and structure.

The pitfalls I've outlined are pervasive in a typical analyst's work product. The best analysts assume nothing and search for quantitative correlated proof of every finding. To accomplish this, *great* analysts

- Have clearly defined objectives (PIRs)
- Use a framework
- Work within the intelligence life cycle
- Document sources and source credibility
- Question assumptions
- Correlate across multiple sources and disciplines
- Utilize peer review and challenge perspectives
- Incorporate feedback mechanisms
- Practice a code of ethics

I applaud researchers and analysts who adhere to ethical principles in a world that seems to reward clicks and notoriety. I know a few people, including DiMaggio, who refuse to publish their work until it meets their rigorous standards. Likewise, I know researchers who are a little too quick to push the publish button. This is dangerous and irresponsible.

Mapping psychological profiling to MITRE ATT&CK is difficult due to the framework's focus on quantitative factors like TTPs. That said, you can impact the prioritization of the framework by mapping the TTPs and applying contextual knowledge of the threat actor, looking specifically at

- Motivations (financial gain, espionage, hacktivism)
- Capabilities (tools, infrastructure, skill level)
- Behavior patterns (preferred targets, typical operational procedures)
- Known campaigns (past attacks, attribution reports)

For example, if the threat actor (TA) uses PowerShell scripts for execution, map this to Execution/Command and Scripting Interpreter/PowerShell. Then, look at the motivations of known TAs who use that TTP and would *likely target* your organization because of politics or ideology. You may find a short list of actors that fit the bill. Take the additional TTPs from that list of actors and apply the appropriate defenses in good measure.

MITRE ATT&CK's lesser-known little brother, MITRE Engage (https://engage.mitre.org), maps out how to use deception and deception technology to learn more about adversaries. This can be a useful method for better understanding the attacker's TTPs.

The challenge remains to get our arms around the psychological attributes of a given attacker. Effective psychological profiling requires dialogue or conversations with the threat actor, not surveys. While imperfect, there is a way to bridge the gap between quantitative TTP analysis and traditional criminal psychological profiling for cybercriminals, and Adam Bregenzer may have stumbled into it.

Adam joined the team five years ago as GroupSense's CTO. Adam is a start-up veteran and previously worked for many fast-growing high-tech companies, the last of which was sold to PayPal. When Adam and I started talking about his joining GroupSense, he was most recently in charge of application development at Venmo.

Adam is good at large, complex datasets, and our data was certainly that. One of the first things Adam did when he came on board was to recategorize our datasets. He immediately began referring to the collection of dark web, open web forums, chatrooms, Telegram channels, and similar as *conversations*.

The dark web, illicit market activity, chatrooms, and channels serve as a nexus for profiling, while incident response investigations and traditional cyber intelligence provide the TTPs. The key is to tie the two together and use other online activities (like OSINT) as supporting evidence.

We can build on the traditional cybercriminal profiling assumption that humans are creatures of habit by appending the knowledge that they do what they know and repeat those actions. This behavior gives us a glimpse into probable future behavior. An effective model uses technology to collect and correlate data and conversations across myriad platforms. With any successful correlation and attribution, the platform can roll these conversations under a single threat actor persona. The conversation data is then joined with OSINT and breach data analysis.

It is most helpful to start with breach data analysis. Most breach datasets are not comprehensive enough, containing only the username, email, password, and/or password hash. This is because these are gathered for a singular use case, account takeover protection (ATO).

A comprehensive dataset will contain nearly all the data from the breach and can be leveraged in numerous use cases. The collection can include but is not limited to the following:

- Name
- First Name
- Last Name
- Username
- Address
- Street
- City
- State

- Country
- Zip
- SSN
- ID Number
- DL Number
- Password
- Password Hash
- IP Address used to access the breached property

GroupSense collects up to 26 different fields from each breach we ingest, allowing us to take advantage of many applications for cybersecurity beyond the typical account takeover protection. One of the most effective uses is pivoting through fields to identify additional handles, emails, or other indicators. For example, if BadActorA has a unique username, something like "SHN-92824," we will search the breach dataset for that handle. Maybe we don't find it in the username field, but we do find several breach records using that exact set of characters for a password. Some further digging into (again, for example) location data, IP data, or similar fields leads us to believe these email addresses in the breach also belong to BadActorA. (Bad actors are in breaches, too, you know?) We run those email addresses through our datasets as well, which might allow us to discover web activity by BadActorA, perhaps even identifying them on a particular forum, certain hobbyist sites, or social media. We now know much more about BadActorA *as a person*. Ultimately, we will have a collection of conversations, behaviors, indicators, and TTPs associated with BadActorA, all of which will become part of our TA Dossier.

The process looks roughly like this:

1. **Identify actor (group)**
    (a) **Assign identifier (ID):** A social media handle precedes a dark web handle. In either case, the property should be part of the ID, i.e., ACTORNAME-PROPERTY. If the actor is active in multiple properties, choose the property with the most activity for the ID.

(b) **Check breach data:** Take the known indicators and reference them against a comprehensive breach dataset. Grab all correlated additional indicators.

(c) **Correlate activity:** Under the assigned ID, correlate other online activity, including open web, forums, social media, dark web, and chat (Telegram and others).

(d) **Correlate and assign any communication identifiers:** This should include DM on platforms, email addresses exposed, and other chat-based systems used, like TOX or Jabber.

2. **Document actor activity** (using the previous indicators as seed)

    (a) Using intelligence tools, identify actor activity based on posts (or, if you have engaged the actor via DM, their conversations). Look for patterns. Patterns and artifacts to look for include but are not limited to

    - **Time of posts/comms:** While this can help identify regions/locations, many actors have unique time schedules when they are active. The most accurate region assignments can be done around every region or country-specific holidays, where the actors suddenly go quiet.
    - **Language use (dialect, language, or grammar style):** *Pay special attention to the time and the language used. This can be used to identify multiple actors behind a particular single moniker.* Also, using AI and open source tools, you can identify attributes of an actor or actor group.
    - **Activity purpose:** This is broad and subjective but can often include initial access advert, credential leak, malware broker, stolen data dump or sale, vulnerability exposure, hacktivist statements, etc. On the open web, assuming accurate correlated attribution, it can include hobbies, favorite foods, favorite music or bands.
    - **Group associations:** This could be particular hacktivist or hacker channels, race or political channels, or association with a particular ideology.

- **Direct message data:** If you are engaging with the threat actor, collect any direct message communications for analysis.
   (b) Take technical indicators and run them through OSINT.
   - Document all additional indicators generated by OSINT.
3. Using a text analysis tool (or generative AI), analyze the conversational data, dark web posts, forum activity, and chat dialogue for insights. The tools should be able to determine with some accuracy traits like demeanor, sex, age, sentiment, dialect or country of origin, native speaker or not, and high-level personality assessment.
4. Inventory any associated known technical TTPs for the TA.
5. The combination of language analysis, behavioral observations, associations, indicators, and TTPs make up the TA dossier.

Below is a rough example of how this system would function.

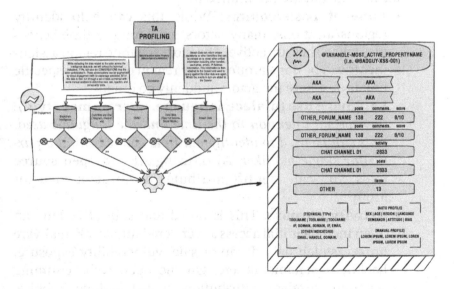

The use case for combining technical TTPs with social and behavioral data can provide additional attribution insights and advise defense measures. For example, if we saw a threat actor emanating from a known TTP domain and using a familiar signature of attack tools against a particular religious organization, we may not be able to identify the specific threat actor by the TTP correlation alone due to the fact that many actors use the same attack infrastructure and the same or similar toolsets. But hypothetically, if our dossier told us that BadActorA was from the region where the time zone aligned with the attack times, is an active member of Telegram channels that are against that religion, is vocal on an open web forum (under another handle) in discussing Middle East politics and showing favoritism toward Iran-backed militias, typically uses the tools that were used in this specific attack, and has been recently active in forums related to initial access and/or tools related to the incident, then we may have some confidence that BadActorA is our adversary. While not exact, the defending organization could put in place defenses, containment, and response measures related to the intelligence and TTPs in BadActorA's dossier.

TA profiling can also yield preventive measures. If an organization could inventory TA dossiers for certain attributes related to its industry, ideology, product focus, and country of origin, then this would help build defense and response strategies. Matches would yield typical attack strategies and TTPs that may be targeting their organization. As you might expect, this same dossier system can be used to engage threat actors. Good intelligence powers successful espionage and negotiation, and our ability to understand with whom we interact informs our entire engagement strategy.

Do not underestimate the correlation probability and value when analyzing a threat actor across mediums. An example of the power of this analysis and correlation is the discovery of an alter ego for the late Alexandre Cazes, the founder of the dark web market AlphaBay. In a multinational sting operation named "Operation Bayonet," investigators linked the leader of the dark web site to another handle used on an open web forum discussing misogynous male pickup strategies. In this case, they were able to not only determine the subject's schedule and daily habits but also psychologically analyze him prior to his arrest. This example is a powerful representation of a clandestine criminal's need to have an outlet for expression. Researchers have powerful tools and data to connect these outlets to their cybercriminal avatars successfully.

I cannot emphasize enough the importance of understanding the psychology driving a cybercriminal. While the field of cybercriminal profiling is nascent, we are beginning to bridge the gap between the technical and human aspects of cyber espionage and forensics. Understanding that our adversaries are not faceless or hoodie-wearing entities but human beings with emotions, goals, desires, and motivations is paramount. This discipline can help foster more creative and adaptive approaches to cybersecurity.

If you do one thing after reading this chapter, begin to shift your lens to a more human-centric view of your cyber adversaries. If you are a researcher or practitioner in private practice or law enforcement and wish to contribute to the development of this practice, please contact me.

Joanna Catherine Burkey

Cyber Recon Leader Profile:

Joanna Burkey

Current Role: Serves on multiple boards of directors

Other Affiliations: National Association of Corporate Directors, Digital Directors Network, former fellow at the Center for Strategic and International Studies

Joanna's Bio

Joanna Burkey is a corporate director, former cybersecurity executive, and the founder of Flat Rock Advisory. She serves on the boards of Beyond Inc. (NYSE: BYON), CorVel Corporation

(Nasdaq: CRVL), and ReliabilityFirst Corp. In her role as principal at Flat Rock Advisory, she provides strategic consulting services to multiple global enterprises. Her three-decade career in cybersecurity and technology spanned engineering, strategy, and digital transformation, most recently as the CISO for HP Inc. and Siemens AG. She holds NACD Directorship Certification from the National Association of Corporate Directors, is a certified Qualified Technology Expert with the Digital Directors Network, and was previously a fellow with the Center for Strategic and International Studies in Washington, DC. She is based in Austin, Texas, and serves locally on the NACD Texas TriCities Chapter board.

Joanna's Impact

I believe that the best teams are made up of empowered people who are united in, and clear on, their function and their mission. Leaders serve these teams best by clearly defining the destination and letting the experts determine how best that destination is reached. Leaders serve their organizations, not the other way around! Leaders exist at every level and can be differentiated from managers because they have followership. Followership is cultivated by individuals who are authentic, who actively listen, who provide meaningful recognition, and who create supportive environments where everyone is allowed to be their whole self.

YouTube URL: www.youtube.com/watch?v=GmG2VgWlsao

YouTube, LLC

Chapter 5
OPSEC or Die

We all know the loud talker with the earbuds. This behavior is one of the most significant risks to corporate confidentiality, yet we do nothing to educate our staff on the risk and suggest mitigating controls. One of my regular haunts in Arlington, Virginia—the birthplace of GroupSense—is NorthSide Social, aka "NoSo." It is a cool, borderline hipster coffee shop in an old building. They offered great coffee and good Wi-Fi and were patient with remote workers who spent excessive time there. Unsurprisingly, it was a cacophony of commercial and government information.

While enjoying my coffee and a PolyFace Farms egg sandwich in the upstairs bar area at NoSo one day, I observed a man in a branded polo coming up the stairs. I recognized the company name on the polo, and the same logo appeared on his backpack. He had the cliché blinky thing in his right ear while he carried on a conversation, carting a tray of food to the room's opposite corner. He then got into a heated discussion with his sales manager or director about the status of various business deals, their likelihood of closing that quarter, and so on. In one case, he had pleaded for mercy on a deal that had not closed because "the product management team had not made the improvement they promised."

Fortuitously, a former colleague of mine worked for the company on the logos as a senior product manager. For fun, I popped onto Skype and messaged my former workmate: "Adam, why hasn't your team delivered this product enhancement for Prospect X; you are negatively impacting top-line revenue. How is Aaron supposed to make his number?"

Shocked that I knew anything about this, Adam didn't censor his response, saying, "How the &%^$ do you know all of this?"

"Your colleague Aaron is like a megaphone in this coffee shop," I replied. Moments later, Aaron's head began swiveling and darting around the room. I went over and shook his hand.

Before the COVID pandemic in 2020, most of us reported to an office and sat side by side or cube by cube with other staffers. Those staffers all probably signed an employment agreement with similar language surrounding confidentiality. This meant talking about internal issues, projects, deadlines, capabilities, customers, and revenue in the open environment of the office was relatively safe. Walking through the office, the chatter was likely riddled with secrets or sensitive information that would be a goldmine to a competitor—or an adversary.

Random paperwork is often left lying around in an office. Workers carelessly discard failed print attempts in nearby recycling bins or leave them beside the printer to use as scratch paper. Bulletin boards in common areas like kitchens or break rooms are littered with important dates and people's names, titles, and other personal information.

These same workers often treated their network and computing environments similarly. While sensitive information might be encrypted as it left the physical confines of the office space, inside, it was unlikely to be obfuscated as it traversed the wired or wireless network. Their corporate directory was likely not even password-protected.

Those of us who adopted the coworking model saw a preview of the post-COVID #OPSECfail world. One could walk through a coworking space and gather information about various companies, topics, customers, revenues, and trade secrets. The common-use printer was a treasure trove of personally identifiable information (PII), and the network was awash with the crown jewels of the community participants.

I remember working in a space in the Washington, DC, area. At the time, I was just starting GroupSense, and we were the only cybersecurity company in the coworking space. A startup in the space was building an online used car marketplace. Seemingly, every time I walked by the printer area, I would witness a stack of customer profiles for their marketplace, complete with pictures of IDs, names, addresses, bank account information, and balances. As often as I had the time, I would pick up the stack of compromising PII, walk it over to their shared space, say "No!" and slam the stack of paper down on one of their fancy standing desks. Similarly, a media startup would give me the news before anyone else. The fundraising goals of my office neighbor were posted on a board visible through the trendy glass walls as if it were the menu at a New York deli. Everyone's business was on public display.

Much later, GroupSense moved into a proper office—a fancy penthouse space with a walkout roof deck. On the top floor, adjacent to our suite, there is a shared conference space available to any of the building tenants. A new startup with recent venture funding used the space for a meeting only an hour before we had it reserved for a customer presentation. I entered the conference space to find three copies of that company's board briefing deck in printed form. It contained their investment strategy, their hiring strategy, their burn rate, information about a legal dispute, and their intellectual property filings. I rushed the copies down to the floor where they resided and asked to speak with the CEO. Her inevitable unavailability sent me back to our office, where I put the board books into a large sealed envelope and returned to the reception desk with a present and a sticky note. "Call me—Kurtis." I did not receive a call.

A month later, I reserved the same space. Imagine my disappointment when the shared audiovisual computer was left logged into one of their customers' private intranet sites. I took a picture with my phone, logged it out, and emailed the CEO, "Call me—Kurtis." We have never spoken. Considering these behaviors can be cultural in a company and are often driven from the top down, I remain concerned for them and their customers.

Post-COVID work environments have opened up a gaping OPSEC hole in many organizations. Most of us are no longer in those confidentiality-clause cubicles and inside the no-need-to-whisper walls of our corporate offices. We are now in coworking spaces, our homes, coffee shops, and condominiums. Yet our corporate policies around OPSEC—if they even existed in the first place—have not been adjusted. The newly expanded corporate workspace—coffee shop conversations, condo conference calls, and hotel lobby Zooms—leaks critical information daily. Here's a pro tip: They are listening, the walls are thin, and someone will always see what you left lying around.

This is especially pertinent when attending industry conferences. We collectively forget that we are in a public place or within earshot of someone who might compromise us or the company. GroupSense, like many other companies in the tech space, attends and exhibits at a handful of conferences each year. Before each conference, GroupSense participants get a stern reminder about CONOPSEC, or Conference OPSEC. They are reminded to use their inside voice and stay clear of crowds or large rooms when engaging in a company call. They are discouraged from using headphones for calls; headphones can give you a mistaken sense of privacy despite our tendency to talk louder when using them. They leverage specific privacy tools when using their computing devices on the road, like screen protectors, VPN, cellular Wi-Fi, and burner phones. Finally, we remind the team of a strict rule: no talking in ride shares. Uber drivers are human beings and probably understand English, so we instruct them to use one-word answers to the driver's questions and remember the drivers are on a need-to-know basis. This was confirmed on one trip where the driver admitted to receiving cash payouts from local investigators for information they gleaned while driving unsuspecting passengers. Passengers assumed that the driver either didn't understand them or wasn't listening. #OPSECfail!

In the case of BlackHat and DEFCON, two back-to-back cybersecurity conferences held in Las Vegas on the hottest summer days, our team does not stay near the conference venue nor in the Vegas Strip hotels. We stay together at an Airbnb a few miles away. BlackHat and DEFCON are notorious for shenanigans on the networks of the venue and hotels, and it is even more critical that OPSEC is maintained at conferences. Yet at any conference in any industry, you are not only in public but surrounded by people from your specific area of focus. The likelihood that they know you, your company, the person with whom you are speaking, and the technology you are there to sell is very high. Don't forget, most hotel walls are very, very thin.

For personal safety, I always try to practice situational awareness. A side effect of this is observing many things that would otherwise be overlooked. I recall during a flight delay on one trip, seeing someone sitting across from me. She was on her phone and had her notebook open. The notebook had an inventory sticker displaying the name of a well-known manufacturer along with some numbers. She was on her phone talking about the company's challenges in closing a sale with a well-known healthcare institution. Talking to colleagues, she mentioned she was delayed, but it was good because Mark was late and hadn't even shown up at the gate yet. As I gathered information, a mildly panicked gentleman squeezed quickly into the seat next to her. "Hi, Mark," she said.

Mark nodded and then acknowledged another gentleman with a similarly stickered notebook. He began to talk to Mark about the sales rep who had not done his job and its apparent impact on the deal that Julie was talking to the colleague about. (Mark had identified her.) It was clear the man on the end of the row was their supervisor, and they were all on their way to attempt to save this important healthcare account. The salesperson they referenced was not present. The boss, Jon, got up to fill up his water bottle and left his laptop *on the chair,* facing me, *unlocked.* I could plainly see an unsent email to the salesperson threatening their job. A few clever LinkedIn searches, and I had all the context and names. Think about how much information I, a complete stranger, gleaned from just sitting in the airport and paying attention. Of course, I did nothing with this information besides discussing my observations quietly with my travel companion. If I knew any of the players, companies, or manufacturers involved, this could have been useful corporate espionage. This kind of thing happens consistently, frequently, and everywhere.

It also happens on the plane. How often have you seen the person's screen next to you, in front of you, across the aisle, and recognized something of interest? There are screen guards that make this difficult, and they are relatively simple to use and inexpensive, but many travelers don't bother to use them.

A common misconception is that information haphazardly made available to strangers is useless to them. While a single piece of information may not be helpful by itself, it can be weaponized when combined with other data. Attacks against people or organizations usually involve the threat actor combining leaked information from multiple sources with open source intelligence (OSINT) or public data. This information cocktail powers impersonation, fraud, identity theft, corporate espionage, and many other risks.

OPSEC Origins and Methods

Not unlike intelligence and possibly because of it, the concept of OPSEC originated in military culture. The attack surface for a military force as it relates to spy activity is massive. Each member of the force is a potential leak of potentially deadly information. As a result, the military carefully protects its data through a combination of compartmentalization, least privilege, and OPSEC training. These principles easily translate to daily life and our professional settings.

Compartmentalization is what it sounds like. The practice is aimed at minimizing data theft or loss in an incident. The organizational assets (data) are divided into isolated compartments, allowing access to only the systems and data needed to perform a specific task or job. As a result, compartmentalization reduces the risk of massive compromises by restricting the reach of potential adversaries.

Least privilege is a byproduct of this practice, limiting systems access to the minimum level required. This concept is often also applied to networks through a concept called segmentation, where the user only has access to the computer networks relevant to their role or task. When implemented, managed, and monitored correctly, all of these concepts are highly effective ways of limiting or preventing data leaks or loss.

At its core, OPSEC is a method (or combination of methods) to identify and protect critical information for a given institution. The U.S. government adheres to a five-stage cycle for OPSEC and often refers to this process as a "periodic assessment of effectiveness." OPSEC is not just a set of rules; it is a cyclical process (see Figure 5.1). The five steps in the OPSEC cycle are as follows:

- Identification of critical information
- Threat analysis
- Vulnerability analysis
- Risk assessment
- Countermeasure application

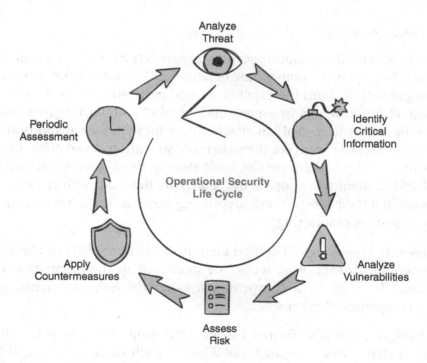

Figure 5.1 OPSEC cycle.

Identification of Critical Information

Critical information in the hands of the adversary can be used to cause harm. Classifying critical information is challenging because a single piece of information, in a vacuum, may not seem necessary, but when it is combined with other data, it could *become critical information*. It is important to note that this classification is independent of security classification. It could be unclassified as far as the government is concerned but still be considered critical information from an OPSEC perspective. The subjective nature of this is challenging for even the most sophisticated organizations to navigate. One relatively simple way to address this is to build a corporate culture that uses best judgment against a blanket need-to-know basis for all information. This policy should be mapped against the core corporate values, and people should be held accountable to that policy.

Threat Analysis

A large part of any mature security program revolves around understanding against whom we are defending. This not only informs the organization about the capabilities and motivations of a would-be threat but also aids in understanding what countermeasures may be necessary to fend off an attack. Any actor with the capability and intent to cause harm is a threat to an organization. As an offshoot of threat analysis, there are five basic steps to threat identification for OPSEC: identifying opponents, analyzing their capabilities, understanding their motivations, identifying possible attack vectors, and continuous monitoring.

Identify Opponents The first step in threat analysis is to identify potential threats. Who would be interested in the organization's data? It could be a competitor, a cybercriminal, hacktivists, or state-sponsored cyber spies.

Analyze Their Capabilities After cataloging the opponents, the next step is to assess the capabilities of each threat persona. This is usually informed by cyberthreat intelligence. Do they have a sophisticated phishing architecture? Do they traditionally leverage social engineering? Are they writing custom malware or using artificial intelligence to obtain information?

Understand Their Motivations So far, the organization is informed as to who may be trying to get access to critical information. Using cyberthreat intelligence, they have a basic understanding of what they are capable of. The next step is understanding the motivations of the threat actors. What is their intent? What motivates their actions? Is it for financial gain, or do they just want to cause damage as a form of protest? Is it industrial or nation-state-driven cyber espionage? This step is crucial because it informs the protector of the critical information and what lengths the attackers may go to achieve their dubious goal.

Identify Attack Vectors The most fun part of this process is identifying how the attackers might succeed. What attack tactics might they use? What are the "low-hanging fruit" areas in the company where the attackers would most easily gain ground? To thwart a bad actor, one must think like a bad actor. One of the best ways to inventory the attack vectors is to carry out a tabletop exercise (TTX), essentially gaming the attack process against the existing mitigation strategies.

Monitor Continuously Utilizing tools like digital risk monitoring, brand monitoring, and cyberthreat intelligence, organizations must continually assess or monitor the threat actor ecosystem and adjust the defense strategy accordingly.

Assess Vulnerabilities

Step 3 of the OPSEC cycle requires a careful analysis of how the previously identified critical information could be exposed. A broad lens should be taken to this approach, as the exposure may surface in many different ways. The most obvious, digital exposure, is also the most difficult to assess. This is because of the interconnected nature of our systems and the ubiquitous use of mobile and personal devices. This means that a user could deliberately or mistakenly transport critical information in an insecure fashion. Other avenues, including physical exposure, human error, and social engineering attacks, should be considered.

Risk Assessment

Step 4 of the OPSEC cycle is performing a risk assessment based on the information garnered from the previous steps. This is achieved through evaluating the vulnerabilities, determining the likelihood of the vulnerabilities being exploited, assessing the impact if that should occur, and then prioritizing those risks. The vulnerabilities could be technical or nontechnical. This means they could be vulnerable software or unpatched code but also policy-driven or human error–prone items. The impact assessment is typically measured regarding financial loss or operational interruption. Finally, the priority will inform the organization which items to address first and what to invest in the mitigation.

Countermeasures

The organization must implement mitigation strategies to prevent loss or harm following the risk prioritization. These countermeasures could be technical, such as a software patch or a firewall; administrative, such as a policy or procedure; or physical, such as locking the information in a physical container or location.

Obviously, this process is referred to as a cycle with the intention that it be repeated perpetually. Each time the cycle is completed, the organization tightens the controls, learns a lesson or two, and increases overall security and safety.

OPSEC is a critical part of any practice, and especially so in the realm of cybersecurity. Whether you are a red team, a blue team, a researcher, or doing forensics, staying on top of your OPSEC game is critical. This is equally important for cybercriminals.

At GroupSense, we are often called on to help identify or perform attribution on threat actors who have crossed a well-resourced opponent. Sometimes, this is driven by a commercial company wanting to file a legal claim against an actor or the country that harbors them; in others, it is federal or national law enforcement bodies looking to make a bust. While each case of #opsecfail leading to successful attribution is different, most of them follow the same pattern. Take Viscily, for example.

Viscily was sufficiently paranoid. He knew that despite the amnesty his home country provided him if his true identity were in the hands of Interpol or their friendly agencies, he would never be able to travel again. What was the point of making all this money if he could only spend it in St. Petersburg?

Years of tribal knowledge made hardn0c (Viscily's dark web persona) an effective clandestine cybercriminal. His ability to script up a scanner and exploit dropper was infamous among his peers, so much so that in the initial access broker (IAB) community, hardn0c's access offers sold at a premium. They always worked and were persistent and undetected in the victims' environments. His most frequent buyers were ransomware operators. The ransomware gangs were willing to pay that premium because their return on investment (ROI) was immense. It was a solid and profitable relationship.

Despite moving away from the questionable area of Kupchino in St. Petersburg, Viscily still favors the Sladkoyezhka (Сладкоежка) coffee shop in the shopping center for remote work. He launched a TOR browser using public Wi-Fi and a VPN, which he had used since his gaming days. He accessed the IAB boards on several different .onion sites and two Telegram channels. Although several law enforcement agencies have taken over boards and TOR exit nodes, TOR is innately anonymized. The VPN was the extra layer of obfuscation. The provider he used was a favorite of the gaming community and offered proxies that even used cell phone handsets as waypoints. Viscily did all these things to prevent anybody from identifying him on the Internet—except we did just that.

As with many investigations, it is never one piece of data that gives away the perpetrator but a collection and correlation of data points. Like so many others, Viscily was guilty of using the same or a similar password across multiple accounts, a convenience many of us use across numerous email accounts we use for different forums and activities. On several occasions, Viscily disabled his VPN when troubleshooting connectivity at the coffee shop.

Combining V's password and credentials in a data breach allowed cyber sleuths to cross-reference his unique password across other breach data. Investigators accessed the credential database of two forums running against a password-cracking system, which allowed them to triangulate V—largely by using visibility into and analyzing traffic on TOR exit nodes—to a particular forum and review his history there. That information and an access log to the forum allowed them to locate V's preferred coffee shop. In this case, as the coffee shop was inside the borders of the Russian Federation, V could not easily be apprehended. Still, we had identified him and could continue to link and follow his online activity across multiple properties.

One day, V took a vacation to the Maldives. The minute he stepped off the airplane, he was met by U.S. federal officers, who took him into custody. They took his laptop, cell phone, and the Nintendo Switch in his backpack. Two months later, V was in a U.S. federal court under indictment, prosecuted for myriad Internet crimes and money laundering.

The story of V shows that it takes only one mistake to get caught, and OPSEC relies on all of us to remember that the bad actors aren't the only ones who make mistakes. There have been countless anecdotes that the threat actors make mistakes as often, if not more often, than the practitioners, from the slip-up of the founder of the Silk Road to the administrator of AlphaBay, who famously bragged about his OPSEC to the community. Or as you saw in Chapter 4, "Whodat?" the bad actors end up in breach databases with reused passwords just like the rest of humanity.

One afternoon a couple of years ago, one of my top analysts (we'll call him Sam) called me in a panic. Sam is a real practitioner, a "white hat" hacker who catches "black hat" hackers, a real Internet sleuth. He has strong OPSEC, so much so that he was the chief author of our OPSEC workbook for the other analysts on our team. I like to refer to the stars on our team as "sufficiently paranoid," and Sam certainly fits this description.

When Sam called me one morning to inform me that the FBI was in his living room, I was surprised. I instructed him to answer their questions honestly but not gratuitously—using yes or no answers, only adding context when asked. In other words, I counseled Sam to provide only the minimum amount of information to answer the questions he was asked. At one point, the FBI agent asked to speak to me, and Sam and the agent called me. I explained what our operation was and what Sam did per the agent's questions. I further pleaded Sam's case as a patriot and a principled man with a solid moral compass who was simply doing his job. Our consistent pro-bono work and the data we provided brought us goodwill. The FBI agents left satisfied.

Once the FBI was gone, I said, "Sam, your OPSEC is broken. Where did you slip up?"

He couldn't recall immediately, so we began trying to reverse-engineer how the Bureau had targeted him, identified that he was active on illegal forums, and found his home. Sam occasionally engaged with threat actors using one of our more than 4,000 curated threat actor personas or sock puppets. When he does this, the other forum or chat community participants think he is another threat actor looking to traffic stolen IP or data. To perform this with the best OPSEC, we insist on adhering to a process designed to prevent anyone in that forum or on the Internet between his research machine and the forum from identifying that the persona is actually Sam, let alone determine his physical whereabouts. After some detective work, we determined that a split tunnel VPN configuration on one of the research machines may have provided the IP address of his home router when he accessed a dark web forum and participated in a conversation that may have been with an undercover law enforcement agent. When the agent could track the IP address to a location in the United States, I am sure they were excited. Most digital evidence typically leads them to a foreign actor in a country without extradition. The FBI needed cyber arrests and wins, and they thought they had one. Unfortunately, we were operating within the law. Sure, there were gray areas, but we often provided the Bureau with gratis data and information during our work, building trust and an understanding of our mission and purpose. Thankfully, this was the case for Sam, but his story illustrates how small a mistake can be to allow somebody to show up at your front door.

Digital OPSEC Tools and Practices

OPSEC practices and sophistication vary, yet many online practitioners have a need to practice it on a daily basis. Remaining unidentified online requires tactics, tools, and discipline. Some of the common tools and methods are as follows:

Network-Based Anonymity Tools   There are myriad ways to disguise where your traffic is emanating from. VPNs, proxy servers, TOR, or a combination thereof make tracing traffic back to its origin difficult. Combining these methods with each other and launching the connection from a public place or public Wi-Fi further obfuscates the user.

VPN   VPNs should be standard operating procedure for everyone, everywhere, all the time. While the personal VPN market has become largely commoditized, not all VPN providers are alike. I am careful to use providers that prioritize the privacy of their customers. Pay close attention to where the VPN provider is based. Assume VPN providers based in unfriendly countries or any of the Five Eyes[1] may knowingly or unknowingly allow government access to your data. I also habitually switch these up on occasion, as well as switch which location I terminate at. I have used Nord VPN and Proton VPN with confidence. Also, if you have multiple computers, use separate VPNs. The goal is to make forensic analysis of your traffic difficult.

Proxy Servers   VPN providers have largely integrated this capability to personal use. The concept of a proxy is captured in the name; it means to stand in for someone. In proxy use, the connection is

---

[1] The Five Eyes is a global intelligence alliance between Australia, Canada, New Zealand, the United Kingdom, and the United States.

terminated and re-created on the outbound as a new connection. For security researchers, proxy providers—and there are many—are necessary to hide where one is coming from when accessing a forum or chat site. NinjaProxy is one I know and trust, as I know the owners personally.

TOR   Remember that The Onion Router network was created initially to provide true anonymity to the user. For the most part, it indeed does so. While TOR has a dirty reputation for being a network of thieves, it can also serve an OPSEC purpose. The downside to TOR is it is very slow.

Email Providers   It is no secret that many email providers mine their customers' email data. Providers like Proton Mail and Tuta keep their customers' data private and do not require you to provide too much personal information to sign up. Both providers now offer enterprise-class features.

Personas or Sock Puppets   False accounts that appear to be real people are used regularly to obscure the real person behind the keyboard. These can be very simple or sophisticated, requiring fake addresses, names, and even fake phone numbers. Tools like Fake Name Generator and This Person Doesn't Exist use AI to generate names and fake headshots for social profiles. Generative AI can also generate fake content, giving context and realism to an online persona.

Encryption   Using end-to-end encryption for communication is a standard operating procedure for maintaining strong OPSEC. Tools like Signal, TOX, Jabber, and Telegram support this. Sometimes, these tools make it difficult for law enforcement to extract details from the application. Full-disk encryption is pretty much standard and is offered by most operating systems. Turn it on.

Device or User Isolation   This tactic creates an air gap between the user and any network. This makes it difficult to facilitate online activities, but it can be useful when hiding from would-be wiretaps or spyware.

Research Computer Maintaining a completely separate computer for your online research efforts is advised. I typically run Ubuntu, a widely used open source form of the Linux operating system, on these computers and rebuild them frequently. This can also be accomplished through virtualization using tools like VMware, VirtualBox, and others. The advantage of virtual machines is that rebuilding to a known good state is simplified.

Sandbox If the research requires downloading objects or files, a sandbox is a necessary tool. There are varying versions/types of these, but generally, they are used to detect malware or malicious code embedded in objects. Some popular sandboxes are VirusTotal, Yara, and Cuckoo.

Burner Phones You can acquire relatively inexpensive burner/prepaid phones and procure SIM cards for those phones tactically. Use these to create accounts for platforms that require phone numbers. If it can be avoided, do not use these phones for operations directly. These can also be used as a backup to a primary phone in a pinch.

Event or Log Cleaning It is a common practice to edit and remove any indication of access to a system and any activities on that system. This hinders attempts at forensic investigation after the hacker has come and gone.

Remaining Unpredictable Avoiding repeated patterns and changing the order of operations can be an effective tactic to avoid detection.

In the cybersecurity space, there are a number of teams where the practice of maintaining strong OPSEC practices is critical.

Red Teams

Talented hackers for hire, red teams, and penetration testers adhere to strong OPSEC principles. These practitioners frequently face operational security teams (blue teams) that can limit their ability to gain access. To remain effective, red teams must keep close tabs on what they expose at every step in the process. This includes soft items like their plans, identities, capabilities, and access levels. Even more so, hard indicators like domains, IP addresses, and credentials must be obscured, or the team risks being detected. Sophisticated targets utilize advanced cyber detection tools capable of correlating massive amounts of log data, connecting dots in real time. These systems make offensive security practitioners work much more diligently on their OPSEC.

Security Researchers

Security researchers and cyber intelligence analysts may have the most pressing OPSEC needs. These Internet spies regularly masquerade as threat actors, utilizing sophisticated sock puppets and fake personas. Should the threat actor community in which they are participating discover their true identity, digital justice would be swiftly served, which is why these teams utilize a combination of old-school spy tradecraft and new technologies to hide their true identities from their adversaries and sources.

GroupSense researchers maintain a personal level of OPSEC but also sit behind an infrastructure protecting them and their cybercriminals' interactions. Our team routinely uses most of the tools just listed, including virtual machines, research hardware, cloud-based computers, VPNs, proxy servers, and burner phones. Combining these tools makes it difficult for anyone to hack or identify the real person behind a persona.

A research machine is often refreshed on a regular cadence, reloading the operating system and toolset. When rebuilding the machine, the researcher will select a location and persona. For example, the researcher may choose Romania. As a result, a Romanian name would be selected for the machine name, like Murzik, which is loosely translated as "afraid." In addition, the user on the machine might be of Romanian origin, like "Catalina Drumbrova." Further, the time zone on the machine should match Romania, and a VPN or proxy setup should be set to exit in Romania.

As an extra layer, they may route traffic through a dark web network like TOR, though this can be quite slow. To a chat server, all evidence indicates that the machine is a Romanian actor, including the IP address and user agent information. Of course, this machine would be separate from the corporate or home user network. Many researchers will use mobile hotspots or something like StarLink for their research nodes. A week later, the same machine may appear to be from Lithuania and be named Mishkukas ("teddy bear").

The prudent security researcher is diligent about possible cross-contamination between the research machine and other business computing devices. In a scenario where the threat actor provides a file, it will be run through a sandbox to determine if it contains malicious elements. In some cases, it may be referenced through tools like VirusTotal to see if it has been associated with any malware or cyberattack campaigns.

Optionally, the researcher, upon segmenting the research machine from other networks, may choose to run all traffic from the research network through a TOR gateway. The Whonix gateway is one method with which you can route traffic through a single gateway or route traffic through the TOR network for anonymity. This is an alternative to using a TOR browser on the research machine or VM.

Other tools make research efforts and obfuscation easier to accomplish. While discussing OPSEC strategy with Jon DiMaggio, one of the top cyber espionage practitioners in the world and author of *The Art of Cyber Warfare*, I was enlightened to find there are cybersecurity research tools streamlining this process and making switching origins, personas, and user agents much easier. Tools like Authentic8 Silo not only make impersonation more efficient, but they can also reduce or eliminate the need for burner phones and other ancillary devices. Silo, for example, utilizes a series of network tunnels that are not associated with commercial VPN or proxy offerings to allow the user to select an origin location and device profile. The researcher can choose to emulate a mobile phone in Tokyo or an office computer in Chennai. This feature is priceless, as many of the forums and threat actor communities have blacklisted

VPN source IPs or consider them suspect (likely researchers), at a minimum. Silo's ability to choose things like user-agent data, screen orientation, and location, and even to emulate real phone numbers is a game changer for the security research community.

Hacktivists

Hacktivists are notoriously focused on OPSEC due to the nature of their work. Hacker groups like Anonymous and LulzSec were perpetually investigated by global law enforcement. As a result, they were particularly careful about leaving evidence that could compromise their identity. One particular hacktivist has eluded identification for decades. The Jester, or "th3j35t3r," is an infamous Internet vigilante hacktivist. He is allegedly responsible for hacks against Wikileaks, Jihadist websites, Westboro Baptist Church, and the Russian government. He has picked Internet fights with members of Anonymous and LulzSec and even possibly assisted in unmasking some of their members. Yet his identity is still not known, while there have been moments when it seemed he would be exposed, he has somehow remained under a clever Internet vale. In recent years, Jester founded the social media platform Counter Social, an alternative to Facebook and Twitter and a "counter" to other fringe social media sites like Parler, Truth Social, and Frankly Speaking. Occasionally taking interviews, Jester reports that he built the site himself and remains the sole employee of the platform. Given his activity and high profile, his platform, and the need to utilize a large amount of Internet bandwidth and cloud computing, it is a miracle that he has not yet been identified publicly. His laptop is on display at the Spy Museum in Washington, DC.

OPSEC for Everyone

Regardless of your profession or place on the Internet, it is wise to practice personal OPSEC. We all face various adversaries on a daily basis. Some of us may be hacktivists, security researchers, or just activists with a strong voice. Others may be law enforcement, public figures, or outspoken advocates for a particular cause. These activities will always solicit enemies, and those enemies will attempt to use our digital footprint against us, whether using our OPSEC failures, such as breach data and poor password practices, to gain illicit access or simply using publicly available data to find out where we live.

My job and passion projects have me facing ideologically opposed persons and international cybercriminals. As you can imagine, I am sufficiently paranoid and careful about my OPSEC. I recommend practicing practical cyber hygiene. Like physical hygiene, these things must become habits and easy to work into your digital and kinetic lifestyle. Among these is good password hygiene. I use a password manager. I use multifactor authentication (MFA) on everything I can, specifically using MFA that requires a token (or MFA application) rather than an email or SMS message. My mobile phone and systems all use VPN, and my mobile phones only use messaging apps with end-to-end encryption.

Rob Shavell, CEO of Abine, has been a longtime personal privacy advocate and is the creator of the "DeleteMe" service. DeleteMe does what it sounds like—it uses software tools and analysts combined with privacy legislation to have an individual's personal information perpetually removed from data brokers. If you have ever Googled yourself, you will find a dozen companies claiming to have your personal information, hawking that information to whoever will fork over $10. DeleteMe makes their job much more difficult and is a priceless addition to any privacy and OPSEC stack.

Sometimes, one's work puts them at more risk than others. Our work with a large municipal government got some unwanted attention. The customer approached the account team and asked if GroupSense could assist with a study to determine whether foreign actors were posing as ethnic citizens within neighborhood-focused Facebook groups. Their theory was that foreign agents pretending to be members of that community were spreading disinformation about elections and healthcare in these private forums. We used our intelligence tools to identify that this was partly true. There were agents in a foreign country pretending to be a part of an ethnic community in the city, posting false and misleading information and memes on the forum. Years later, our analysts picked up conversations in politically charged Telegram channels, where my name and the names of our board members were mentioned. They were attempting to do reconnaissance on us using OSINT tools and posting it on the channel. The perpetrators claimed that we were part of the deep state and that we were spying on U.S. citizens. It turns out they learned of the report through the Freedom of Information Act (FOIA). I cannot prove that I am not part of the deep state because *I do not know what that is*. I firmly believe our work was legitimate and to protect U.S. citizens from foreign influence. Nonetheless, it put a spotlight on us again. As a result, we continue to practice OPSEC with diligence.

We also provide OPSEC. GroupSense offers a VIP Digital Protection Service to protect high-net-worth individuals, public figures, and celebrities from online attacks and spying. This premium solution monitors social media and underground channels for chatter about the customer and offers insight and remediation by a trained cyber analyst. If you are a public figure, then you are making enemies. You need to know when those enemies are organizing against you and plan accordingly. You may believe you are not on the radar if you are an executive at a company and this may be true, but you are not in the clear. One of our VIP customers was a senior executive at a large bank. For the most part, she does not show up on the digital underground radar. However, her nephew was an avid gamer and was active in some hacker communities. One afternoon, he made enemies with LulzSec. Not good! This made him a cyberattack target, and his aunt would be collateral damage. Our systems detected the activity and alerted her to their intentions to dox (hack her systems and dump her personal information publicly) her and her family. Our analyst team quickly worked with her corporate security to tighten the defenses and put a laser focus on logs and security alerts. In the end, Lulz did release some of her information, but that information had already been exposed in an earlier breach. Lulz knew of the relationship between the nephew and the banker through social media.

Daily Life OPSEC

How does the average person maintain personal OPSEC in a world where sharing pictures of what you had for dinner with the world is normal? Culturally, sharing personal information on social media has become the norm, and most people do not realize the impact of doing so. We have devices in our homes and pockets tracking our movements and recording our conversations. Obviously, connecting dots like family relations, learning habits, travel, work, school, and other personal information is one of the risks. New risks arise daily as governments, scammers, fraudsters, and other cyberthreat actors have advanced tools like generative AI at their fingertips.

Connecting to the Internet, being social, or performing a public-facing job all have associated risks, but you can manage them by taking some basic steps. The key is to build habits and consistency around these practices and make them part of your daily routine.

You don't have to be a security researcher to benefit from some of the tools we've listed:

- Everyone should have a personal VPN on their computers and mobile devices.
- Everyone should use a password manager.
  - Avoid using cloud-centric solutions and browser plug-ins.
- Everyone should enable MFA wherever it is offered.
- Everyone should use end-to-end encryption software.
- If you must talk on headphones in public, leave one headphone out to maintain situational awareness and meter your volume.
- If you must use your device on a plane, use a screen protector.
- Do not have private conversations in ride-shares or taxis.
- Do not leave private information lying around on printers or the seat of your parked car.
- When traveling abroad, use end-to-end encrypted phone calls through apps like Signal, WhatsApp, Telegram, or Wire.
- Use services like DeleteMe to remove your data from the data brokers. This year, we saw the data broker US Public Data get

breached. The data breach exposed 2.9 billion U.S. citizens' records, including names, addresses, and account information. My data was not in it because of DeleteMe.

Scams

I recently gave a talk to a few hundred retired seniors at a local university. My talk was called "Digital Danger: How to protect yourself from cybercriminals and scammers." I was inspired to do this talk because I had been taking inventory of how many cyberattacks and scams were being perpetrated on American small businesses and the public. I was and am convinced it is a national economic and security issue, yet local law enforcement can or will do little about it. I have been working on ways to solve this but wanted to take some immediate action. This talk was one of those actions.

I was inspired to invite this audience by a conversation with Colorado State Representative Rick Taggart and Mesa County Sheriff's Sergeant Ross Young. They informed me of a record number of cases targeting seniors, and many of them were losing their retirement savings. I partnered with Cheryl Squire of D.A. Davidson, a local wealth manager who had seen this happen to a number of her clients. She convinced me to assist when she told me that a few of her clients, whom she had helped save for retirement over more than two decades, lost all of it in a single click. We rented a space and got the word out.

One of the most effective scams I spoke about is often called the "Grandparent Scam." This is where the victim gets a phone call from someone claiming to be their grandchild. The caller ID says something like "Las Vegas Police Department." The person sounds *exactly* like their grandchild. They inform the grandparent that they are about to be put in prison and that they need them to deposit money in a special ATM so they can get out. They beg the victim not to tell Mom and Dad. Then they put the "police officer" on the phone, who confirms the story and sends the victim to a Bitcoin

ATM near where they live. I think you know what happens next. The caller uses AI to sound just like their grandchild; it only takes a few-second sample of someone's voice for AI to duplicate that voice. They get these voice samples through social media. They find out about these victims in the first place through data brokers and data breaches.

Surviving Social Media

The easy button here would be not to use social media, but we know this is not a realistic suggestion. If you must use these platforms, there are a few basic steps you can take to minimize your risk.

Tightening up your social media permissions around those who can see your profile, posts, data, and pictures is a good first step.

Being selective with whom you connect or converse with is key. Trust but verify. For example, when you receive a connection request from someone you believe you are or were already connected with, contact that person to see if they have had some issue with their profile before accepting. Most of the time, these are cloned accounts, impersonations, or account takeovers that would give the attacker full visibility to your profile. Guides and tools are available to assist in this process for most social networks.

Do not participate in surveys or games on the platforms. These are often tricks to give third parties access to your data. I avoid them altogether as a result.

On professional platforms like LinkedIn, limit access to your profile to first-level connections and police those connections carefully. Do not allow any connections to see your list of other connections. I suggest removing your location information, phone number, and email address from view. Finally, do not accept messages from non-connections if possible.

Most importantly, do not post information that could compromise your or your family's safety. This includes information about your location, travel plans, daily commute, gym, and so forth. If you must post about your location or "check-in," do so after you have left the location.

Personal Device OPSEC

Your personal OPSEC involves the care of your personal devices. Of course, run malware and endpoint detection on your devices, mobile, and desktop/notebook. Update the operating system and other software when the vendor suggests it, and do so immediately. In these cases, the software vendor has typically discovered a mistake in their code. They are offering you a fix to that mistake before an exploit is used against you. Stop playing "Words with Friends" for a minute and take them up on it.

Your personal device has your life on it, so be careful with whom you trust with it. Taking your notebook to the Genius Bar at Apple or the GeekSquad at Best Buy and leaving it with them is like taking a filing cabinet with all of your financial information, the codes to your safe, the keys to your safety deposit box, your personal journal, and some family pictures and leaving it with the person who changes your oil. Further, when a computer has reached its end of life, trading that machine in, recycling it, or throwing it in the trash is similar to the above metaphor. The disk drive on that machine is a goldmine of personal information. I use disk wiping software to clear the disk before I do so. Depending on the machine, I sometimes remove and physically destroy the disk.

The apps, microphone, and camera on your mobile phone are siphoning away your privacy. Use only the necessary apps, and be deliberate on what permissions you grant them. Most mobile operating systems now have a permission review feature; make a habit of running that and reviewing what access each app has.

Alexa, Google Home, Apple HomePod, Samsung Smart TVs, and other connected devices around your home are always listening. If you must use these devices, do so with deliberate intention. Put them in rooms where it is unlikely they will hear compromising conversations. If they have features to limit the listening, enable those features.

If you insist on using a fitness tracker, disable any real-time tracking features. Enable them only when necessary. Avoid posting your workouts to social fitness platforms.

The companies that sell these devices are not necessarily using them to spy on you, but they are collecting the data. Are they good stewards of the data? You should be as concerned about those companies suffering a breach as you should be about their misuse of the data. Remember the Ashley Madison breach? The users of Ashley Madison never considered that the application would be compromised and have their data displayed all over the Internet. Now, imagine that your Alexa's data was compromised, including every conversation you had in front of that device. Behave accordingly. Remember, one piece of information or data seldom exposes or identifies you; it is the amalgamation of those indicators that accumulate and de-anonymize you.

Personal Digital Attack Surface

It is wise to consider what is at stake if someone successfully hacks your systems. Consider the risk and what would be exposed (the identify critical information stage of the OPSEC cycle). For many, it will be their communications. Consider the exposure to years of email, texts, messages on chat platforms, and so forth. Do you need to keep all of this data? I would argue the risk associated with the exposure greatly outweighs the impact of that data being compromised. No matter how well-meaning, well-spoken, or politically correct an individual is on a daily basis, the exposure of messages out of context in a public forum can make them look bad and potentially ruin a lifelong positive reputation. Delete old messaging data. If the tool supports it, set an auto-purge on data older than a certain time frame. Whatever you are comfortable with will be better than retaining all data for all time.

AnonymOS

Colleagues of mine were once covered in *Wired Magazine* for the privacy-based bootable CD they had developed called AnonymOS. Developed by the kaos.theory team, the live CD integrates strong encryption and anonymization tools, making privacy accessible to every day, less sophisticated users. It was based on one of my favorite operating systems, OpenBSD. New versions of AnonymOS are in the works, and I am encouraged that technology like this can be made in a way that is almost seamless to the public.

Extra Measures

In today's connected, data-driven world, it is almost impossible to remain anonymous. There are, however, steps that one can take to obfuscate their personal data and information. Here are a few tips on how to cover your tracks from OSINT-capable adversaries.

LLCs and Trusts

Create an LLC to put your personal property under. This includes your house, vehicles, and other large purchase items. You may want to create multiple LLCs to separate certain items. For example, if you collect motorcycles, as I do, you may create an LLC that owns those motorcycles that is separate from the LLC that owns your personal residence. This creates a firewall in the event that one area of your life creates a unique signature. Use the LLC or an alias for utility bills or cell phone contracts.

In the United States, certain states are known for their strong privacy laws regarding LLC registrations, allowing members and managers to remain anonymous. These states do not publicly disclose the ownership or partnership information of LLCs. Register your LLCs in these states. States like Delaware, Nevada, Wyoming, New Mexico, South Dakota, and Alaska do not list the LLC partner information in public databases.

Use living trusts if you plan on purchasing firearms or firearm-related equipment.

For more obfuscation, you can layer the entities—for example, an LLC owned by a living trust.

For the Extra Paranoid (I love you!)

Anonymous Travel Use alias names for hotel and airline bookings where legal.

Home Privacy Enhancements Install high fences, avoid street-facing windows, and use unlisted phone numbers for utilities. Install digital cameras with recording capabilities.

Secure Purchase Records Pay in cash or cryptocurrency for personal items when possible.

By combining these personal privacy practices with digital OPSEC, you can create a comprehensive security posture that reduces exposure to threats in your personal and professional life.

PO Box or Private Mailbox

You can link your LLC to a private PO Box or mailbox at a UPS Store or similar. Use this address for everything you can. For frequent packages and purchases, purchase them with the private bank account or a fillable prepaid debit card and have those packages shipped to a designated drop store. Amazon has the best support for this.

Following the success of the personal security and anti-scam seminars, I assisted my colleague Chuka Eze in building a program to continue the education and protection mission. Chuka's burgeoning company, Protectiv, aims to educate and protect individuals from scams and fraud nationwide.

If you do one thing after reading this chapter, think carefully about your personal OPSEC. Where might you be providing evidence or gratuitous information about yourself? Who can see you on your social media? Do you reuse passwords? Do you employ proxies or VPNs? Do you talk about business operations in public spaces?

Cyber Recon Leader Profile:

Heather Antoinetti

Current Role: Founder & CEO, Ah-Ha Marketing

Other Affiliations: American Marketing Association, Digital Marketing Institute

Heather's Bio

Heather Antoinetti is a creative force in marketing, known for translating technical ideas into business value. With 20 years of global experience, she's made a career out of simplifying complex topics—especially in cybersecurity—and turning them into messages that spark connections. As CEO and founder of Ah-Ha Marketing, Heather helps cybersecurity firms cut through the noise, build absolute authority, and drive results that matter.

Before starting Ah-Ha, she led high-impact marketing efforts at NTT Security, Elastic, and Security On-Demand (now Deep Seas). Now, she's at the forefront of the generative AI wave, building privacy-friendly tools that help marketing teams move faster and smarter.

Through her Reputation Architecture course, Heather shows technical leaders how to share what they know in an authentic way that builds credibility. Her work helps experts become trusted voices and make a name that sticks.

Heather's Mission

I stand for clarity in a noisy world—and for helping experts lead with substance, not spin.

I believe trust is earned through honesty, consistency, and the courage to show up as you are. That the most powerful brands aren't built on personas, but on real people owning their voice and using it with intention.

I believe in elevating others—not with gimmicks, but with strategy, empathy, and stories that connect.

I value simplicity, momentum, and doing the work that matters. I challenge ego-driven marketing and the idea that louder is better. Instead, I advocate for thoughtful visibility—where influence is rooted in value and impact.

My mission is to help technical leaders turn their ideas into influence and their expertise into movements. Not by making them someone else—but by making sure the right people finally hear them.

YouTube URL: https://youtu.be/L0ci_VDyCZI?si=a9q57w1rEwzidFJ-

Chapter 6
How Not to Go to Jail, Hell, or Worse

"Another security researcher contacted our client's incident response firm and suggested he could purchase the dataset from the threat actor. He claims to be in a conversation with the TA," the voice on the phone said.

"Can you tell me who this is?" I asked.

"We would rather not."

"If I guess correctly, will you affirm?"

"Unofficially? Sure."

"Victor."

"Damn, you guys live in a small world. How did you guess that correctly on the first try?"

"Because I know Victor, and I know his methods. I also know he offered your client a rate that was a percentage of the negotiated buy price versus what is being advertised now. He also attempted to contact your client, and when they did not respond, he reached out to the well-known incident response firm, safely assuming they were on retainer with your client for incident response."

"He didn't contact our client."

"Yes, he did."

"No, we checked." He seemed sure of it.

"Check again," I insisted. "Check *info@ admin@* and *webmaster@*. Have the IT leadership check their LinkedIn messages. Without question, Victor has been voraciously trying to contact your client."

"Regardless, should we trust him to do it?"

"I don't think so. Here is the deal: If the TA really has the data and he thinks he can do a deal with Victor, he may, but Victor is not well respected by these actors, and there is a chance they will screw both him and you. If you want to buy the data, the TA will eventually post it on the marketplace. My team can then engage the TA and get samples—then we decide whether we pay anything. This TA is not well known, and this could be shit data."

This was my conversation with a prominent law firm about one of their clients. Their client contacted them after the IR firm let them know a researcher had evidence some threat actors in a private channel were claiming to have *terabytes* of their customer data. When the law firm asked their client to check their emails and LinkedIn messages, they found many messages from the researcher, as I knew they would. In the end, this played out as I predicted: The TA eventually posted on a forum; my team engaged and got data samples, determining that the data was from a third party and did not contain the critical client information the TA claimed it had. In the end, the victim organization decided not to pay the TA to delete the data.

This is a regular occurrence in our line of business. In other cases, we are asked to negotiate with a threat actor and advise the client on how to transact with the bad guy to prevent data from being sold to anyone else. As you can imagine, this is a dicey operation. Indeed, it seems like a digital spy versus spy, choose your own adventure, or a digital Q from James Bond, but is a normal day for us. (Granted, I may have been sipping on a martini during this particular case.)

I have repeatedly spoken to university students about business ethics. There is even a video series by the Daniels Fund featuring me speaking on the topic. When I do speak at ethics courses, I often start my talk with something like: "I help good guys pay bad guys, so let's start there."

> The Daniels Fund is a nonprofit organization established by cable television pioneer Bill Daniels. The Fund gives money to universities and other nonprofits with a focus on ethics. Find out more at https://danielsfund.org/Ethics/Collegiate and www.youtube.com/watch?v=zvRNfPY01Eo.

I am and have always been on the side of the victim. Not only do I not want to pay bad guys, I don't think we should. Yet, I believe it is an unfair situation. Most businesses are under what I refer to as the "cyber poverty line," and the government has done little to prevent attacks or help the victim organization recover or survive.

One of my favorite keynotes is "The Software Won't Save You." It is a talk about self-reliance, education, and how our capitalist system churns out cybersecurity tools that are unusable by the bulk of the market. (See Chapter 1, "Why Spy on Bad Guys?" for more detail.)

As you should understand by now, our cyber adversaries rely on a well-organized, well-funded apparatus to attack our citizens and businesses with impunity. Some of those adversaries are members of foreign military, specially equipped and trained to hack our systems. If Russian soldiers were parachuting onto the lawns of our corporations or Chinese special operations forces were tunneling into our critical infrastructure, Seal Team Six would be all over that shit. Yet these countries engage in the *digital* equivalent of those things, and the U.S. government barely lifts a finger. Small businesses, you get a pat on the head and a weak "Good luck fighting Russia."

Thousands of small businesses are hit with ransomware and extortion from foreign actors daily. Usually, they have only two options: pay a ransom or go out of business. Until the government realizes that the backbone of the U.S. economy is dying by a thousand small cuts and mobilizes to support them, the digital bloodbath shall continue.

This widespread bloodletting does not justify paying ransoms, but it might help one understand the psychology of why we would consider doing such a thing. Many of these ransoms would still be paid if negotiators did not exist; the companies would just pay more. It is not lost on me that we may fund awful things when we make these crypto payments. Ransoms paid in cybercrimes fuel illegal activity, empower our enemies, and consume global money laundering efforts. I wish there was a clear answer, but I know telling the victims to take one for the team is not it.

As my workload increased over the years, opportunities to do ransomware response work and help other victims in other ways kept surfacing. I was uniquely positioned to help many people and felt a responsibility to do so. I took on more pro-bono jobs and free advisory work than I could handle, and this deep sense of purpose rose within me. Over a three- to four-year period, I helped nonprofits, microbreweries, a granola manufacturer, dispensaries, logistics companies, small government contractors, municipalities, and schools navigate cyber incidents and recover or restore their operations. I helped the National Guard in several states respond to cyberattacks on their constituents.

Some of the most impactful work I did was with law enforcement. It became apparent that most victims, personal or business, had no one to go to for help from a legal perspective. Local law enforcement agencies were and still are not equipped to handle these kinds of cases or their rapidly growing volume on a city-by-city basis. I took the time to investigate this problem and met with the law enforcement leadership, who informed me of the bombardment of digital crime cases and that they lacked the capabilities to solve these crimes or even to assist their citizens. In most cases, they would fill out the intake form and immediately check a box at the bottom: "Exhausted All Investigative Resources."

Most victims were referred to the Justice Department's IC3 Internet crime reporting website, where they disappeared into a black hole along with millions of other victims' reports. The FBI and Secret Service are overrun with these cases and cannot assist their municipal counterparts. My volunteer work required additional skills, and I learned them while I helped. I learned how to do cryptocurrency tracing and follow-the-money financial investigations. I learned how to draft compelling subpoenas and understand chain-of-custody processes. I observed that in addition to ransomware attacks on small businesses, U.S. citizens were being relentlessly attacked by fraudsters and scammers on behalf of sophisticated organized criminals.

Throughout this journey, I met some amazing human beings who, like me, saw the onslaught of cyberattacks and fraud as a call to action. David Lutz, an anti–money laundering (AML) specialist, helped banks with compliance during the day and chased crypto scammers at night. Erin West, a prosecutor in Santa Clara, California, at the time, was building a network of digital crime fighters after she finished her day job. Paul Marinnan, a former international law enforcement agent, supported folks like David and Erin from his perch as the top intelligence person at TRM Labs. Jason Ingalls led a national incident response (IR) practice while volunteering to help secure our nation's elections on the side. Through Jason, I met Josh Dann and Allyn Lynd, who were knee-deep in digital forensics for helpless victims while building their own IR practice. Lt. Colonel Sarah Frater, former active duty Army and active National Guard, drove incredible results in Wisconsin, going above and beyond what her job called for. Each time I felt overwhelmed by the additional work I was putting on myself, I remembered these people and buckled down.

While speaking at conferences, I found myself approached by an increasing number of wonderful people who wanted to make a difference. Their determination and energy for saving victims from digital attacks were palpable. As practitioners and cyber defenders, we all have a responsibility to do something.

This chapter will explore the landscape and players in this space, their purpose and mission, the ethical dilemmas they face, the unspoken promises they make, and the legal environment surrounding all of this.

I mentioned in the ransomware chapter that there are those who masquerade as good actors but who are actually fraudsters and ambulance chasers profiteering from victims. The so-called data recovery companies are among these players, fleecing cyber victims of their already meager resources. They are in strong company with some independent consultants, people who call themselves "response specialists," law firms, and even the insurance industry taking a bite.

When GroupSense entered—somewhat unwillingly, I might add—the ransomware response space, we were deliberate on how we monetized and performed that work. In a world where our opponents are largely anonymous and rarely face consequences for their actions, where the amount of money being litigated is largely arbitrary, and where all of the communications happen between two parties in a dark web chat room, there is plenty of room for fraud. There was room for the *accusation* of fraud, and we observed a number of companies and consultants who were charging a percentage of the amount they saved the victim in the negotiations. This seemed unfair to us, as the amount of money the threat actor was demanding was made up, at least it was at that time. We came up with a flat fee we felt honored the level of effort and expertise required by these negotiations and built processes to give the victim organization control and visibility into the threat actor engagement. We involved the victim in the strategy, explained every chess move, and ensured they understood those moves' risks; as a result, no message was ever sent without the victim's approval and understanding.

Any kind of incident response work, whether kinetic or digital, is a difficult job. In the kinetic world, many of the responders are purpose-driven people immersed in rescue disciplines: certified emergency medical technicians (EMTs), firefighters, nurses, doctors, and so on. Most of these people have a soft approach when addressing victims or victims' families. It is not just a part of their training but a part of *who they are*. Cyber incident responders can be quite different. The type of person who enjoys and is good at combing through logs, malware reversal, and the like is often not necessarily good with people. This is, of course, not representative of all technical incident responders. I have met and worked with some amazing technical liaisons in the business, like Jibran Ilas of Mandiant, Josh Dann of DL Cyber, Jason Ingalls of Ingalls Cybersecurity, David Carrion of Carrion Group, Steve Ocepek of Kroll, Dave Cunningham of Alvaka, Joseph Greenfield, and one Taylor Banks, who is not only a technical responder but also a certified EMT and firefighter. These folks break the mold and bridge the gaps between the technical nature of the event and the nontechnical emotional impact of the event.

Our approach to ransomware response seemed to resonate with the clients, so much so that we often became the de facto project manager for many of these incidents. The presidents, principals, and CEOs of the companies would call us at night and on the weekends to vent or rant about their situation, putting us in the position of being therapists as well as responders. To this date, we have achieved success in every single case we have taken in that our clients in the ransomware response sector are not only happy with the services we provide but have a tremendous amount of trust in GroupSense.

Breach Consultants

There are plenty of stand-up professionals engaged in this line of work when businesses choose Option 1 (pay the ransom). I am not talking about those fine individuals in this passage. However, cyber incidents' chaotic, emergency-driven nature presents opportunities for those who wish to line their pockets. One large issue for cyber response work is that there isn't a good litmus test as to the qualifications of the breach responders. There are a few certifications, and certainly, big brands like Mandiant are widely trusted. However, most victims are not sophisticated enough to understand or even have an awareness, which opens the field to consultants who ambulance-chase by calling victims and offering support only to sell them useless advice. Others are like the "Victor" I mentioned in a previous chapter. Still, others make back-channel deals with the bad guys to ensure the appearance of success while locking in a profit. The main issue is a lack of transparency; when you engage a consultant, be sure to look out for the abstraction of their actual activities. If they are going to talk to bad guys for you, request screenshots of the conversations. Even better, get in on a screen share while they perform the act. If they will facilitate cryptocurrency transactions for your company, you should ask for the transaction IDs and any related logs. Use a crypto intelligence tool like those provided by TRM Labs to validate every transaction. Watch out for those who operate on your behalf without your oversight.

Data Recovery Companies

There are some good data recovery and breach recovery companies. I consider Alvaka to be one of the best, and Carrion Group are remarkable at what they do. Unfortunately, if a cyberattack victim Googles "how to decrypt ransomware" or "how to recover from cyberattack," the paid ads will often turn up fraudulent companies. We cover their methods in Chapter 7, "Negotiating with the Enemy." They were also exposed in a ProPublica investigation. In addition, they were covered in Dan Golden and Renee Dudley's book, *The Ransomware Hunting Team*. These firms have also served a dubious purpose for public sector leaders who want plausible deniability. You will find many law enforcement and municipalities among the data recovery company's satisfied customer list, primarily so that the chief of police or the mayor may tell the media and public that they did not pay the ransom. They paid a "data recovery company" to "unencrypt the data" using "special software."

I continue to see these companies advertised on search engines, and they seem to be doing good business. This is a shame, and I will continue to report them and try to stop their activities. My friend Dave Cunningham of Alvaka has a great template he emails to anyone considering using one of the data recovery companies. I have stolen his template and made it my own. Thanks, Dave.

Security Researchers and Security Research Firms

There is a class of security research and research firms you may have heard from. They will email or call you to explain that they have encountered a large amount of your or your customer's data, and that for a small consulting fee, they will tell you how they obtained it. The message between the lines is that the data will ultimately be exposed if you do not pay. These actors obtain access to the victims' data in myriad ways. Some have automated tools, such as scanning the Internet and looking for vulnerable databases or open cloud storage. When they discover one, they exploit the database via a SQL injection (SQLi) or simply copy the cloud storage's contents. Others have purchased or obtained the data from dark web activity, ransomware dumps, or initial access brokers. Our friend Fred in Chapter 4, "Whodat?" operated such a firm.

If it feels like you are being extorted, that's because you are being extorted. It is difficult to address these situations, as the threat actors already have the data, and you may not know how they got it. Your options are to pay and learn how they did it or tell them, "No, thanks." In either case, you have a data loss situation to deal with both from a technical perspective and a legal one.

If you choose to tell them "No thanks," look closely at your cloud storage infrastructure and run some vulnerability tests against any publicly facing databases for SQLi vulnerabilities, as these are two of the most common exposure areas. Unfortunately, the third most common exposure isn't even you; it is your business partner. The issue with the business partner leak is your constituents probably won't care or know the difference. If your partner leaks data they were allowed to have but it contains your private information, the public will likely still fault you. This is why careful data classification and a strong third-party risk program are important.

The ransomware epidemic and their practice of double extortion have worsened third-party data exposure. When a company is hit with ransomware and they choose not to pay or negotiate in good faith with the ransomware actors, the actors will almost always leak the stolen data on a "shame site." Our customers would hear about a ransomware incident resulting in leaked data from a business partner in the news and then submit an RFI (request for information) to our team to detect whether the breach exposed their data. This happened so often we responded by building a tool called FileRecon to download the leaked data from the shame site, check it for malware, extract it, pull out all file types, scan the data according to our customers' prioritized intelligence requirements (PIRs), and produce a report detailing everything the customer needs to know. Figure 6.1 shows the layout of a typical ransomware shame site.

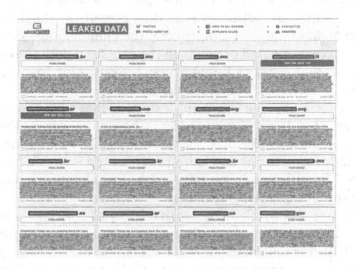

Figure 6.1 Typical ransomware shame site.

Law Firms

Law firms serve a meaningful role in the incident response space. Given the complexity of breach compliance and notification laws, I recommend having a retainer with a law firm that has breach response practice. That said, many law firms have attempted to enter the technical response, digital forensics, or negotiation areas of incident response without the requisite talent to do so. This is unfortunate for victims who will do nearly anything their lawyer tells them during an incident. In several cases, the victim contacted us to support them through an incident only to have their law firm tell them not to use our services because the law firm would perform the work. Needless to say, they did not get the best results.

In response, GroupSense developed a ransomware negotiation course in partnership with Max Bevilacqua's company, Mindful Negotiation. We have had many law firms and IR firms take the course to become better at ransomware negotiation. After taking the course, several of the attending firms have entered into an agreement with GroupSense to act as a coach during incidents.

Insurance Companies

Like law firms, cyber insurance is a practical way to transfer risk when building a cyber program, but in many ways, it is bittersweet. In the earliest days of cyber insurance response to ransomware, the narrative was that insurance companies were making the ransomware situation worse when they simply paid the ransom. Of course, they were just doing what their (deeply flawed) actuary tables told them to. When the insurers realized their math was not working, they began attempting to enforce good cyber practices on their clients. This is actually a positive outcome. Not so many years ago, a company applying for a cyber insurance policy would get a questionnaire about its cyber protections and processes. Now, the insurer *checks* to see if those controls are in place. Companies began to cross their digital Ts and dot their cyber Is to get an affordable policy.

The insurance companies began to curate "panels" around incidents and ransomware responses, which are essentially lists of approved suppliers and vendors. The panels kicked off a quick race to the bottom. Because the insurers cut the checks, the incident responders needed to be on those panels but to get on those panels, they had to cut their rates. This had a tangible impact on quality. The strong talent began to leave the response firms, and the outcomes are now suffering. In 2024, I witnessed more failures in incident response than ever before, which, of course, was unfortunate for the victims. Many of the victims are hit again almost immediately after closing an incident. Others call us in a panic to help redirect their ransomware negotiation due to incompetence from their insurance-supplied vendor. It is incredibly difficult to explain to the victim that the ransomware actors do not care if we "switch pitchers." I cannot jump into the existing dialogue and ask to start over just because I am new on the scene. Nonetheless, I have taken these cases and driven better outcomes than the expected trajectory. The more IR firms we see sign up for our Ransomware Negotiation Training, the better I will feel about this.

In addition to threat actor engagement failures, these response firms are dropping the ball on their alleged core competencies. Lately, I have witnessed several cases where, after closing a case and restoring a network, the threat actors quickly hack back in and lock the network down again. This not only further damages a company's ability to operate but further ruins their reputation, costs them even more money, and is poisonous to the morale of the staff.

These failures *have* to be registered on the cyber insurer's actuarial radar. I am hoping for a shift for quality over quantity and to reach a point where we pay the responders what they are worth. I know the rest of the industry and the policyholders wish for the same because this race to the bottom has spawned a cadre of providers who refuse to work with the insurance industry. These folks believe in quality work for quality pay. Their clients are the uninsured or the insured willing to pay a little more to keep their insurer honest. Good for them, I say!

CISOs and Cybersecurity Leadership

While I am hesitant to put them into buckets or label them, there certainly are "styles" of security leaders. I have met chief information security officers (CISOs) who have never been on a shell prompt. I have also met CISOs who get on the dark web and argue with threat actors about their claims. I am acquainted with and have met hundreds of cybersecurity leaders throughout my career. I remember admiring the dedication and spirit of cyber leaders all the way back to Dwayne Moehl, who ran the IT department at Northwestern Memorial Hospital (NMH) in 2002 when I was a punk systems engineer. In the basement of NMH, Dwayne managed a ragtag team of engineers who kept one of the largest hospitals in Chicago running against all odds.

One of my favorite CISOs is Richard Rushing, who became the CISO of Motorola Mobility and Lenovo USA when Motorola acquired Air Defense in 2008. Richard was the co-founder and chief security officer of Air Defense prior to the acquisition, and he was legendary for his technical prowess and hands-on approach to leadership. Now one of the longest-tenured CISOs in the industry, Richard still shows up to work in jeans and a "The Punisher" T-shirt, running circles around his talented staff. Once, after interacting with a Chinese state-sponsored threat actor on the dark web, Richard found their office address and sent them a self-help book as a joke. At a lunch meeting with Richard, he presented to me a book on Chinese poetry they sent him in return. It was epic!

On the other end of the spectrum are CISOs who prefer to avoid technical weeds and focus on policy and politics with their board. Of course, Richard also does these things, but in his own unique way. This is not a slight on those CISOs; this approach is necessary. I see the leaders get caught up when the focus is too much on compliance. There is a difference between securing an organization and being compliant. There can be a stark contrast between being a good steward of your employees' and clients' data and being compliant. This can become a religious discussion around the minimum effort needed to show due care balanced with budget and business priorities. Add risk management and risk transfer to the discussion, and people will pull out the sharp objects. All of this is to say that running cybersecurity in any organization is a noble profession, and these champions deserve our respect and empathy.

Some CISOs excel at business management, politics, and technical leadership. Kelly Moan, the CISO of New York City, is one of these people. Her ability to navigate convoluted politics and provide tactical, technical leadership during an incident is admirable. Kelly also possesses among the highest emotional intelligence quotients (EQs) of any cyber leader I have met. Considering that the largest metropolitan city in the United States is a prime target for threat actors, it is amazing that she sleeps at night.

There are very high-paid CISO positions, for sure, and I would argue even those people aren't paid enough. The job of the CISO—defending an organization against organized crime and nation-states—is one of the most difficult jobs in the world. The CISO role is a labor of love and a purpose-driven position, so hats off to those who choose to do the work, and thank you to those who do it as a public service.

The Threat Actor Code

Regarding the overall ethics of cyber incident response, most participants in the response business live and act by a strict code. They are in this line of work because they have a sense of purpose and responsibility. Their primary goal is to help those who cannot help themselves secure and defend the defenseless against a formidable adversary. I know my team at GroupSense feels this way, and our ethical goals are codified in our company's core values. We don't like the bad guys and have pledged to act as good stewards of our country's digital assets and as protectors of our fellow citizens.

The bad actors have ethics, too, or at least they have the appearance of a code of conduct. Years of espionage, social interaction, and transactions with threat actors have uncovered some of these largely unwritten rules. Most threat actors operate under some

How Not to Go to Jail, Hell, or Worse 151

variation of an honor system. Reputational systems and escrow functions reinforce some of this honor within illicit markets, but some transcend technology. In ransomware cases, one of the most asked questions is, "Will they honor the ransom payment?" Nearly 100 percent of the time, the answer is yes. This is partly because if they did not, people would stop paying ransoms and partly because they view their work as a business. The ransom payment is a business transaction to them—you are buying a product in their view.

In access broker circles, it is widely understood that double-selling access is a bad practice. This means that if you have advertised some illicit access to a particular system or network and someone pays you for that information, you cannot sell it to anyone else and, indeed should not even attempt to do so. There are certainly actors who violate this, but their careers in those marketplaces are short. In one case, we purchased access information from a broker who often offered our team private menus of victim organizations. The next day, the actor apologized. Another team member had unknowingly and simultaneously sold the same access information. They offered us a refund.

When threat actors violate these rules, they become pariahs in the underground community, which will certainly damage, if not end, their ability to do business. Exit scammers are hunted down, forums and sites are hit with denial-of-service (DoS) attacks, and people are SWATted. When the leader of LockBit's ransomware, LockBitSupp, didn't honor a payment to his software developer, the developer leaked the code base. Later, when the same actor was hacked by law enforcement, his affiliates avoided him like poison.

SWATting is when someone calls in anonymously to local law enforcement and convinces them that a target is performing some dangerous act, causing the police to storm the target's house, weapons drawn. The first instances of this practice involved SWAT teams, which is where the name comes from.

The threat actor's code extends to their victims in other ways. When we have issues with a ransomware decryptor, the ransomware group often provides technical support up to and including screen shares to assist in the troubleshooting process. When we come to an agreement with a particular ransomware group, we ask them to provide a report on how they gained the access as part of the terms of the payment. Most of the groups honor this and provide a detailed description of how they thwarted the security systems.

One area where they do not honor their word is deleting stolen data. We have seen stolen data resurface and be used as a seed in follow-on attacks. Further, storage is cheap, and I believe there is a quid pro quo where they must provide that data to their home country's intelligence service.

Cybersecurity is a strange business; it is one of the only private sector roles where you have an actual *enemy*. I do not mean competition—I am talking about someone who intends to harm you and your organization, and it is your job to defend the organization against that harm. Yet our opponents are human, too. I recall the story about when the British army in World War I engaged in an unsanctioned truce over Christmas when the Germans were heard singing "Stille Nacht." Soon, the British soldiers joined in the singing, and they eventually came together in No Man's Land and gave each other gifts like chocolate and cigarettes. They played games and laughed together. It makes me believe that we would behave differently if we knew the people on the other side.

How Not to Go to Jail

I am not a lawyer; nothing in this book should be considered legal advice. Further, the legal landscape on these topics shifts almost daily.

Espionage

The act of creating a false persona to gain access to an online property lies in a large gray area. While it likely violates any number of terms of service for the property, it is not illegal. That said, if access is gained through hacking the property, one can be in violation of the Computer Fraud and Abuse Act (CFAA). Access gained through an invitation or some other form of self-provisioning would not violate CFAA. Similar laws exist globally, so it is important to know them. For example, misrepresenting or impersonating someone to gain access may be considered fraud in other countries, and depending on the person being misrepresented or impersonated—such as a law enforcement officer or government official—it could well be illegal in this country as well.

Since those conducting espionage violate the terms of service of a given property, it is important to consider civil liability implications. Further, practitioners should familiarize themselves with eavesdropping and interception laws. Joining private conversations in closed forums may violate wiretapping or interception legislation. This is especially sensitive if communication occurs over encrypted apps like Telegram. Data protection laws may dictate that collecting information about forum participants could violate privacy laws like GDPR or CCPA. Precedents around the expectation of privacy may assign private forums as spaces where participants have a reasonable expectation of privacy, and engaging in these practices could be considered wiretapping in some jurisdictions.

All those reasons are why law enforcement, both local and federal, are hesitant to participate in or subscribe to this kind of data. These challenges and chain of custody complications are why many illicit activities in forums continue with impunity.

Entrapment is an area where cyber intelligence companies can get themselves in hot water quickly. One simple rule helps keep the practitioners on the right side of these things: *Do not solicit a criminal act.* In practice, this means one cannot go on a dark net forum and *ask* for access, data, or information. For example, let's say a cyber spy was committing espionage against Acme Airlines. The spy had infiltrated a particular forum trading similar stolen access and information, so they posted, "Does anyone have any credentials for Acme Airlines?" That act may *cause* someone to commit a crime; that someone may not possess the credentials, but in seeing an opportunity to make money, may then go obtain them illegally. Just like a police officer cannot ask a criminal to get them narcotics, cyber espionage practitioners cannot solicit illegal activity.

Ransomware Payments

In the case of ransomware, there are many legal hurdles and complications to navigate. There are longstanding and developing breach notification laws that vary by jurisdiction. Some U.S. states have exceedingly strict laws, like California's Consumer Privacy Act (CCPA). Notification, in general, seems to cause many problems for the victims, so much so that threat actors know this and use it as leverage. This is also the area from which many civil lawsuits stem. One of the most common and biggest mistakes I see ransomware victims commit is communication. The failure to communicate what is occurring in a timely manner to their internal and external constituents ultimately leads to future civil and class action lawsuits.

Sanctions are also relevant to ransomware response. The U.S. Treasury Office of Foreign Asset Control (OFAC) maintains the sanctions list. One must exercise due diligence and care to ensure one is not paying a sanctioned entity. When dealing with a non-U.S. victim or a victim with a global presence, foreign sanction laws are in play. There is a process to get an exemption from the Office of Foreign Assets Control (OFAC) for ransomware incidents, and in these cases, contacting OFAC early in the process and working closely with them will help. The Treasury Department strongly discourages the payment of ransoms and recommends that every victim self-report.

In most cases, paying a cyber ransom is not against U.S. law, but new legislation is being considered that may change that. Federal ransomware acts like the Ransom Disclosure Act aim to force disclosure. Some federal policymakers have suggested outright bans on ransomware payments, though, as I stated, these are short-sighted. We have to hope the U.S. government will provide us with more options. At the state level, the approach to governing ransom payments varies from state to state. North Carolina made it illegal for public entities or entities funded with public tax dollars to pay ransoms. New York has batted about similar laws for both public and private entities.

Internationally, the updated NIS2 Directive in the European Union (EU) requires stricter security measures and reporting for specific critical industry sectors. Staying on top of international laws can be challenging as every nation approaches the problem differently. The United Kingdom has proposed legislation mandating nationwide reporting while joining the United States, 46 other countries, and Interpol in signing a joint policy statement saying their government institutions will not pay ransoms.

To make matters more complicated, ransoms are typically paid via cryptocurrency. Given that the ransom amounts can range from four figures to eight or nine, the payer may be sidestepping a number of financial laws. In an effort to curb organized crime and money laundering, the United States Financial Crimes Enforcement Network requires reporting transfers above $10,000. Additionally, the victim or the crypto broker facilitating the payment may violate Know Your Customer (KYC), AML, and money transmission regulations. Finally, some countries have specific cryptocurrency laws or outright bans on the use of cryptocurrency. In response to these regulations, many crypto brokers and exchanges refuse to participate in a cyber ransom transaction. Others still specialize in complying with these laws relative to making ransom payments.

This murkiness, volatility, and confusion around the legal landscape can be a landmine for the responder, let alone the victim. Regular touchpoints with legal counsel are paramount to maintaining a proper response apparatus and response plan. Organizations should maintain updated and specific policies, keep good records, and develop a response plan that aligns with their values and legal responsibilities.

One area that remains a touchy subject and equally murky is the collection of breach data. Cybersecurity vendors offering cyber intelligence and ATO continue to collect massive amounts of breach data. Considering that most breach data contains personal information, laws like California's CCPA and the European Union's General Data Protection Regulation (GDPR) may apply. The spirit of those laws is to prevent reckless use or unnecessary loss of their citizens' PII. The laws have features like "the right to be forgotten," where the constituent can request that their personal data be deleted from the database. Breach data, however, has already left the building, so to speak, making it difficult to understand how those laws may apply.

GDPR requires cybersecurity companies to establish and document a lawful basis for collecting breach data, whereas the CCPA requires transparency about data usage. Under both laws, cybersecurity companies must limit their collection to include only data that matches their approved application or use case. Cyber companies must also respond to consumer requests related to access and deletion, with a few exceptions regarding fraud. Perhaps one of the more difficult requirements is GDPR's requirement that EU PII data cannot be transferred or stored outside the EU.

We must realize that our adversaries are not concerned with these mandates. In fact, they use disclosure laws and regulations like the Health Information Portability and Accountability Act (HIPAA) as leverage against their victims. This is so effective that some ransomware groups have discontinued the use of file encryption and simply rely on exfiltrated data for extortion. This will continue to evolve as our laws and regulations catch up with technology and digital crime. These laws have been enacted to protect the public, but it remains to be seen if the United States can take other measures to protect its citizens. We continue to watch companies die, and citizens lose jobs because the government has yet to realize they have a responsibility to act.

I sometimes give a talk called "World War III: The War You Didn't Know You Were Fighting." The premise of this talk is that the days of conventional warfare are diminishing and that the new battlefield is obfuscated or amorphous. We are in a new world where countries like Russia and China carry out large-scale cyberattacks designed to steal money, intelligence, intellectual property and critical infrastructure information through proxies. These countries not only allow these attacks on Western nations and their allies but also enable and support them. How does a small business in Springfield, Illinois, stand a chance of successfully fighting this adversary? How is a municipal water district with municipal tax funding responsible for building an effective cyber defense against a nation-state? As I write this, we are in the middle of the Salt Typhoon attack, which targeted telecoms and put messaging privacy at risk. This attack, perpetrated by the Chinese Cyber Military, compromised some of the most sophisticated and well-funded telecommunications companies in the world. If this can happen, it stands to reason that most of the rest of us don't have a chance at avoiding these kinds of attacks.

To make matters worse, dozens of cyberattacks, scams, and frauds are perpetrated on U.S. citizens, most of whom do not know how to protect themselves or cannot afford to do so. In nearly every case, the impact is multifaceted: disruption, stolen information, and stolen money in the form of cryptocurrency. The stolen capital leaves the U.S. economy forever and is used to fuel future attacks, both kinetic and digital. Meanwhile, the government and local law enforcement can do nothing to prevent it or even help in recovery efforts. This will boil over when municipal candidates are not elected or re-elected due to being unable to address the digital crimes being levied against their constituents. The title of a book by Nick Furneaux sums it up pretty well: "There's No Such Thing as Crypto Crime." In other words, it's just crime. Or, in this case, war.

At the moment, the best thing we can do is take care of ourselves and each other. I continue to challenge my cybersecurity colleagues to do more. Do pro-bono work, train your family and your friends, and volunteer at your local Chamber of Commerce. We can make a difference within our own circle of influence and, collectively, the country. *If you do one thing after reading this chapter*, familiarize yourself with the cyber incident process reporting in your community.

Cyber Recon Leader Profile:

Maureen Kaplan

Current Role: Chief Revenue Officer, SilverSky

Other Affiliations: SC2, ISSA, board member of Exit12 Dance Company and lifetime member of Girl Scouts USA

Maureen's Bio

Maureen Kaplan is an executive-level leader, focused on growing cybersecurity companies for over 25 years. She has extensive experience in corporate strategy, sales, marketing, operations and acquisitions, driving growth for mission-driven companies ranging from start-ups to multinationals. She is a Black Belt in Lean Six Sigma and holds CISSP and GSEC certifications. Maureen excels in operating amid ambiguity to deliver on ambitious goals and takes bold visions and executes tactical implementation, operationalizing teams, and engaging the customer base to gain traction for new initiatives.

Her passion is helping people uncover their hidden talents and utilizing those newfound skills in creative ways. Maureen enjoys diverse volunteer activity such as STEM leadership program mentoring and helping young women starting out in their careers, guiding the corporate direction for a dance company focused on healing military veterans with trauma from war, and nurturing entrepreneurs in their quest for building the next great company.

Maureen's Mission

I believe in the power of community to tackle challenges, nurture the best in us, support each other, and embrace diverse perspectives. I seek out thorny problems, looking for ways to bring teams

How Not to Go to Jail, Hell, or Worse

together to drive solutions, building strength in organizations while delivering a positive outcome and streamlined experience for customers and employees alike. Pulling together requires recognizing unique capabilities, attributes and contributions from others, and, in some cases, discovering elements they didn't know they had and also celebrating small victories along the way. Growth requires flexibility and courage. Be comfortable with discomfort. Sharing your talents with others fuels your soul. There are both power and pride in leading great teams; it becomes a virtuous circle of contribution and growth.

YouTube, LLC

YouTube URL: www.youtube.com/watch?v=4-B-YX9w2yo

Chapter 7
Negotiating with the Enemy

GroupSense's initial foray into the ransomware response market was accidental. On the front end of the COVID epidemic, a series of events pulled us precipitously into the center of the ransomware universe.

In the course of monitoring illicit internet activities for risks to our clients, our software and our analysts consistently uncover threats to non-clients. In the margins of our analysis, we see negative impacts on other organizations. In the early days, we would point these out in our weekly meetings and express our pity for those victims but continue about our work. In a couple of instances, we knew someone at the victim organization or knew someone who knew someone, and we would attempt to notify them. Needless to say, notifying a large organization about anything approaching the concept of a breach was an art form. We learned some hard lessons, including several instances where we sounded a fire alarm and experienced the "swiveling empty chair" syndrome. This was where the people we were meeting with would abruptly leave the meeting with no explanation. Something about the "b-word" was causing this.

The frequency with which our analysts would see these indicators of compromise (IOCs) related to non-clients continued to increase year after year. We eventually developed a process we called the "Open Findings" process, in which we identified a victim, assessed it for impact, and stack-ranked a list of those we would notify. Then our team would each assign themselves a target and attempt to reach them. Often this fell on deaf ears since most cyber teams were inundated with "security researchers" who were "trying to help" but were actually ambulance chasers or outright attempting to extort the victims. In the event we did reach someone who was open to listening, we would provide the digital artifacts and evidence. If needed, our analyst team would then assist the victim with the next steps. This often involved our team engaging with the threat actor in question, using one of our personas to validate the situation, gain samples of the data, or proof of the threat. Sometimes those victims became clients, but most of these companies ignored us entirely or offered at best a sincere "thank you."

We have navigated cases that required us to deliver the data in person at a military base. We have done open findings that landed me at Department of Justice headquarters. Once, one of my executives had to bring the evidence on a USB stick in person to the Joint Special Operations Command (JSOC). One cannot fully appreciate the breadth and scale of the stolen data that is pilfered around the Internet's dark places. As a U.S. citizen, it concerns me, but more on that in another chapter.

One Open Findings process had us stumble into our first ransomware response case. My team had notified the C-level cyber executives at an affected company. Our intel determined that a threat actor (TA) had persistent access to that company's network. The GroupSense team had already engaged the TA and validated the access, including screenshots that included command windows displaying unique RFC 1918 (internal and private) IP addresses. It was real, and it was not good.

The deputy chief information security officer (CISO) reached out to me shortly after. He said our outreach was timely, as they recently experienced a ransomware event. He wasn't certain, but just in case our open findings notification and the ransomware incident were related (we later determined that it was more likely a coincidence), he would like to retain our services. He suggested a 30-day contract to investigate the TA and perhaps draft some additional intelligence around the incident. While GroupSense does not normally do one-month engagements, we felt it was in our best interest to support him and his team through this difficult time.

A few days after inking the 30-day agreement, I received another call from him. "We are in real trouble here, and the board wants to negotiate with the TA. We would like you to do it."

"I don't do that," I replied.
"But you guys talk to bad guys all the time."
"Yes, but they think we are other TAs; we don't sit on the other side of the table, so to speak," I said, continuing to back away.
"Do you know anyone who does this kind of work?" he asked.

About a year prior to this conversation, I had dinner with a well-known cybersecurity practitioner we'll call Victor. Victor reached out to one of my investors and advisory board members, asking for an introduction. I obliged, and on my next business trip through his city, we met. His primary agenda was convincing me to buy his company. He had a small (I think just him) cyber consulting company and some software that dabbled in the dark web intel space. I always try to keep an open mind, so I saw the demo and got some sample data. In the end, it wasn't going to be a good fit—plus, my team did some background intel on Victor and found that he had a pretty poor reputation with virtually all of his past coworkers. But that night, during dinner, he told me stories of negotiating with ransomware actors on behalf of victims. At that time, I had not heard of such a thing, and I was fascinated. By his account, he was quite good at it, even getting the ransomware actors to unlock the victim's files for free on occasion. I decided that I could assist the client better with Victor's help.

"I am acquainted with this guy, Victor; I don't know him well, but he is allegedly practiced at this. Would you like me to introduce you to Victor?" I asked.

"We need to move quickly—subcontract Victor under your agreement with us and bring him to the web meeting tomorrow. We want to start engaging the TA in the morning," the CISO replied.

That afternoon, I contacted Victor and briefed him. I proceed to get the necessary confidentiality agreements and subcontracts in place and prepare him for the web meeting. Everything seemed on track. The next morning, I joined the Webex. The victim company is well known, and some of the executives—the CEO, for example— are semi-celebrities in the business world. I sat patiently, watching the squares populate one by one, like the opening sequence from *The Brady Bunch*. The CEO, CFO, CISO, Deputy CISO, internal and external counsel, a representative from the cyber insurance company, someone from the incident response firm, a PR person, an agent from the FBI, and me—everyone showed up relatively on time except Victor. Earning his reputation as an unreliable fellow, he failed to show altogether; strangely, no one on the call asked where he was. They simply asked me what to do. In a moment of weakness, I convinced myself of three things: We had to get through this call, I would somehow find Victor, and he would provide me with a perfectly reasonable excuse for his absence. Maybe he fell in a manhole. Maybe his kids were sick. Perhaps he was grazed by a passing bus and was recovering in the hospital.

We were unable to reach Victor throughout the entirety of the case. Lucky for me, I am a quick study, and I had surrounded myself with legit professionals who understood the science of negotiation and cybercriminal engagement. Several members of my team at the time were former law enforcement, some even undercover operatives, who had been formally trained on the craft. I relied heavily on them for feedback and spent every spare minute getting smart on negotiation science. The CISO and Deputy CISO were collaborative, helping to drive the outcome. I later learned they poked fun at me on a personal level, but I had to admit to myself that they were right—it *was* funny.

In the end, we reduced the ransom to an amount that the insurance company was willing to pay. The threat actor honored most of the agreement, save providing a video of the file deletion. Afterward, cyber breach law firms and insurance companies came calling and a new world opened for me and GroupSense.

Weeks later Victor sent an email to me and to my client as if no time had passed asking basic questions about the incident. I immediately called him and he picked up.

"What are you doing?" I demanded.
"What do you mean?" Victor asked.
"Dude, you were MIA for weeks!"
"Oh yeah, I'm sorry I missed that call; I had a late night the night before on an investigation," Victor said.
"It has been *weeks*," I said, seething. "Victor, I am sure you have a perfectly logical reason why you ghosted us, but I need you to do me a favor."
"What's that?" he asked.
"Remove mine and my customer's contact information from your devices and don't call again," and with that, I ended the call. Unsurprisingly, that wouldn't be the last time Victor and I would cross paths. This industry is small, and Victor will visit us again in another chapter.

Based on this forced experience I became fascinated with the discipline of negotiation science. I studied the great books on negotiation, old and new. I read blog after blog on the topic and took a master class. In some ways, I was uniquely suited to the mission. While many skills can be learned, practiced, and developed, there are key elements to negotiation that are more soft in nature. Such skills are hard to teach, difficult to test, and demanding to develop. Chief among these skills is empathy. As we built out our practice, this was one of the soft skills most people either had or didn't have, and developing empathy would require vast expense, a tremendous amount of time, a mental health professional on retainer, and a trainer skilled in altering lifetimes of mental perceptions.

I want to be clear that I am not talking about sympathy. Empathy and sympathy are often conflated yet have vastly different meanings and connotations. Most often, I do not have sympathy for my opponent in a ransomware negotiation—but I can put myself squarely in their shoes. I know who they are, where they come from, how they are compensated, how and why they justify their actions, and I can almost predict their emotional reactions to what I am about to say. I am talking about deep, powerful empathy, an innate ability to understand what *I* would do in their situation. I find this makes me very effective at negotiation, and that capability remains a big differentiator in our ability to drive meaningful outcomes for our clients.

We also quickly learned companies subjected to these kinds of cyberattacks needed more than a negotiator. Most of them needed a coach, a leader, a therapist, a business consultant, a liaison for law enforcement, a translator, and someone who knew how to put themselves squarely into their opponents' shoes. We rose to the occasion on every front. I led the team down a path that ultimately became a burgeoning full-time practice for GroupSense, complemented our core digital risk mission, and increased our reputation for effective threat actor engagement.

Ransomware Response and Negotiation

Should I pay?

One of the first and most common questions victims ask is, "Should I pay the ransom?" This is a difficult question and is largely a business and financial decision, yet there are other items to consider that play into the equation. At GroupSense, we are committed to helping victims of cyberattacks answer this question. First, there are a couple of key gates, starting with whether or not it is illegal to pay the ransom. Depending on where your company is based or operates and its primary business, there will be regional and federal laws that dictate whether you can pay a cyber ransom. In the United States and many EU countries, there is a list of companies that thou shalt not transact with. For U.S.-based companies, this list of sanctioned entities U.S. citizens and companies are forbidden to do business with is maintained by the Treasury Department's Office of Foreign Asset Control (OFAC). Much of the list consists of adversarial nation-states, companies backed by those nation-states, organizations known to fund terrorism or terrorist organizations, banks doing business with or assisting in laundering money for those nation-states and terrorist organizations, and so forth. The list also includes ransomware operators and ransomware groups. The groups on this list have associations with the aforementioned entities or have committed a serious crime against the United States. Checking the OFAC list is simple; visit https://sanctionssearch.ofac.treas.gov in your favorite web browser. This site allows you to run text-based queries against the list. This, of course, is a silly way to check, as the actors and their groups change frequently, but it's a start.

The GroupSense process is more comprehensive, and we strive to show due care and diligence beyond just running simple searches against a keyword list. As a cyberthreat intelligence company, we know plenty about bad guys. We know them individually and as groups. We know where they live and hang out. We know what tools they use and from whom they obtained them. We use all of this data and more to determine who we might be dealing with in each case, which informs how we search the OFAC list. Further, when we do get the cryptocurrency address to which the actors want us to send payment, we will run a trace to see what we can learn about that wallet. While many of the wallets are fresh or newly created, we occasionally can learn about recent transactions involving that wallet as well as other wallets with which those transactions have been involved. Cryptocurrency trading software vendors also maintain intelligence about wallets, and some of the open source tools have community input and tagging for those wallets. With these tools, we can determine when and where the wallet was created, what transactions it has been involved in, typical victim payment amounts, and if the wallet is involved in fraud, scams, or other Internet crimes. We might even be able to determine if the wallet is sending its proceeds to unfriendly or OFAC-sanctioned entities or countries. We document everything carefully for due diligence purposes because after dealing with all the stress, drama, and cost associated with the ransom incident, no one wants to get an angry letter from the DOJ or the Treasury Department.

The next gate is much softer and often more difficult to navigate: Does paying a cyber ransom violate your values as a company? While it seems a simple question, I often have to advise companies to take this seriously. If you have a set of core values for your company, they should stand for something. Those values should stand the test, regardless of circumstances. Compromising these at this time will have long-lasting effects on employee morale and their sense of purpose in your organization. If you are using your core values well, they are *the* non-negotiable litmus test for hiring, firing, promoting, demoting, punishing, or rewarding your team. If you violate them, then those guideposts mean nothing. On the other hand, if you use this moment to reinforce those values, this can be an incredible teaching moment for the organization and team. It can be used to strengthen the bond and purpose of the team and the leadership. Real trust is built through shared experience, and this experience is a unique and powerful one. Choose your path carefully.

Leading Through Values Reinforcement

I remember sitting in the conference room as our VP of WW Sales briefed the executive team on the sales pipeline. The VP was a proven sales leader and had run sales organizations for some of the most successful and largest tech companies in the world. We were blessed to have him join our ranks. He was not one for sandbagging—that is, hiding the real value of a deal until the last minute—but in one particular case, he did just that, and it was inarguably justifiable. That day there was a project on the pipeline that he informed me was in a proof-of-concept phase, and he was confident we would win it. He explained that the team had been working on it for some time and that we were doing much better than the larger and more well-known competitors. He forecasted the deal at an average price for our service, so it didn't raise any flags for me. I asked some routine questions on his strategy and we moved on to the next deal.

In the next week, we were informed we won that opportunity, and it was much larger than the average deal size he forecasted—exponentially so. Of course, I was excited to win a deal of this size, but was concerned about how it was managed and how I would explain to the board that we misforecasted by such an amount. (Even coming in much higher than predicted is frowned upon because it indicates we are not accurately running the business.)

Over the weekend, I reviewed the lengthy legal agreement and got to know the customer. Due to compliance on their end, they required us to use their tedious and complicated contract instead of our standard agreement. The contract was for an organization working on a multibillion-dollar project in a foreign country. While the country was friendly to the United States, and it would certainly pass a sanctions review, I had some concerns, starting with whether the data we provided that organization with could be shared with other nation-state actors within the country and used to cause harm. I asked the team involved with the opportunity how the proof of concept was carried out and who from the customer side participated. I was made aware of the fact that the country's intelligence operation members were indeed present. My concerns were valid, but the sales team was not happy with my concerns or questions.

Ultimately, we decided to say no to the deal. This hurt my sales VP's feelings and initially upset the team that had successfully competed and won the proof of concept. Further, my advisers and board members—with one exception—advised me to take the deal. They argued that I could not make business decisions on moral gray areas, asking how I would litigate future deals. They were right; it was a difficult tightrope to walk. I thought long and hard about it. I meditated on it.

The controversial country in question had a history of harming humans that stood in its way. I was deeply concerned that in the course of our normal work, our data would be used to identify and target civilians in that country or others. We later learned that the hypothetical scenario I used as a discussion point on whether they would use the data to harm people who disagreed with their strategy or direction was actually happening on the ground, in real time, as the once-prospective client pursued its project.

I saw this as a teaching moment for the GroupSense team and sent an email to the entire company: "First, I want to thank all of you who contributed to the success of this opportunity. It is a testament to how our small organization can compete and win against much better-funded, big-brand competition. You should be proud. We have ultimately decided that we will not be accepting the contract. This will have a substantial impact on our revenue and will result in a burned bridge or two between our partners. I am sad about these outcomes, as I am sure you are. I have consulted with our board and advisers, who warned me that making business decisions like this, based on values and morals, is a slippery slope and will set a difficult precedent for us. I do not deny this. After much consideration, I have come up with a litmus test for our future engagements. While imperfect, it is a bellwether for us. GroupSense will not do business with any organization we believe will use our data to materially or physically harm human beings. Yes, that will preclude us from business with certain federal government entities. But I will sleep better at night knowing that we are focused on good. We prevent bad things. We will continue to prevent bad things. That is our job. We do not cause them. We prevent them."

That moment turned out to be huge for our company culture. It reinforced our values in a way that cannot be done with simple words. We backed those values up with sacrifice and action. Priceless.

Back to ransoms.

Once the first two hurdles are cleared, we must decide if we can afford to pay the ransom. This is where the difficult business math begins. Getting our arms around the total business impact, both immediate and long term, is a difficult task, but drives our decisions on engagement and strategy.

The ransomware gang/operators often follow a standard operating procedure for ransom incidents. Once they gain persistent access to your systems, they will patiently widen and strengthen their access. They will watch over weeks, months, and sometimes even years without executing the actual ransom attack. During this time, they are accomplishing two primary objectives: stealing/copying as much of your critical information and data as possible (with special attention to documents containing intellectual property, contracts, designs, incident response plans, cyber insurance policies, and key financial documents); and learning how your internal IT processes work, like backups, provisioning, and network connectivity to other nontraditional systems, things like IP phones, HVAC, cameras, physical access control systems, etc. It is only after they feel they have succeeded in these efforts that they execute the malware processes to lock all of your systems and files.

The amount of leverage that this affords the threat actors is practically immeasurable—practically, but it can be measured. Most companies have a rough understanding of the immediate business impact, which is often tied to an operational interruption. Understanding the extent of that interruption and how the attack impacts the business operationally and financially is a key part of our equation. The soft costs and longer-term business impacts are more difficult to quantify. I often refer to these things as the "ransomware blast radius." In trying to get our clients to dig into these issues, we ask them a series of questions, including the following.

- If this incident is prolonged, what will impact the morale of the IT and security staff?
- What will be the impact on the morale of the greater team?
- If, due to this incident, you cannot do accounting and thus payroll, will there be attrition?
- What will be the cost of recruiting and re-hiring for lost staff?
- What is the cost of brand damage to the broader market?
- What is the cost due to loss of customer or partner trust?
- And perhaps most importantly, what is the cost to the business from lost intellectual property (IP) or trade secrets?

That last question didn't occur to me until a specific incident many years ago. It is widely known threat actors like to execute their attacks on holidays and holiday weekends to maximize the time between onset and detection and to take advantage of typically lower staffing levels. One of our law firm partners brought us a new case one Christmas. It was a large manufacturer, and they were down hard. We went through our rigorous process and ultimately negotiated the ransomware actors down to about 30 percent of their original ask. In exchange for the payment, we received the decryption software, unlocked the files, and got the TA's commitment that they would delete the exfiltrated data. (Of course, there is no guarantee that this will occur, which is why companies involved in these incidents should use some form of monitoring post-incident.) After we agreed to a deal, transferred the cryptocurrency, and unlocked the last file, the CISO and I had a phone conversation to wrap things up. He expressed a deep concern that had not occurred to me prior.

He said, "The financial and operational impact of this cyberattack was measurable and painful for the business, but that pales in comparison to another concern I have. We have been the leading manufacturer in our category for over one hundred years. The materials and process in which we build our product is our very confidential trade secret. The IP getting in the hands of one of our competitors or an upstart in Asia could have a devastating impact on our business five years from now."

These business outcomes must be considered and factored into whether to move forward with the ransomware gang engagement/negotiation. Further, these items should be assigned a quantitative value in order to start to define a budget for any possible payment.

Also, the impact quantification step reinforces why it is important to work with a professional. Understanding what the threat actors in question typically ask for and typically settle for is paramount. If, for example, the threat actors ask for 5 percent of the advertised annual revenue of a business and, on average, settle for 80 percent of that number, but the business runs a low margin, then it may not make sense to engage at all. While we have successfully educated threat actors during negotiations on profit and loss in

Negotiating with the Enemy 173

order to reset their expectations in our favor, it is difficult to do and takes time.

By now, we know three important things. First, the hypothetical company is not violating core values by paying a ransom. Second, it is not illegal to pay a ransom. Finally, we understand how to approach the impact and establish a ransom payment budget.

The next two steps happen in parallel. We need to make the first outreach to the ransom actor, and we also need to determine the financial logistics of making the ransom payment.

How we interact with the ransom actor depends on the ransom group. Typically, the ransom note will dictate the communication method. That method is often via the dark web, but sometimes it can be via an anonymous email address or an anonymous chat tool like TOX. Take, for example, the redacted ransom note in Figure 7.1.

```
Hello!

If you are reading this, it means that your system were hit by Royal
ransomware.
        Please contact us via : [REDACTED].onion

In the meantime, let us explain this case.It may seem complicated, but it is
not!

Most likely what happened was that you decided to save some money on your
security infrastructure.

Alas, as a result your critical data was not only encrypted but also copied
from your systems on a secure server.

From there it can be published online.Then anyone on the internet from
darknet criminals, ACLU journalists, Chinese government(different names for
the same thing),and even your employees will be able to see your internal
documentation: personal data, HR reviews, internal lawsuitsand complains,
financial reports, accounting, intellectual property, and more!

        Fortunately we got you covered!

Royal offers you a unique deal.For a modest royalty(got it; got it ? ) for
our pentesting services we will not only provide you with an amazing risk
mitigation service,covering you from reputational, legal, financial,
regulatory, and insurance risks, but will also provide you with a security
review for your systems.

To put it simply, your files will be decrypted, your data restoredand kept
confidential, and your systems will remain secure.

        Try Royal today and enter the new era of data security!
        We are looking to hearing from you soon!
```

Figure 7.1 Redacted ransom note.

Most ransom notes look like the one in Figure 7.1. They are usually sent as an unencrypted text file on one of the systems affected by the threat actors. Sometimes, the messages will come via email and sometimes as a pop-up window. Regardless of the medium, they have some common attributes.

They announce what has occurred (systems were encrypted and thus unusable).

They announce who they are ("You have been hacked by RANSOMGROUPNAME").

They tell you what not to do. "Do not rename or move files," "Do not shut down your systems," and my favorite, "Do not attempt to use third-party decryption software to decrypt the systems or files." (That is because there is no such thing. I will discuss this later.)

There is a time frame specified or a deadline.

They tell you what to do, which often translates to "contact us."

They give you very detailed instructions on how to contact them. Most often, this is a short tutorial on how to get on the dark web.

If the dark web is the communication method, they will provide a dark web URL.

Negotiation

When we started the negotiation practice, I led the negotiation process, supported by my analyst and research teams. One member of my staff was a former undercover law enforcement officer with some negotiation experience and training. I leaned on him often for advice, and later, he became a leading ransomware negotiator himself. I reread some of the best books on negotiation, both old and new. Books like *Getting to Yes* by Roger Fisher and William Ury and *Never Split the Difference* by Chris Voss. I found a Venn diagram overlap between business negotiation science and hostage negotiation science encompassing ransomware negotiation. It was both at the same time. Figure 7.2 shows a Venn diagram of the overlap between negotiation styles.

Negotiating with the Enemy

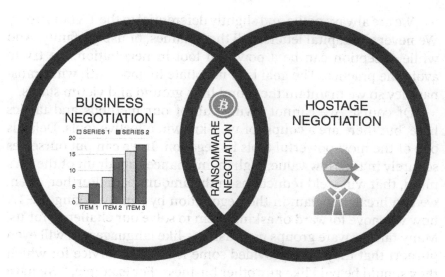

Figure 7.2 Venn diagram.

We quickly developed some basic rules for how to engage with the actors, rules that have proven effective and meaningful as we navigated case after case. First, we do not identify ourselves as a third party. There was a time when this may have made sense, but the threat actors soon became aware of firms like ours and put forward public threats to delete the decryption keys and leave victims unable to recover if they found out professional negotiators were involved. Being a third party is useful, as you can foreshadow or use a foil to signal during the negotiation. For example, "Oh, man, I don't know if my client can afford that," or "I can ask them, but I doubt that will fly." If you do not announce that you are a third party, the actors will likely assume you work for the victim organization. If this is the case, you still can use some form of foil foreshadowing. "I don't have the authority to approve this, and I must run it by the board." I suspect ransomware actors probably assume it is someone appointed by the cyber insurance company or the law firm they are speaking with. In some cases, they do ask. We typically ignore this ask and go about our strategy, and it falls by the wayside. Ultimately, the threat actors just want to get paid.

We are always polite and slightly deferential to the TA but strong. We never use capital letters, call them names, or use profanity. And while deception can be a powerful tool in negotiation, we try to avoid the practice. The goal is to negotiate in good faith with transparency so we maintain the moral high ground and victim status.

Of course, we cannot divulge all of our methods and tactics here, but there are a couple of well-known, effective tools. Delay is one of the most powerful tools in negation. If we can put ourselves squarely in the "low value, high maintenance" quadrant of the TA's mind, that will yield reductions in the amount paid. Further, often, we can break a logjam in the negotiation by simply asking the TA how we move forward or asking them to solve our challenge for us. Many ransomware groups use business-like language and will even purport that they have provided some legitimate service for which they should be paid like any other business. For example, "We have performed a security audit on your business. Contact us to discuss the fee." I have found that when they do this, it is in our best interest to pretend right along with them that this is simply a business transaction.

Here's an example:

We are the RansomHub.

Your company Servers are locked and Data has been taken to our servers. This is serious.

Good news:
    - your server system and data will be restored by our Decryption Tool;
    - for now, your data is secured and safely stored on our server;
    - nobody in the world is aware about the data leak from your company except you and RansomHub team;

FAQs:

Who we are?
    - Normal Browser Links: `https://[REDACTED]`
    - Tor Browser Links: `http://[RECACTED].onoin/`

Negotiating with the Enemy

Want to go to authorities for protection?

- Seeking their help will only make the situation worse, They will try to prevent you from negotiating with us, because the negotiations will make them look incompetent, After the incident report is handed over to the government department, you will be fined <This will be a huge amount, Read more about the GDRP legislation: https://en.wikipedia.org/wiki/General_Data_Protection_Regulation>, The government uses your fine to reward them. And you will not get anything, and except you and your company, the rest of the people will forget what happened!!!!!

Think you can handle it without us by decrypting your servers and data using some IT Solution from third-party "specialists"?

- they will only make significant damage to all of your data; every encrypted file will be corrupted forever. Only our Decryption Tool will make decryption guaranteed;

Think your partner IT Recovery Company will do files restoration?

- no they will not do restoration, only take 3-4 weeks for nothing; besides all of your data is on our servers and we can publish it at any time;

as well as send the info about the data breach from your company servers to your key partners and clients, competitors, media and youtubers, etc.

Those actions from our side towards your company will have irreversible negative consequences for your business reputation.

You don't care in any case, because you just don't want to pay?

- We will make you business stop forever by using all of our experience to make your partners, clients, employees and whoever cooperates with your company change their minds by having no choice but to stay away from your company.

As a result, in midterm you will have to close your business.

So lets get straight to the point.

What do we offer in exchange on your payment:

- decryption and restoration of all your systems and data within 24 hours with guarantee;

- never inform anyone about the data breach out from your company;
    - after data decryption and system restoration, we will delete all of your data from your servers forever;
    - provide valuable advising on your company IT protection so no one can attack your again.

Now, in order to start negotiations, you need to do the following:
    - install and run 'Tor Browser' from https://www.torproject.org/download/
    - use 'Tor Browser' open http://[REDACTED].onoin
    - enter your Client ID: [REDACTED]

There will be no bad news for your company after successful negotiations for both sides. But there will be plenty of those bad news if case of failed negotiations, so don't think about how to avoid it.

Just focus on negotiations, payment and decryption to make all of your problems solved by our specialists within 1 day after payment received: servers and data restored, everything will work good as new.
    ****

A few months into the practice and with many cases under our belt, a gentleman named Maxwell Bevilacqua reached out. A Fulbright scholar, Max had been involved with the Harvard Negotiation Project, taught negotiation at Harvard Law School and Tufts University, and ran a consulting firm that teaches negotiation strategy to law firms, U.S. government leadership, the Army, Marine Corps, and others. Max asked if he could work with us to strengthen our strategy and sharpen our tools. Of course, we said yes, and a partnership was born. To this day, Max is on my speed if I want to navigate a complex interpersonal situation, ransomware or otherwise. His ability to label and verbally diagram any communication scenario is on the genius level.

Over time, I connected with other professional negotiators. I became acquainted with and learned from FBI negotiators, professional hostage negotiators, crisis management negotiators, undercover law enforcement, and some of the top minds from

MIT, Berkeley, Northwestern, and others. A couple weeks prior to speaking at the NYPD Counterterrorism and Cyber Intelligence conference in New York, I received a phone call. I recognized the voice immediately: Chris Voss, a former FBI hostage negotiator. Chris's book *Never Split the Difference* had a number of negotiation tools that had proven invaluable to me. I watched his masterclass and followed the blog he published on behalf of his growing consulting operation, Black Swan.

"Hey, Kurtis, I just listened to your Wall Street Journal Tech podcast," Chris said. "I really dig your methods."

"They are your methods, Chris," I said, and a friendship was born. At the NYPD conference, Chris and I shared the stage with Shawn Henry, chief security officer at CrowdStrike, blowing the audience's minds (see Figure 7.3).

With the help of Max, his team, and a network of leading negotiators, GroupSense quickly grew into a world-class ransomware response and negotiation firm trusted by the largest and most

Figure 7.3 NYPD conference.

prestigious law firms and cyber insurers in the world. Sadly, the skills I perfected at the hands of Chris, Max, and others would only work on the bad guys. I still paid too much for my Tacoma.

The Ransomware Negotiation Experience

Most often, ransomware gangs present a dark web website the victim must log in to for their interactions. This site is usually customized for each victim case, and because the site is unique, the ransomware actors know who they are talking to. The sites vary in design, complexity, features, and purpose. Some dark web sites look just like regular websites, complete with tutorials, FAQs, blogs, and an embedded chat window. Others are styled to look like old CRT monitors or Unix terminals and have minimal functionality. The sites commonly present some time frame in the form of a countdown clock or something similar, associating the clock with some type of threat. "If this clock reaches zero and we have not been paid, we will delete the decryption keys and your files will be lost forever." Or they may approach the situation in a less ominous fashion, stating, "If you do not pay by the time the clock runs out, we will double the price." Either way, these clocks serve the simple purpose of creating a false sense of urgency. Like the ransom amount, these clocks and their associated threats are always negotiable. Figure 7.4 is a screenshot of a ransomware group, Sarcoma, victim site.

The chat window is where the action is. This is where we conduct our "business." Since the ransomware groups are hierarchical organizations, it is fair to assume the first person you interact with in the chat window is of low rank. These folks often have poor English-language skills, and they are usually pasting in script segments handed down from their superiors. You should use very simple language when communicating with these folks. They are probably taking the words you send and putting them through a translator to understand better. It is important to keep the messages simple to use, plain, unadorned language to avoid any confusion over context or meaning that can happen when run through a

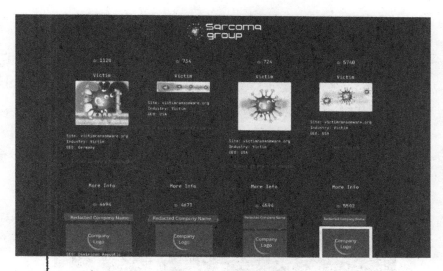

Figure 7.4 Redacted image of ransomware victim site.

translation program. Figure 7.5 shows an example of a ransomware negotiation chat dialogue. In this case, the chat is with the ransomware group Akira.

Chats with threat actors often follow a playbook or pattern. We quickly became intimately familiar with each group's cadence. Most often, the victim is typically presented with the ransom demand within the first couple of messages. We have found these amounts to vary greatly. Some of the groups have adopted a formula (i.e., 5 percent of top-line revenue), but they do not have a robust understanding of a balance sheet. We have found ourselves giving micro business classes to the actors to explain things like margins and assets, leasing versus owning, and so on. This usually works but is time-consuming and difficult. Other groups are rather arbitrary and just throw big numbers at the wall, having been emboldened by the data they have or an article or marketing feature on the company they found on the Internet. Even still, there are groups who will have successfully obtained a copy of the victim's financial records or perhaps their cyber insurance policy. This can drive large, bold, and specific ransom amounts. Even in these cases, there are proven strategies to reduce the ransom payment.

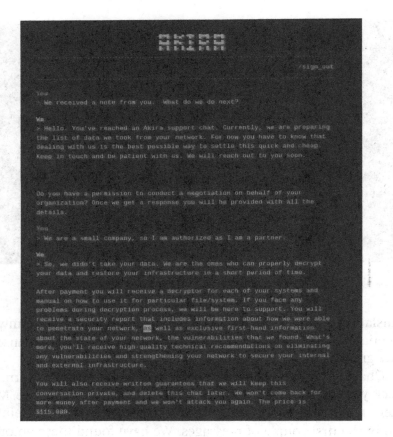

Figure 7.5 Ransomware negotiation chat dialogue.

Ransom cases vary in time to settle as well, but an unscientific estimate would be five to seven business days from contact to close, provided the victim organization's bank cooperates. It is important for the victim to get in front of any financial hurdles or speed bumps early in the process. Due to some saber-rattling from the SEC and the Treasury Department, banks have begun implementing more restrictive measures regarding transferring FIAT capital from their institutions to any form of crypto broker or exchange. This becomes increasingly difficult as the amount goes up. Understanding these policies and their impact on the overall timeline is crucial. The threat actors aren't very patient once an agreement has been reached. Our team has experience navigating and shortcutting this process. Our transaction team goes to work once we kick off the initial contact and receive the ask amount. We work with trusted over-the-counter (OTC) cryptocurrency brokers and exchanges. We are careful to follow all of the reporting and sanctions rules put forward by the aforementioned governing bodies while producing gratuitous evidence for any future proof or diligence related to the case.

Once we reach a final agreement with the threat actors, the GroupSense negotiator sends a list of what we expect in return for payment. It is best practice to ask for as much as possible in exchange for the ransom payment. This list includes, but is not limited to, the decryption keys or software, proof of deletion of the stolen data (this can be a video or log files), and a promise that the ransomware actors will not attack the victim again, will not announce or broadcast any details of the incident, and so on. Obviously, there is no way to guarantee any of these things, but our success rate in getting the decryption keys/software is near 100 percent. As with the notes and communication, it is at this stage some of the ransomware groups will once again pretend they've engaged in a legitimate transaction, providing their promise to deliver in choppy, legal-sounding stanzas. "WHEREFORE we will provide the keys . . . HEREIN, the payment will be considered complete . . ." No kidding!

Transparency and Scams

Considering that the ransomware ecosystem is fueled by anonymity, it is going to be rife with scams and fraud. The dark web (TOR) affords virtual invisibility to these actors and anyone communicating with them. Further, the transactions are done over the blockchain, typically utilizing Bitcoin or sometimes Monero, an even more private token. While the blockchain is transparent, the wallets and tokens can be unattributable.

Due to the difficulty in attributing wallets and tokens, GroupSense insists on being as transparent as possible about our customer negotiation and payment processes. We saw the opportunity for fraud, or at least the accusation of fraud. As a result, we set up a system where the client can review and approve every single message we craft. We explain the purpose and desired outcome for the message we are about to send and even allow the client to weigh in—the client sometimes has a brilliant idea or suggestion. Ultimately, we work for the client and will send the message they want to send, with some limitations. We have refused to send messages containing threats and profanity, for example. Though I understand why the client might want to send those messages, they do not serve the purpose of a successful negotiation. When a client overrides our suggestions, we carefully explain to them what we believe the result will be from the message they crafted. If the client accepts these caveats, we will send it.

We once had a client who was more involved in the message crafting than others. We had long, drawn-out conversations about the messages, the wording, and the timing of when it should be sent. One night, after carefully crafting a message with the client and scheduling a later time to send the message, the client called me.

"Kurtis . . . have you sent the message yet?" he asked.
"No, sir," I replied. "We agreed I would send it at 8:26 p.m. local time."
"I would like to adjust the message slightly."
"Okay, what did you have in mind?" I asked.
"I would like to change this word to 'onerous.'"
"With respect, sir, I can't say how 'onerous' will translate in tone and context in Ukrainian." I suggested leaving it as it was.
"Good point," he said.

Once the messages are agreed upon, we execute. For transparency's sake, the messages on the dark web, whether email or chat, are captured and saved for future reference and proof of execution.

One common scam that occurs is the data recovery company scam. We ran into evidence of this early in our practice. This has also been written about in ProPublica, in the *New Yorker* piece on me, and was explained in Renee Dudley and Dan Golden's book

The Ransomware Hunting Team. (A good book and worth picking up, by the way.)

Victims usually come across the data recovery scam by Googling "how to decrypt [ransomware variant name]." This is a completely natural thing to search for when you have been hit by ransomware, but unfortunately, many of the initial results you will see are not real solutions. Data recovery companies claim to have "special software" that can decrypt the ransomware. All they need to do this is your ransom note and a couple of sample files.

Our first experience with this occurred when a victim called our hotline the evening before Thanksgiving—another holiday attack. They expressed that they had hired a data recovery company to unlock their files, but the company had gone dark, and they were now in a hurry. Unfortunately, they had already paid the recovery company a retainer fee of a few thousand dollars, but the ransom attack made this seem like a minor loss. When they explained that the recovery company claimed to have special software that could decrypt the files without paying the ransom, I knew something was amiss. I asked the client what had happened so far with the data recovery company. He explained that they wanted the ransom note and two files to test their software on and that they would get back to him. He provided this, but they had not gotten back to him or returned his call in a couple of days. I asked him why a data recovery company needed the ransom note and asked for the same document. I knew what I would find when I got to the ransomware victim site. Unsurprisingly, logging into the chat on the ransomware victim site, I saw a chat history going back a few days where the data recovery company had apparently impersonated the victim and negotiated for the decryptor themselves without the victim's knowledge or consent. I could see they had negotiated the amount to $12,000. By the time I captured this evidence and called the victim, they had already heard back from the data recovery company. The data recovery company informed them that they needed to do some special coding on their super-duper decryption software for their case, and it would cost them $65,000 in professional fees and licensing to decrypt their files. That is quite a markup. Unfortunately, it was too late to reverse the situation in this case. The ransomware group thought they had made a deal with the victim but had made a deal with the swindling middlemen instead. There was no going back to the negotiating table.

These fake data recovery companies are still out there, defrauding and hurting victims. One of them even has a prominent former public official as their spokesperson! I took the time to find this person and called to confront them. They categorically denied everything, despite the existence of a promotional video on the front page of the data recovery company's site and their name in the "Advisory Board" section. I followed up by filing a complaint with the FBI, the FTC, and the District Attorney in the state where this company is headquartered. As far as I know, they are still in business.

One year at DEFCON, the venerable hacker and cybersecurity conference in Las Vegas, I found myself sitting on the main stage panel discussion with members of the Ransomware Task Force, cyber thought leaders, policymakers, and academics. Ironically, while on stage, I was in the middle of a negotiation on my phone with a ransomware group. The victim was a small business, and my participation was pro bono. The panel discussion led me to an epiphany that these efforts from Washington, DC, are missing a major point. Exacerbated by the fact that the Ransomware Task Force at that time did not have representation from the *victims*, there was a dissonance around the macro-level impact of the problem. Following up with a cyber think tank member after that panel, I became irate. The think tank member dismissed my concerns for small businesses, stating that the focus should be on protecting critical infrastructure. I passionately reminded him that small to medium businesses (SMBs) make up half of the U.S. gross domestic product (GDP) and more than half of the jobs. Collectively, SMB *is* critical infrastructure and ransomware attacks on SMB is death by a thousand cuts—and no one is paying attention. The U.S. economy is being irreparably harmed by the ransomware epidemic, with businesses shutting down, critical and secret data being pilfered, and funds leaving the U.S. economy forever, often flowing to an unfriendly country. This is a soapbox you will find me on frequently, in life and throughout this book.

Ransomware and cyber extortion continue to wreak havoc on businesses and the U.S. economy. *If you do one thing* after reading this chapter, update your systems, and enable MFA anywhere you can. Bonus if you draft or revisit your incident response plan.

Cyber Recon Leader Profile:

Max Bevilacqua

Max Bevilacqua

Current Role: Founder, Managing Director, Mindful Negotiating; Professor, Tufts University

Other Affiliations: Program on Negotiation (Harvard Law), Fletcher School of Law and Diplomacy, Tufts University Prison Initiative, Planet Indonesia, Lynn Calm Team Community Advisory Committee

Max's Bio

Max Bevilacqua is the founder and managing director of Mindful Negotiating, a global organization that trains U.S. military, incident responders, lawyers, executives, and startups to navigate negotiations skillfully.

Prior to founding Mindful Negotiating, Max was a senior trainer at Vantage Partners, where he advised Fortune 100 executives, business development teams, and U.S. Special Forces. He has taught negotiation at Harvard Law School, Boston University, the Fletcher School at Tufts University, and a medium-security prison.

Max believes negotiation is a civic responsibility tied to adult development and rooted in family systems theory. He's passionate about empowering people with the skills to navigate high-stakes decision-making.

When not negotiating, Max enjoys racket sports, making pasta, rolling Brazilian Jiu-Jitsu, and playing music.

Negotiating with the Enemy

Max holds a B.A. in Religious Studies from Wesleyan University and an M.A. in Law and Diplomacy from Tufts University.

Max's Mission

I believe there is constructive and destructive conflict. I'm interested in cultivating the wisdom to discern between the two, the bravery to engage in conflict constructively, and the creativity to close the gap between what is and what could be.

YouTube URL: youtu.be/42_xp2mSdSc?si=a1ESivdqLkNXWKBY

YouTube, LLC

Chapter 8
You Don't Have to Be a Doctor to Know How Not to Die

"Good evening. I am sorry that we are meeting under such circumstances," I said as I appeared in a Zoom call, my oversized talking head on an 80-inch flat screen in a corporate conference room. The ransomware attack occurred only hours earlier, impacting much of their business operations. They could not use email, make phone calls, take orders, ship products—and worse, they couldn't make payroll.

I worked through the procedural questions I asked at the front end of every ransomware engagement. I asked about the time of discovery, who found the note, and the current understanding of the impact. I asked if anyone had contacted or planned to contact law enforcement and where they were in their incident response process and plan.

Silence.

"Well... about that. It is... encrypted."

This Fortune 1000 company probably paid hundreds of thousands of dollars to PriceWaterhouseCoopers or Deloitte to help them build, draft, and test their incident response plan, only to have it rendered unavailable during the actual incident because no one had access to a printed copy. Ransomware is a different kind of cyber event, and one must prepare for it differently.

I am a big fan of Stoic philosophy. As a young man, I practiced many of the lessons in Stephen R. Covey's classic book, *The 7 Habits of Highly Effective People*. I didn't know then that one of my go-to pieces of wisdom in that book was derived from Stoicism. The idea behind one's sphere of influence is that one should focus on only the items within their immediate control—and only the items they can tangibly impact at that moment. Everything else is a distraction, taking away from the energy needed to execute. This philosophy, whether you credit Mr. Covey or Marcus Aurelius, is central to reducing ransomware attacks, business email compromise, and other cyberattacks. We may not have the power to stop the attacks or change international policy toward Russia's amnesty for the threat actors. It is not within our reach to arrest many of the perpetrators of these attacks. What *do* we control? *Ourselves. Ourselves*, my friends, is all we control.

I have been called to Washington, DC, to be interviewed by congressional committees and congressional leadership. I have spoken to the White House Office of Management and Budget, which drafted the Biden administration's Cybersecurity Strategy documents. I have met with CISA leadership, the United Nations, and leadership around the globe. When asked the inevitable question of how to reduce or stop these attacks, I always give the same answer: *prevention and education*. Those two things are squarely within our sphere of influence.

My position on federal and state policy remains constant. If this were looked at from a macro level, there would be a clear return on investment (ROI) for the U.S. government in participating in and subsidizing prevention, education, and recovery efforts. My answer when being probed about whether paying ransoms should be made illegal is often "No! Absolutely not!" Victims, many of which are below what I call the "cyber poverty line," are faced with either paying the ransom or going out of business. If we made paying a ransom illegal, the payments would still occur but will be reported less often. As responders and policymakers, we want to collaborate with the victims and learn about the impact. Let's give these victims a little help, a third option: recovery without paying a ransom. Only then will the ransomware actors choose another profession.

The cyber poverty line is a byproduct of our tech economy, much of which is fueled by venture capital (VC). While there are many positives to the VC approach to growing a tech business, it has some negatives. Over the years, companies subsidized by VCs have adopted a particular strategy that is antithetical to the cyber needs of the larger economy. The VCs have a prospectus, often a certain multiple return in a certain number of years from their portfolio companies. They are awarded a board seat at the company as part of their investment agreement. Their influence on the boards of these companies drives the companies into a trajectory that matches their prospectus. That trajectory requires them to get big quick with as much profit margin as possible. The result is high-tech, high-margin tools marketed as security solutions. To maintain these margins, the products have to be self-administered by the buyers. The VC-backed company, in order to keep costs down and margins high, cannot provide advanced services with the software or hardware products. As a result, these products are not solutions; they are tools, and tools need operators.

The cybersecurity market has suffered a talent deficit for a decade, which has driven salaries sky-high for anyone who can spell "malware." This leaves the bulk of the market and small-to-medium businesses with little hope of using the most sophisticated technology to defend themselves. Only recently have we seen some shift toward SMBs in venture investment—starting with private equity's interest in managed IT providers. Perhaps this recent shift, in combination with the U.S. government's interest in protecting critical infrastructure, including the backbone of the economy (SMBs), will change the paradigm. Until then, cyber hygiene and basic prevention are the key.

I sometimes give a keynote speech called "The Software Won't Save You" on this topic. I ultimately get asked a repeat question: "Kurtis, do we all need to become cyber experts now?" My answer, often while smirking mildly, is, "No, we don't. Just like we don't all need to be doctors in order to know how not to die."

Myriad resources illustrate the steps an organization can take to avoid being the victim of ransomware or other cyberattacks. GroupSense gets a pretty clear picture of how the threat actors gain access to the victim networks in each ransomware response case. We have distilled this down to a personal and organizational cyber hygiene guide, which can be found here:

What we have learned is that most cyberattacks are preventable by implementing some basic changes in behavior and small software tweaks—not necessarily by buying new expensive cyber defense toys. The rest of this chapter will be familiar to cyber professionals, but the information will be useful to those new to or unfamiliar with the nuances of cyber defense strategy.

When thinking about organizational cyber defense strategies as they relate to ransomware, it helps to understand better who the adversary is, what their motivations are, and what tools they use. Most ransomware operators are running a business, and they operate like any small business. They have margins, cost of goods, quotas, and bonuses for their staff. This means they want to gain access to the victim systems and networks as inexpensively as possible to increase their margins and make their quotas—and go to the president's club. Not kidding!

We know this in part because a few years ago, one of the most notorious ransomware gangs, Conti, decided to write a post on their blog about their support for the Russian invasion of Ukraine in 2022. Unfortunately, they forgot that some of their key and senior members were Ukrainian; the blog post offended those members, and they dumped the transcripts of their internal chats for the world to see. With a quick parsing of the JSON files and native translation work, the intel community learned much about how Conti operated. What we saw validated what our intelligence had indicated. These cybercriminals were like a medium-sized business with all the business mechanics and even office drama you would expect.

That cybercriminals use a traditional business approach to run their ransomware operation indicates these threat actors are not spending time writing custom vulnerabilities to attack their victims. They are not purchasing zero days on the dark web. Instead, they take advantage of the average organization's poor cyber hygiene using deliberately simple and inexpensive attacks.

Let's run through how to improve cyber hygiene quickly and inexpensively. The following are steps any organization can implement to protect themselves and significantly reduce the likelihood of a successful ransomware event or other cyberattack.

Good credential and password policy: A good credential policy includes using complex passwords that are rotated (ideally using a password manager) regularly. This is something we have known for a long time. It should also enforce a policy that prohibits the use of corporate credentials or email accounts for use on any application or site unrelated to the business. Credential monitoring will ensure that policy violators have their password reset and are notified in writing of their policy violations.

A good credential and password policy helps prevent cyberattacks because in many cases, the bad actors don't "hack" into your systems—they simply log in like anybody who already works there. This is especially effective because all the security systems are designed to detect unusual activity or software, and logging into a device is hardly unusual.

Here is what happens all too often: Someone from a commercial organization uses their work email address to sign up for a third-party website or application that has nothing to do with the business. Let's pick on iloveknitting.com. The employee uses their corporate credential to sign up for iloveknitting.com. The nice lady who runs iloveknitting.com isn't great at security and neglects to update her web software for a known security vulnerability. She believes bad guys don't care about iloveknitting.com, so she doesn't prioritize it. Unfortunately for her (and the corporate employee's company), the bad guys are opportunistic. They have written a scanner to pore over the entire web for this specific vulnerability, and when it finds one, it automatically executes the attack. The results of that attack are the transmission of all the usernames and passwords used on the site to the attackers. Now the bad guys have all the usernames and passwords from iloveknitting.com and maybe hundreds of other websites with the same vulnerability. Of course, the majority of these are personal email addresses, but the bad guys are clever. They write a script that goes through the thousands of user credentials they've collected and removes the personal ones, discarding anything ending with @gmail.com, @aol.com, and so on. What they are left with is all the commercial email addresses from all of those sites. They also have a script that they run these remaining addresses through; this one just pulls the company name out of the domain in the email. So if the credential is john.doe@companyname.com, they separate john.doe and companyname. The script then takes companyname and runs it against a database of IP spaces and returns a range of IP addresses. Next, it scans those IP addresses for remote access systems like VPNs or remote desktop ports, like RDP. It then uses john.doe and attempts to log in to those devices. And guess what? The employee or john doe used the same or similar password on iloveknitting.com as they used at work. Many of these attempts will fail, but enough of them succeed to cause real damage, and it requires virtually no effort or time from the threat actors.

To monitor for violation of this policy, utilize digital risk protection services (DRPSs) or brand monitoring services. The bad actors

You Don't Have to Be a Doctor to Know How Not to Die 197

will often trade and even openly share these credential lists on the dark web, Telegram channels, and other unsavory locations. DRPS and brand monitoring solutions monitor these bad actor channels continuously, looking for their customer credentials. When they see them, they notify the company, which in turn alerts the offender, reinforces the policy, and resets their corporate passwords.

Password managers: Implement a password manager at the enterprise level. This will ensure the staff are using different passwords for all systems. It can also be used to deprovision users from third-party applications and sites when they leave the company.

The human brain is an amazing computer. It can remember the equivalent of petabytes of information, yet as a multipurpose computer, it can remember complex strings of characters only for short periods. We store these complex strings in short-term memory. As a result, we would have to use them often for them to transfer to long-term memory. Since we have passwords across so many different sites, we are incapable of remembering different complex strings for each of them. This is why we reuse them so often, as illustrated in the scenario earlier, where the threat actor simply logs in. Some people are diligent about trying to use different passwords, using a technique neuroscientists call "chunking." This breaks down those complex strings into "chunks" of smaller, easier-to-remember information. Unfortunately, humans recombine the chunks in different orders to make other passwords. The threat actors' tools are wise to this and use "fuzzing," a way to quickly try different combinations of passwords. Eventually, they get the chunk order correct and are off to the proverbial races.

Password managers allow the user to use one complex password for the manager itself and then use the password manager to generate different random complex passwords for every site and store them for automatic retrieval via an application or browser plug-in. This means the user often does not even know what the password is to any given site. They simply use the complex password to access the password manager, which supplies the relevant site password. As a result, we have different passwords for every single site. If one site (iloveknitting.com) gets popped, the credentials taken from that site are useless for any other web properties related to that user.

Some in the information security industry consider password managers risky due to the "eggs in one basket" concept. We store the passwords to every site we have credentials for in one place. I understand this is a risk, and some password manager companies *have* been breached, but to date, those breaches have not exposed the actual passwords. In one case, the credential database was taken, but it was encrypted. This is still a concern, as governments have the computing power to reverse the encryption over time. Regardless, the risk that your credentials will be taken in a breach of a third-party site and then reused on other properties is higher. In fact, it is practically guaranteed, and it doesn't require nation-state computing power and 10 months to execute. I am convinced that the password manager is the best solution currently available.

A number of high-profile attacks involved using user credentials that should have been deprovisioned or deleted when the user of those credentials left the organization. As we learned in an earlier chapter, these are called orphaned accounts. Orphaned credentials have been leveraged in attacks involving industrial espionage, financial theft, data theft, and ransomware. For example, the Colonial Pipeline attack in May 2021 had measurable kinetic impacts, leaving millions without fuel on the eastern seaboard of the United States due to the password reuse of a user who no longer worked at the company. Their credentials had not been removed from the VPN remote access system long after they had left the organization. Most enterprises utilize identity and access management (AIM) systems to assist with this. AIM systems are effective but they're complex and expensive to acquire and implement. Enterprise password managers can remove or reset the passwords for the sites the users in an organization use for work after they leave the company, effectively rendering them useless to the user and any attackers.

Multifactor authentication (MFA): Implement the use of MFA everywhere possible. Choose third-party vendors (apps and SaaS) who support this feature over those that do not. Utilize app- or token-based MFA systems, not SMS or email-based ones.

Where AIM, password managers, and credential policies fail, MFA comes to the rescue. MFA is combining something you know (a password or PIN) with something you are (biometrics) or something you have (a token or generated code) or both. The safest implementation of these tools involves avoiding the use of easily manipulated or compromised protocols or systems like email or SMS. A best practice is to use an authenticator app or a token on your phone. The authenticator apps are often free and function by generating a new numerical code on a synchronized cadence with the system being accessed. The token is a separate device that has the synchronized code and functions solely for that purpose. This solution provides another layer that would prevent an attacker from gaining access even if they have correct credentials. MFA prevents so many cyber incidents that many cyber insurance companies require it to be implemented on key systems before underwriting an organization's policy.

Effective vulnerability and patch management: Update your systems regularly. This means training your users to update their browsers, operating systems, and mobile devices when possible. Prioritize updating and patching externally (Internet) facing systems, especially remote access devices like VPN.

Any company can achieve vulnerability management by regularly scanning systems to determine what services are advertised by the system and whether those services are susceptible to a known exploit or vulnerability. This is critical because software vendors *always* have flaws in their code that threat actors are eager to take advantage of. Determining if the organization has implemented systems with these flaws and actively mitigating the risk of executing exploits against them is fundamental to a cyber security program. Large organizations will struggle with the sheer volume of vulnerabilities because of the huge number of systems involved in operating the company; we refer to this as the "attack surface." Effective vulnerability management programs include vulnerability patch priority, which means understanding which vulnerabilities are actively being exploited in the wild and at what frequency will determine which systems to patch first. Regardless, it is inevitable that software suppliers will make mistakes that lead to security risks. It is critical to either patch those mistakes or, when that is not an option, put in mitigating controls to prevent or contain exploit activity.

User training and a security-focused culture: Create an organizationwide culture of prioritizing security and secure behavior. Implement regular user security training. Train staff about the dangers of clicking links in emails, instant messages, or texts. Teach users about the latest social engineering attacks and tricks the threat actors are leveraging against companies.

The biggest risk to the cyber safety of an organization is human beings; they are simultaneously the best defense. Threat actors know this and use our humanity to get around cyber security solutions. It is counterintuitive to impress upon a company culture to distrust communications from peers. This is why threat actors are so successful at using social engineering to weasel their way into an organization. It is not about distrusting one another as a team but about distrusting our communication medium and systems. In the past, this was largely limited to email communications, but it has quickly expanded to include instant messages, internal chat tools, and even phone and video communications. It is important to train staff on how these attacks occur and build effective business processes to thwart them.

A close friend and colleague once gave a talk at Defcon that serves as a great example of how threat actors can use their systems against users. Taylor Banks and Michael Silvers designed a talk called "On the Hunt: Hacking the Hunt Group" where they tricked the staff of a large call center into willingly downloading malware onto their systems. Before giving the talk, they executed this attack on a real call center as a proof of concept. To execute the attack, they would call the call center's main number and when the employee picked up the phone, they would immediately three-way call the same number. Another staff member would pick up and bridge them together. The confused call center employees would chat briefly about what was happening; they would exchange names and information, which Taylor and Chris Silvers would record for future use. They did this repeatedly over the course of a couple of weeks. The staff began concluding there was some kind of glitch in the phone system. As it repeated, the staffers would talk longer and discuss how the IT and phone system managers weren't addressing the problem. They would name those team members and refer to the phone software on their computers they used to record information about their calls and their callers. Taylor and Chris now knew all they needed to know to execute the attack. They created a website mimicking the site of the phone system manufacturer and included some information about the call center company. They added a download section labeled to reflect a troubleshooting scenario and put in a piece of remote access software (RAS) labeled with a filename reflecting the diagnosing of phone systems on that link. They then called the call center and chatted up the staffer, stating they were from the IT department. They referenced the recurring problem and discussed how they had met with the IT and phone system managers by name. They referenced the software on their computer and explained they were calling to attempt to troubleshoot the problem. They directed the user to the website and asked them to download the software. Of course, the user obliged and they were in.

This could have been prevented through a number of methods, including basic user training, technology, and a business process. If you had implemented *all three strategies*, this type of attack would have been nearly impossible for the attacker. Training users to fully authenticate who they are speaking with would have potentially stopped the attack. This is necessary now more than ever, as generative artificial intelligence can enable attackers to fully emulate a person's voice with as little as 15 seconds of sample material. (The required sample time is going down quickly!) Technology that limits execution, access, or detects the RAS software would have set off alarms and limited the program's capability. Also, using limited access, role-based access, or Zero Trust methodologies may have prevented the user from downloading or executing the program. Finally, a business process that required the user to get permission or prevented the user from visiting the site and interacting with the third party could have prevented this.

Business email compromise (BEC) attacks get fewer headlines than ransomware but are responsible for more financial damage worldwide. Business email compromise is a form of attack where threat actors insert themselves into an email thread or communication and typically direct a person in the communication to take an action that compromises the organization. These attacks are typically carried out in stages. In some cases, the attackers have access to legitimate email accounts; in others, they simply use a domain name similar to the victim's and spoof a known employee. They typically have done significant reconnaissance and open source intelligence (OSINT) work in the latter case. The goal is to trick a staffer into clicking on something, downloading something, or even changing the bank wiring information for a particular customer, partner, or transaction. A combination of technology, training, and business processes prevents these costly attacks. Training users to look for domains that don't look right, to be aware of unusual behavior and requests, and not to click on or download anything from an email would make this more difficult for the attacker.

Technology can detect when an external non-sanctioned domain communicates with an internal user and visibly warn them. It can also detect malicious files and links. However, the best backstop for these kinds of attacks is business processes—processes preventing employees from changing any financial information without proper approval and validation. This may include looping in another team member to vet the change and/or calling the party asking for the change via an approved contact list.

One of my close and trusted colleagues had a BEC incident and called me to ask what they should look for in the aftermath. An attacker inserted themselves in an email thread between their staff and a partner. A transaction was looming, and the attacker saw the opportunity to capitalize. They ultimately had my client change the bank routing information for the transaction, transferring their money to an offshore account. The money was simply gone. While speaking with the CTO, someone I knew well, I asked about their business processes related to changing such information. She informed me they *do* validate account numbers and routing changes by calling the requesting party. Unfortunately, the staffer responsible for the validation call called the number in the email signature rather than using an approved contact list for the partner. Of course, the number in the signature was that of the attacker. The attacker, to no one's surprise, approved the change.

The business processes must be ironclad, with no deviations accepted. Employees must understand what is at risk and respect the process. Threat actors using BEC attacks are sophisticated and well-resourced organizations. Remember, they only have to be right once to make their yearly salary. They can afford to be patient and methodical. Make their job difficult with layers of training, technology, and processes.

Another more advanced business email compromise attack leverages generative AI to trick its target. Threat actors case the company website, taking note of the leadership and board members. They read the news section and maybe the investor relations section. They use LinkedIn to learn about the organization, specifically focusing on people in the finance departments. They feed a carefully crafted narrative aligning with recent events or investor activity to a generative AI engine, then use the AI to create a fake email thread between the members of the executive team and the board of directors, complete with realistic-looking email headers. The attack begins by looping an unsuspecting staffer into this email thread. The ask is for a financial transaction modification or an emergency wire. The staffer scrolls up to see the highest levels of the company discussing this in the email chain. There is an urgency and an appeal for secrecy. This is effective because the staffer, humbled to be trusted by the senior staff and board, will ask fewer questions and execute the request in secrecy.

What to Do When an Attack Occurs

After checking the boxes on basic cyber hygiene, let's prepare for "getting sick." Preparing for the eventual attack, planning, and practicing how we will respond is priceless on the day when an attack slips through our cyber hygiene–related defenses.

When an attack does occur, it can be a jarring and emotional event for everyone in the organization. The leadership may feel panic and embarrassment, and the IT staff may feel vulnerable and violated. The organization at large may feel overwhelmed and afraid. Instituting a plan for response and communications will assist with navigating this tough situation.

Retain the services of an incident response (IR) firm simply because you don't want to meet these people for the first time on the day of an incident. Your team is good, but they don't do this every day—IR firms do. They have seen every recent attack tool and angle, and they have the forensics tools and knowledge to help you identify the threat and recover quickly. They also understand chain of custody requirements and the legal ins and outs of cyber investigations. Some IR firms have experience with negotiation, but most do not, so you will want to put a ransomware responder on retainer as well. Unfortunately, many firms have raised their hands and claimed to be able to negotiate effectively. There is no litmus test for ransomware negotiation outcomes, so it is difficult to know how effective they are. Certainly, ask questions about their negotiation team's pedigree and experience. If they have assigned someone as a negotiator who was doing malware reversal last week, you might want to look outside that firm for your negotiation team.

As discussed in this chapter, your IR plan should include a matrix for calculating the overall impact of the attack. The results of this calculation will drive response, priorities, and, if necessary, a ransom payment amount.

If you have cyber insurance, the IR plan should take this into account. Most cyber policies have fine print about what should be done upon discovering an incident. A specific sequence of actions is often specified in the agreement. Failure to follow these in order in the correct time frame may result in non-reimbursement. Further, your cyber insurer will probably have an approved panel of partners. Consult your insurer on whom they approve for incident response and ransomware response. If your insurer provides an authorized IR firm, ask to speak with the IR firm. If possible, have the insurer's preferred IR provider participate in your tabletop exercises.

Take care to develop a parallel but complementary crisis communications plan. This document is used in conjunction with the incident response plan and catalogs who will be contacted, in which order, plus what will be communicated at which stage of the incident. Enter into a retainer and work with a crisis public relations (PR) firm or specialist. I am not a lawyer or a PR firm, but I have seen this play out firsthand. The best communication strategies I have witnessed are ones communicating as transparently as possible—without speculating—to the constituents, often within the current knowledge boundaries. Remember, when the incident is over, you and your organization are going to need a tremendous amount of goodwill from the community. The quickest way to squander that goodwill is to make them feel like you are hiding something or lying to them. This goes for external constituents *and* staff. If you want to lose the respect, trust, and admiration of your staff, lie to them during a ransomware event. They will eventually learn what is really happening—not to mention that some ransomware groups use call centers to contact your staff directly. The message is usually something like, "Your executive team are not being good stewards of your private information. We have offered them a fair price to protect your information and they have refused. Now your information will be posted on the dark web." Needless to say, HR gets quite a few calls when this happens. Better to read them in on what is going on early and often. Ideally, you employ people you respect and trust, so treat them that way.

By the way, the incident response plan you've had filed away since 2005 is no good. Times have changed, people and technology have changed, and as illustrated in this chapter's opening story, ransomware is fundamentally different. Incident response plans are not a checkbox solution.

As a result, I advise conducting cyberattack tabletop exercises (TTX) at least twice annually—but do them quarterly if you can. Typically, these are divided into parts. One is highly technical and talks through how to contain the threat, assess the impact on systems, engage the incident response firm, and other matters related to the network and systems involved. The other is at the executive level and revolves around escalation, threat actor engagement, communication, emergency changes to operations, and other considerations. Additionally, have your incident response firm participate in the TTX. The more exposure they have to your plan and your organization, the better things will go when an incident does occur.

GroupSense has participated in executive and technical TTXs with enterprise companies for years. Part of the value of these exercises is bringing in pseudo-random scenarios to test the incident response plan's effectiveness. These are called "injects." Our experience in the ransomware response space has given us a strong library of real-world scenarios to inject during TTXs. In late 2024, we began priming an AI large language model (LLM) with the different scenarios. Priming simply gives the LLM context around the user's use case or intent. We also primed the LLM with best practice examples of incident response plans and some example use cases. After priming the AI LLM, which we named Tracey in honor of our TraceLight platform, we used it to create the injects for customer-facing TTXs. This worked well and provided a more real sense of surprise.

Here is some additional advice for those involved in a ransomware attack:

1. Don't panic!
2. Engage your law firm to get your arms around breach notification and legal impact.
3. Have a financial or business impact calculator to determine whether you should engage the threat actor.

4. Follow your incident response and crisis communication plan.
5. The bad guy's advice in ransom notes is sound. Do not move or rename files and do not restart any of the affected machines. Do not contact companies claiming to have decryption software; this is *always* a scam.
6. Do not contact the ransom actor or visit the dark website until you consult a professional responder. (Usually, the ransom site is custom to your attack, which means that simply visiting the site will make the threat actors aware that you received the note and are online and at least remotely interested in talking. This sometimes triggers a countdown clock with additional threats attached to it.)
7. Engage a responder to be the lead on the incident.
8. If you intend to make a payment, ensure you or your responder follows the legal and international sanctions guidelines. They should also be well versed in cryptocurrencies, how to make test transfers, and other aspects of these types of transactions.
9. Engage public relations experts to craft communications, both internally and externally.
10. Optionally, if it is mandated, notify law enforcement.

You have 3 days, 02:37:31
* If you do not pay on time, the price will be doubled
* Time ends on

Current price   1578.282 XMR
                ≈ 200,000 USD
After time ends 3156.564 XMR
                ≈ 400,000 USD

Monero address: * XMR will be recalculated in 2 hours with an actual rate

INSTRUCTIONS | CHAT SUPPORT New   ABOUT US

How to decrypt files?
You will not be able to decrypt the files yourself. If you try, you will lose your files forever.
To decrypt your files you need to buy our special software - General-Decryptor
* If you need guarantees, use trial decryption below.

How to buy General-Decryptor?

Buy XMR with Bank
○ Kraken
○ AnyCoin (EUR)
○ BestChange

Buy XMR locally with cash or online

If organizations and individuals took steps to prioritize some of the changes suggested in this chapter, threat actors would have a much more difficult time disrupting our businesses, holding us hostage digitally, and taking our money. Our continued work in the cyber response space affirms my belief that every dollar spent on prevention and planning is paid back exponentially in reduced risk and during an incident.

Also, don't fall into the "we can build it better here" mentality. Big egos are pervasive in IT departments and cybersecurity practitioners, but the organization that recognizes its core competency and strength versus weaknesses will fare better in the long run. This is one of the primary reasons we offer the GroupSense Digital Risk Protection service. We know the average organization cannot afford to run a cyber intelligence program in-house. Outsource to the experts whenever possible, but be picky about your partner.

I believe the cyberattacks being levied against our citizens and commercial organizations is a matter of national security. I am confident that real and permanent damage is being done to our economy, and for these reasons, I firmly believe that practicing good cyber hygiene is a civic and patriotic duty. Look at what is happening: Foreign actors from unfriendly countries are breaking into our systems and stealing our private data. They are disrupting our systems and our way of life. They demand ransoms. When they are paid, that money goes to an unfriendly foreign country. We don't know what they do with this money, but it is unlikely it ever makes its way back to the U.S. economy.

And another thing: I have been shouting at the top of my lungs to whomever in the government will listen. In ransomware attacks, the threat actors take as much of the data from their victims' networks and systems as possible before executing the ransomware malware. In each ransomware settlement, they "promise" to "delete" the data they stole. But what actually happens? The majority of ransomware attacks emanate from Russia, where Vladimir Putin and his cronies have offered an unofficial amnesty to the ransomware actors. As long as they do not target Russian or Russian-friendly assets, they are free to do as they please. No one in Russia is complaining about the economic harm to the United States or the money being spent in Russia from those attacks. Rest assured, their amnesty comes with a quid pro quo: The FSB/GRU (Russian intelligence groups) get a copy of the data. These double extortion attacks have been happening for more than five years, which means the Russian spy machine has exabytes of U.S. corporate, public sector, military, and municipal data. That data is a powerful seed for future cyber war efforts against our country.

You and I have a civic responsibility to be better stewards of our data, to take better care of our systems, and to practice good cyber behavior. Organizations must prioritize cyber security. Collectively, if we all start paying attention to these basic cyber hygiene practices, it will make a meaningful impact to national security and protect our economy. Don't just do these things for yourself; do them for your country.

If you do one thing after reading this chapter, please start using a password manager. Enable MFA. Update your software. (Yes, stop playing Wordle and update your phone.)

And stop clicking on things. Please stop.

Cyber Recon Leader Profile:

L. Taylor Banks

Current role(s): Global Cybersecurity Sales & Marketing Executive, DEFCON Operations Security Director, & Volunteer Firefighter

Other Affiliations: Founder of DC404, Director of Floor Operations SOC GOONs – DEFCON, Volunteer Firefighter and EMT-IV – Pagosa Fire Protection District, Mentor and Full-time Hacker – Cyber Summit Co, Contributor – SAMAEL (Follow-up to Anonym.OS)

Taylor's Bio

Taylor Banks has built a career on both breaking and securing systems, shaping modern cybersecurity through education, research, and leadership. He has trained thousands of security professionals and developed tools that advance privacy and security worldwide. From training elite teams at the CIA and NSA to negotiating with ransomware actors and advising security startups, his career reflects a relentless pursuit of knowledge and public service. A frequent speaker at DEFCON, ShmooCon, and other top security conferences, Taylor approaches every challenge with technical expertise and a hacker's curiosity. He's also a dedicated firefighter, EMT, and mentor, embodying service beyond cybersecurity. Taylor is continually inspired by those who push the field forward, including Kurtis Minder, whose leadership in cyberthreat engagement has set new standards. When not immersed in security, he's volunteering on search-and-rescue missions, firefighting, or mentoring the next generation of security leaders.

You Don't Have to Be a Doctor to Know How Not to Die

Taylor's Mission

I'm dedicated to building a stronger, more resilient, and more connected cyber community. As a founder, leader, lifelong hacker, and volunteer first responder, I believe real progress happens when people come together—sharing knowledge, fostering trust, and challenging each other to grow. Whether mentoring new talent through DC404 or serving my community as a volunteer firefighter and SAR team member, my commitment is the same: empowering others, strengthening networks, and ensuring people are better prepared to face whatever challenges lie ahead. At the heart of it all, my mission is simple: Strengthen communities and make a lasting, positive impact on people's lives.

YouTube URL: www.youtube.com/watch?v=dzIdamZoYXQ

Chapter 9
Robots, Digital Money, and Teleportation

"I will not prevaricate. I will get straight to the point."

That was the first sentence in a diatribe from a ransomware actor. The message was exquisitely written and in a longer form than we are used to seeing from a threat actor. Until this message, most ransomware actors had scripts with which we had become familiar. During negotiations, responses were curt and sometimes poorly written. This message was more than 600 characters long and written quite well, so much so my team had to pull out the dictionary. My negotiation team brought it immediately to my attention.

> "Have you seen this kind of behavior?" one of them said. "I had to look up *prevaricate!*"
> "It does seem a bit cerebral for someone who doesn't speak the language, doesn't it?" I commented.

I took the text and ran it through a tool that measured the likelihood that generative AI wrote the content: 96% likely.

This was the first time we saw our adversaries using generative AI in this fashion. It makes sense, and we see it more frequently now. Prior to this, we experienced threat actors using AI primarily to create synthetic content for phishing campaigns, web landing pages, and other attack vectors. It seemed a logical next step to use it to better understand large datasets. I had speculated they would eventually start using AI to help them find the needles in the haystacks of exfiltrated data.

One of the challenges they have long faced is the sheer volume of data they steal from their victims. Finding evidence in stolen data they can use to extort a victim is quite an effort. Through our response work, we knew which actors were better than others at this, and I was becoming more certain they had help from the magic cloud robots. It was perhaps naive that I had not anticipated they would use gen AI to interact with victims and negotiators. Or at least if they did, they would know better than to use words like "prevaricate" or change their communication patterns entirely.

Generative AI is transforming the way everyone does business, including our adversaries. As a result, we have to adapt how we defend ourselves. At a macro level, the cyber defense landscape was initially impacted by the use of AI to create synthetic content. The days of poorly written phishing emails riddled with spelling errors are disappearing fast. The new content is crisp, clever, and very realistic. To get our arms around how to defend against these AI-enabled cyberattacks, it helps to think like the attacker.

I ran an experiment where I primed AI with information about me. I used publicly available information anyone with basic OSINT knowledge could gather. I used information from my LinkedIn profile, fed the engine my blog content, and threw in some breach data and data broker information. This culminated in the AI bot knowing quite a bit about who Kurtis Minder is. It understood where I worked, what my jobs were, my overall demeanor, and even my hobbies. (My blog content talks about my affinity for camping and motorcycles and even links to articles I wrote for motorcycle publications.) I asked the AI questions about Kurtis. "What does Kurtis do in his spare time?" The answers were surprisingly accurate, so much so that I might ask it what to do this weekend. Then, I asked the AI to write a spear phishing email that Kurtis would *absolutely* click on. It produced a mesmerizing message from a motorcycle shop that had read my blog and wanted my opinion on a marketing campaign they were about to launch. The message alluded to their need for me to consult for them and produced a link to some supposed marketing images. Click!

The entrepreneurial journey of building GroupSense offered repeated opportunities to take significant venture capital investment. Ultimately, we did take a small amount of seed capital but refrained from the large A-round path. One of the reasons we did this was because the incredibly smart financial minds were always looking for ways to increase the margins on our solution. Don't get me wrong—I am all for this; it is fundamental to running a healthy business. It was the *way* they suggested we achieve it that proved challenging for us.

> "Kurtis, how can we replace your researchers and analysts with AI?" they would ask.
> My answer was always the same: "You can't."

I still firmly believe that AI cannot fully replace HUMINT operations. Retaining the same level of trust and customer service would be difficult if we attempted to replace our analysts with AI. As gen AI became more capable, we augmented our research, analysis, and customer service methods with the technology. We will continue to iterate on this, but it cannot replace the human element in cyberthreat intelligence.

Nevertheless, we have successfully applied AI in some areas in our digital risk and intelligence practice. We still use cloud-based multi-tenant large language models (LLMs) for sales and marketing materials, content creation, and other aspects of day-to-day business. We built a gen AI model in-house for anything related to specific customers or our internal datasets and named the model Tracey in honor of our TraceLight platform.

We started by allowing the analysts to use Tracey to assist in the context and narratives of the finished intelligence reports. To enhance our Cyber Intelligence Advisories, we trained the LLM on what good reports looked like and from where we sourced our context data. Each advisory we assembled made the model a little smarter. This worked well, and we will continue to iterate on it.

It is feasible that there will be a point in the near future when the advisory's contextual content will be 100 percent delivered by AI, but this in no way means we need fewer analysts. Rather, it means the analyst has to slog through fewer remedial and repetitive tasks. As we disengage repetitive and programmatic tasks from the analyst, they can spend more time hunting bad guys and supporting customer outcomes.

Allowing Tracey access to our platform data was transformative, and the use cases are seemingly limitless. Our 10-plus-year collection infrastructure had populated a massive data lake. The data lake contained a number of individual warehouses for the day-to-day application of our technology. Those warehouses comprise rich data around conversations, OSINT, and breach data. Tracey's ability to find patterns across the warehouses and connect dots between Telegram and dark web conversations, indicators of compromise (IOCs), and breach information has had a powerful impact on our ability to both predict behaviors and perform attribution. While it's still in a nascent stage, I envision clear benefits to applying AI in cyberthreat intelligence and cyber espionage.

One robust use case is leveraging the speed of the AI to do analysis. For example, on multiple occasions, we have obtained lists of companies breached as private menus from initial access brokers. Often, the lists are long and comprise a single attack vector, like a known VPN vulnerability. We can connect the list to online activity, conversations, and breach data while compiling an individual outreach advisory for every company on the list at once. We can direct Tracey to divide the victims by country and create notification letters for the appropriate regulatory or law enforcement agencies.

Here is a brief summary of the areas where AI has enhanced our programs.

Collection

Many illicit sites use various technologies to detect automated collection or scraping activity; they also have bot mitigation tools like CAPTCHA and similar. We have successfully worked around these defenses using AI. For example, AI can collect data in a way that emulates a human being simply clicking and browsing the site.

Analysis

The ability to recognize behavioral trends across the dataset. For example, we can now observe the weaponization of a particular CVE and potentially quantify its impact over time. We can see when a particular trend emerges across mediums and can more easily see when a customer is being referenced. Using this visibility, we can prioritize response and recommend mitigation strategies.

Prediction

We can predict attack vectors, timelines, or certain periods of time (events) susceptible to elevated risk. We can also see attack campaigns much faster.

Automation

Our advisories to clients can be automatically classified by risk level, with the context and enrichment done automatically. For specific types of threats, we can automatically recommend an appropriate mitigation strategy.

Augmentation

Our analysts can use the technology to automate repetitive tasks and content creation. The analyst team can use Tracey to automatically pull definitions and context for CVEs, IP addresses, domains, security certificates, and more.

Program Support

Tracey helps us better document and develop our baseline PIRs (PIR-Zero) and suggests additional PIRs for individual customer scenarios. We can also use Tracey to evaluate the maturity and quality of third-party information, API data, and external intelligence.

Cyber Espionage Support

We have been using AI for some time to help us build more realistic sock puppets and personas. This is accomplished by creating false content, web pages, profile information, and activity. We have used Tracey for language analysis and negotiation strategy and have solicited suggestions on conversational techniques during actor engagement.

Training and Simulation

As a part of our ransomware prevention practice R3S, we chair, participate in, or curate tabletop (TTX) exercises for our clients. I have been using AI to provide the injects or scenarios during TTXs for some time. This makes the exercise more realistic and unpredictable.

Threat Actor Profiling

As discussed in Chapter 4, we can use information gathered from dark web, open web, social media, and chat data to seed threat actor profiling. Using the AI engine to in an automated fashion as data is collected to correlate and identify behaviors and qualities.

While my UI designers may disagree with me, I would like to see this data presented like a baseball card to the analysts and customers. (By the time this is published, I will have won or lost this design argument.) The TA-Dossier will be titled with the threat actor's handle and the primary property, the primary property being where they are most active, then immediately followed by all other monikers and handles the TA uses. Below the handles is a comprehensive list of the other properties in which the actor is participatory, accompanied by activity statistics on each property—how many times they have posted, their comments, how many items they've sold, and if the forum supports it, their reputational score. Of course, these are taggable for investigation and association support. The data supporting the TA-Dossier concept is made possible, scalable, and more accurate through the use of AI.

These are some of the immediate uses for AI on intelligence datasets. While I won't rule it out, I have a hard time envisioning the use of an AI bot actually autonomously performing the threat actor engagement. Anything is possible, but the espionage discipline is so deeply rooted in human psychology, emotion, and instinct that it will be difficult to replace with a robot. Perhaps someone more clever than myself will prove me wrong someday.

Regardless, the best thing about this technology is that if you manage it properly and provide the proper guide rails, it improves over time. We have been applying AI to our practice for only about a year as of this writing. I cannot imagine how much better and how much more efficient the technology will be a year from now.

Cryptocurrency powers a cybercriminal boom and fosters creative solutions for the defenders.

> "... you pay us 100k USD BTC, or 75k USD Monero discount..."
> –Ragnar Locker Ransomware Gang

Cybercriminals existed long before the advent of blockchain technology and cryptocurrencies, though moving their money was challenging. Ransomware was a thing, but it relied on money order services and cash or gift cards like Ukash and PaySafeCard. The illicit market economy was nascent but operational, often relying on wire transfers, money services like Western Union and Moneygram, or prepaid debit cards. Many online criminals simply went with cash by mail, value transfer, or bartering.

Electronic payments occurred through services like PayPal but used stolen accounts. Attackers also leveraged early attempts at digital currency; one example is a service called E-Gold, which used digital representation of value backed by actual physical gold. U.S. regulators eventually shut this service down due to suspicion of widespread money laundering. Liberty Reserve, an early version of digital currency that required no verification, was used until authorities arrested its operators and seized their assets for similar reasons to E-Gold. Other digital payment systems were more regional in nature, like Webmoney and Perfect Money, but they died rapidly after Satoshi Nakamoto arrived on the scene.

> Satoshi Nakamoto is the pseudonymous person or persons credited with developing Bitcoin.

Before Bitcoin (BTC), online criminal activity was difficult due to the traceability of most currency exchange options. The available methods prior to BTC were also extremely inefficient, requiring significant manual operations and long periods of time for reconciliation. BTC showed up and offered a solution that immediately fixed many of these challenges.

BTC doesn't require real-world identities, has global reach, and is extremely efficient. At its onset, Bitcoin was independent of traditional banking systems, so no one could interrupt, freeze, or reverse transactions. BTC flew above all of the international laws around fund transfers, including the limitations, monitoring, and reporting. It was a perfect solution for cybercriminals.

Blockchain and digital currencies opened a new world for ransomware operators, too. The early days of ransomware were rough for everyone involved. Sending a MoneyGram to unlock your desktop computer was frustrating, considering the extortion and the time it took to make it happen. The other side of the transaction was equally frustrating. It took forever to get your money, and there was a chance it could be traced back to you. Bitcoin increased the speed of payment, glided over the top of international money transfer laws and tracking, and made attribution of the receiver incredibly difficult, if not impossible.

Paradoxically, BTC and blockchain are 100 percent transparent because every transaction is there for the world to see. The early days of cryptocurrency adoption by online criminals were obfuscated by sheer volume and noise. Today, there is a burgeoning industry of blockchain intelligence tools that, when used correctly, can trace every penny. As a result, the bad guys built infrastructure like Mixers to make tracing transactions more difficult.

Bitcoin Mixers (or Tumblers) throw the tracing tools off track (see Figure 9.1). The function is relatively simple: The illicit funds are transferred to the Mixer, where they are combined in a large pool of other, unrelated funds. The Mixer funds are processing many outbound transactions, so when the illicit input funds are sent out, it is difficult to identify them. This is further enhanced with features like prescribed delays, fragmenting the total payment across multiple wallets, and other techniques. While this is sometimes effective in obfuscating the identity of the receiver, many blockchain tracing tools have become smarter. Companies like Elliptic, Chainalysis, and TRM Labs use algorithms, heuristics, and cluster analysis to mitigate Mixers.

These same tools can be used for intelligence and compliance when dealing with a threat actor. Our team routinely uses blockchain intelligence tools to gain insight into a particular threat actor's

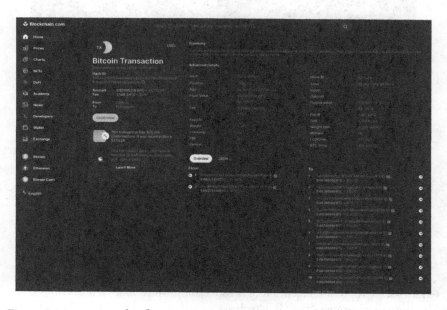

Figure 9.1 An example of Mixer activity on the Blockchain Explorer.

wallet. For example, we might gather data on the wallet's balance, recent transactions going in and out of the wallet, and whether there are any destination wallets tagged with criminal or sanction violations. This process tells us a few essential things, like the average payment (what should we pay?) and whether we would violate international law by making a payment. Figure 9.2 shows a trace from the Mt. Gox hack on the crypto intelligence tool Breadcrumbs.

While threat actors benefit from blockchain technologies, the defenders are finding applications to use against them. Blockchain's permanence lends itself to immutable or irreversible event logging.

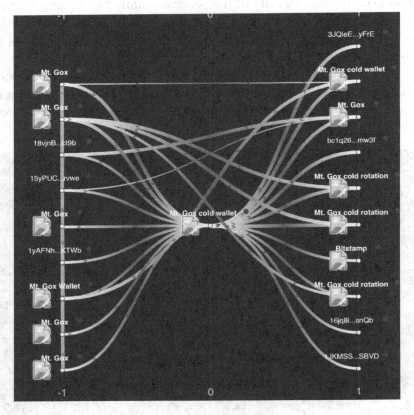

Figure 9.2 Crypto intelligence tool Breadcrumbs, which maps transactions. This is an illustration of the Mt. Gox heist.

A handful of technologies have been developed to take full advantage of this, ensuring sneaky threat actors cannot easily cover their tracks. Similar applications have been developed to record, track, and secure bank transactions, health records, government contracts, and other critical information.

Blockchain applications have also been leveraged in the cyber intelligence space. For example, PolySwarm is a blockchain-based threat intelligence feed. The decentralized feed is entirely powered by Ethereum smart tokens, crowdsourced malware analysis, and threat feeds with blockchain's irrefutability. The platform's "proof of work" is threat detection accuracy and rewards for contributors who submit their malware analysis and samples via the Nectar Token (NCT). NCT shows a value of $0.0249 as of this writing. There is still time to get in!

Blockchain technologies will continue to underpin budding cybersecurity architectures while simultaneously providing threads to sew the hoodies for enterprising, digitally savvy cybercriminals. This is the way of technology. The genie is out of the proverbial bottle, and it cannot be put back in. It is possible, however, that it can be torn limb from limb by a new apex predator technology.

Even in the early days of Silk Road and Mt. Gox, politicians and regulators freaked out about cryptocurrency's inevitable impact on the financial industry. They saw something they didn't fully understand, heard terms like "dark web" and "untraceable currency," and sought to put an end to it all. (The leadership at the Bitcoin Foundation quickly corrected the "untraceable" accusations, pointing out that it was very much the opposite.) Nevertheless, the fear that many evil things could manifest when combining anonymous networks with anonymous and decentralized currencies was justified. Of course, these technologies have also been leveraged for many world-changing positive use cases, from protecting dissidents from authoritarian regimes to providing a non-government-driven, practically inflation-proof monetary system. The very nature of these technologies makes it difficult for governing bodies from any country to regulate them out of existence. Yet another budding future technological leap could do just that.

I would be negligent if I pontificated on new technology and didn't at least mention quantum computing. Considering the amount of attention and effort put into quantum computing worldwide, development and adoption will continue accelerating. Not unlike our approach to generative AI, it is also likely we will innovate ourselves into a problem. Some of those future challenges are easily predictable, but others will no doubt blindside us. Regardless, the quantum age is coming quickly, and it will profoundly impact our technology, financial world, and cybersecurity.

Quantum computing is a new form of computer processing based on quantum mechanics. The processing capability of quantum computers is not necessarily more powerful than our traditional computers today; quantum just processes information *differently*. Today's computer chips process everything in binary; that is, every computation is either 1 or 0. These are bits. This linear process requires computers to attack each problem step by step or in parallel. Quantum computers have qubits, 1, 0, or *1 and 0 at the same time*. This is called a superposition. Quantum computers take advantage of superposition and entanglement to process many possible problems simultaneously, which makes them incredibly powerful for specific types of solutions. One of those solutions is cryptography.

Much has been written about quantum cryptography and quantum computing's potential impact on our current encryption capabilities. This has fostered a sort of quantum arms race between nation-states and their academic partners. The idea that a sufficiently powered quantum computer could chew through and produce a decryption key for AES256 encryption is terrifying. When this is achieved, it will unhook virtually all the privacy technologies that exist in 2025. Top secret encrypted files, peer-to-peer encrypted messaging, and the public/private key infrastructures (PKI) will all be rendered useless. Other technologies that rely on cryptography to function will also be vulnerable to manipulation or attack, including cryptocurrencies.

Bitcoin uses an implementation of PKI called the Elliptic Curve Digital Signature Algorithm (ECDSA) to secure digital wallets. BTC also uses a form of cryptographic hashing called SHA-256 for mining and the creation of new blocks on the BTC blockchain. The integrity of both of these solutions are at risk with the adoption of quantum cryptography. A quantum computer could quickly solve the mathematical problem behind ECDSA. This would allow the quantum attacker to move funds around on the blockchain at will, impersonate wallet owners, and forge transactions. The math behind SHA-256 is uncrackable by current quantum capabilities, but we are in the early days of quantum computing, and it is plausible that future technology will be able to reverse SHA hashes.

Technologists around the world are working feverishly to build new post-quantum or quantum-resistant cryptography algorithms to reinforce or replace our existing crypto stacks. In some cases, the implementation would mean a full overhaul of the current implementation. Other cases are investigating hybrid models. In the case of cryptocurrencies, a rewrite of the protocols governing the securing of wallets and the building of the blockchain blocks will be required. This is a major task and will impact each blockchain differently. Regardless, quantum computing will foster a major sea change in all things crypto, causing a major upheaval across the world.

NIST's Post-Quantum Cryptography Standardization Project is working on standardizing post-quantum and quantum-resistant technologies. Likewise, universities and academic labs are aggressively researching methods to transition from today's cryptology to quantum-enabled cryptography. Governments are putting funding forward for the same purpose. I have assisted in the U.S. Economic Development Administration's Elevate Quantum project; it is one of the largest quantum ecosystems in the world. Tech industry leaders like IBM, Google, and Microsoft are working on both quantum solutions and defense strategies against quantum. In December 2024, Google announced Willow, their newest quantum chip, claiming that "Willow performed a standard benchmark computation in under five minutes that would take one of today's fastest supercomputers 10 septillion (that is, 1,025) years—a number that vastly exceeds the age of the Universe" (see https://blog.google/ technology/research/google-willow-quantum-chip). I am not doubting Willow's ability to guess my password. In cryptocurrency circles, blockchain developers for BTC, Ethereum, and others are working on models for quantum-safe upgrades to wallet security and blockchain functions. Everything is going to be okay. That is what I keep telling myself, anyway.

The simultaneously frustrating and amazing thing about technology is that by the time this book is printed, everything will have changed. The technology landscape continues to increase its momentum while those who would use it for illicit purposes continue to adopt it in parallel. Laws, investigative technology, governments, financial institutions, and average people remain inevitably behind the (elliptical?) curve. If you are interested in getting smarter on quantum mechanics or computing, Wiley Press offers myriad books on the topic.

If we ever meet on the street, at a motorcycle rally, or at a trendy wine bar, be sure to ask me my opinions on whether superpositions are a form of time travel (they're not) or if quantum entanglement is akin to teleportation (it's not). Regardless, I am a joy to talk to— I promise.

In the meantime, *if you do one thing* after reading this chapter, familiarize yourself with at least one of the cloud-based generative AI platforms. While many see gen AI as a threat to their vocation or a tool for cheating, I have found it to accelerate the things I am already good at. Used correctly and with righteous intentions, gen AI is a powerful tool.

Cyber Recon Leader Profile:

Jason Ingalls

Current Role: Chief Cybersecurity Officer of C3 Integrated Solutions and founder of Ingalls Information Security

Other Affiliations: Adviser to Louisiana State University Alexandria (LSUA), Louisiana State University Shreveport (LSUS) Computer Science Departments, Central Louisiana Technical Community College (CLTCC) Curriculum Adviser

Jason's Bio

Jason is the founder and CEO of Ingalls Information Security, an incident response veteran who has led or contributed to the resolution of some of the largest data breaches in history. With over 20 years in IT and more than 14 years in cybersecurity, Jason has provided penetration testing, forensics analysis, remediation, and security monitoring for clients ranging from the White House to TJX Companies. His career began with designing and integrating Multi-level Security systems for the F-22 Raptor Program. Jason's team played a key role in securing the WhiteHouse.gov website using Drupal, contributing to the widespread adoption of open source technology across U.S. government agencies. As a trusted consultant for legal and government entities, he has advised on crisis management, cybersecurity insurance reimbursements, and high-profile breaches. Jason is dedicated to training the next generation of cybersecurity experts and providing subject matter expertise for undisclosed, high-impact incidents.

Jason's Mission

I stand for empowering people and organizations to defend themselves through knowledge, innovation, and collaboration. I'm driven by the challenge of staying one step ahead of adversaries, protecting what matters most, and guiding the next generation of cybersecurity professionals to navigate an ever-evolving threat landscape confidently.

YouTube URL: https://www.youtube.com/watch?v=KimyZefbC1k

YouTube, LLC

Chapter 10
Digital Novichok

Much to my then-wife's frustration, the master bedroom in our new fancy apartment in Schaumburg, Illinois, did not have a bed. It was 2000, and we had just relocated to be closer to one another. She had moved into the dorms at Northwestern University to finish her PhD in electrical engineering. I had taken a cost-of-living pay cut, moving up from Springfield, Illinois, to work for Ameritech Datacomm. The apartment we chose was off Roselle Road, near the Schaumburg Mall, a feature I quickly despised. It had vaulted ceilings, a fireplace, a deck, and French-style double doors leading into the master. In that bedroom, I started honing my threat actor engagement skills. At the time, I had no idea if anyone else was doing what I was doing. I certainly didn't realize I was ahead of the curve on many of my activities. I would routinely get home from work and grab a can of Ballz ginseng energy drink (I bought it by the case from ThinkGeek.com) and huddle in that room, sometimes until 4 a.m., when I would shower to get ready for work again. It was not the healthiest lifestyle, but I was obsessed and young.

The bedroom buzzed with the sound of power supply fans, clicked and snapped from disk activity. It was outfitted with four 6-foot folding tables, covered in slightly dilapidated, unusual computing systems like a Sun SPARCstation 1000 Enterprise (complete with the 1,000 Disk Array), Sparc IPC, DEC Alpha, and a handful of home-built mini-ITX PCs running various flavors of Linux or BSD. My desk was in the center of the room, rectangular with a light maple surface and metal draftsman-like frame. Wires hung visibly from the front of the desk, dangling from two massive 30-inch Sun Microsystems CRTs flanked by a flat(ish) LCD monitor—cutting edge at the time.

Six years after my first interaction with a threat actor, I had advanced my methods. In my master bedroom/cyber lab, I had configured an old PC with two network cards, OpenBSD, and network-sandwiched it between my lab Internet router (separate from my apartment's high-speed DSL) and another PC running an older unpatched version of Microsoft Windows. The OpenBSD PC was configured as a "bump in the wire," effectively invisible to others by functioning as a layer 2 switch between the router and the Windows machine. On the OpenBSD box, I ran the open source intrusion prevention system (IPS) Snort in one window while running the command-line packet sniffer tcpdump in another. This, combined with OpenBSD's packet filtering capabilities (which worked on the traffic despite the layer 2 bridge configuration), gave me full visibility and control of any traffic to and from the Windows machine and the Internet. Then, from the Windows machine, I logged on to Internet Relay Chat (IRC).

IRC was just starting to fade as a popular communications medium in favor of peer-to-peer platforms like AIM, ICQ, and Jabber, among others. But ICQ was still heavily used by illicit actors selling stolen software, music, and movies, as well as trading malware and hacking techniques. My sock puppet, which I created months prior, was emulating a young kid at a high school wishing to get better at "hacking." He would routinely comment on others' posts with rather pedestrian comments, signaling his lack of knowledge. I popped on one of my regular hacking-themed channels and typed, "Got this new Windows box, can I haz warez lol?"

Within a few minutes, the tcpdump screen was alive with scanner traffic. Moments later, the Snort screen threw a couple of signatures that matched, and I watched as my IRC "friends" took over my Windows computer.

This experience was invaluable, as I became a security subject matter expert (SME) for SBC (who bought Ameritech shortly after I joined) across a five-state region. I understood the complexities of packet filtering using tools like PF, IPF, and iptables. I would buy used firewalls and proxy servers from eBay, wipe them, reconfigure them, and sell them back on eBay only when I thought I knew the platform backward and forward. However, I would often try to load NetBSD on them first; I was convinced NetBSD could be ported to run on a toaster.

I had also found other security nerds nearby. I befriended Paul Whittenburg (the person who convinced me to start GroupSense), and we started a local hacker group we called the "LAN." We held regular hacking events where we would use our combined intellect to make some hardware do something it wasn't intended to do, like taking a Bay Centillion switch chassis, filling it with the management modules (which were basically Sparc 5s), and trying to turn it into a Beowulf cluster. LAN had a concept called "friendly fire," where we would try to hack each other and report our successes and failures at the monthly meetings. This practice, by the way, really upset my wife, as we had moved into a smaller condo near the university and all my servers were again in the bedroom. I would hear the disk spin up, jump up, look at my watch, try to remember when the cron jobs were scheduled, and race to the keyboard.

Around this time, I also began to understand the cyber poverty line issue. I built my own version of a unified threat management device and deployed it to small businesses around Chicago, charging them a relatively small monthly fee to maintain it. A friend and I wrote a logging interface for that system and later were asked to write a similar system for a Snort front-end company, AppliedWatch (later acquired by Endace). Those skills won us contracts writing software for the state of Illinois and Bluecoat Systems.

I broadened my view of the cyber landscape with every customer and every project, and it appeared my adversaries were doing the same. The closer I got to the battlefield, the more sophisticated the adversaries became. It would be a few years before it would become clear why this acceleration in criminal cyber-craft was accelerating.

Without question, the digital attack surface expanded in every direction, like the universe after the Big Bang. The Internet of Things (IoT) and operational technology (OT) became part of the lexicon long before the idea that we needed to secure those things did. The U.S. government, giddy over its discovery of this soft digital underbelly, quickly adapted its strategies to heavy investments in "cyber weapons." Of course, the government neglected to make parallel investments in cyber defense, which is one of the reasons why we are where we are today.

The adversaries became many, and their cyber capabilities advanced at an alarming rate. The lines began to blur between cybercriminal and cyber warrior—cyber defense and cyber offense. It even became less clear who the enemy was, to determine who was planting the spy tools in our everyday digital tools. It could have been the cybercriminal, the "researcher," the nation-state proxy cyber warrior, or even our own government. This confusion, a kind of "fog of war," eventually led me down the path that started GroupSense, a company with the objective of getting closer to the bad guy and taking the fight to them. As I pulled my listening ear up from the digital ground, I had an epiphany.

I began giving a talk called "World War III: The War You Didn't Know You Were Fighting *and Losing.*"

How Did We Get Here?

Around the time knowledge of Stuxnet became public, I realized something was wrong. Stuxnet was developed by the U.S. government (and arguably Israeli intelligence) and designed with the sole purpose of disrupting the Iranian Natanz nuclear facility's ability to enrich uranium. It succeeded. The mystery around what happened and who developed such an advanced cyber weapon quickly became clear. On one hand, I was proud of the capability of our U.S. cyber warriors. On the other hand, I wondered about the self-propagating worm that looks for Siemens PLC controller software. What stops it from continuing to propagate? What stops it from being backward-engineered and used against *us*? The problem was we had developed the world's most advanced cyber weapon and let it loose on our adversary yet had done virtually nothing to inoculate ourselves against it. We still haven't.

In my many media interviews and public talks, I speak about the U.S. military's defense culture. The U.S. defense culture is *offense*. In myriad ways, this makes sense for kinetic warfare because there is an ocean between us and our foes. They aren't going to easily sneak up on us. Our strategy of taking the fight to them is a solid one. As a result, the Department of Defense's budget is primarily a department of *offense* budget. We build long swords and spears to blow things up. We don't need heavy shields because our adversaries aren't coming over here.

Yet, sadly, they *are* here, and they've been here for a while. There are no oceans in the cyber realm. The ability for a cyber actor to disable our systems does not require them to get on a plane or a boat. It doesn't require them to *leave their chair* on the other side of the world, safely on the other side of either ocean.

This problem is compounded by the inverted way the U.S. manages itself politically, economically, and from an infrastructure perspective. The federal government has the bulk of resources and capital, but as you get closer to the individual living in a municipality, the money, resources, and authority diminishes. It is at these municipal levels that the responsibility for securing our power, water, and critical infrastructure often lies. It is at this municipal level that law enforcement is responsible for protecting the citizens from and responding to crime.

The United States is built on a beautiful system; the concept of localizing the issues to the state and local level is a promising one that puts the legislation around these issues closer to the individuals. On the surface, it makes a lot of sense. A person in Chicago has very different needs and priorities than a person 200 miles away in Morrisonville. A person who lives in Ely, Nevada, perhaps has different life priorities than the person living in Las Vegas. Yet, the infrastructure that provides them with their power and water and the police who protect them from harm are universally important. The election infrastructure supporting their votes is universally important. The funding does not reflect this reality.

Midway through the history of GroupSense, I began providing pro bono services to small businesses and law enforcement agencies around the country. When possible, I partnered with educational institutions to help scale my work. I learned many of the higher education systems were echoing the offense-as-defense paradigm. There were many classes on red teaming, penetration testing, and capture-the-flag (CTF) activity, but few on incident response, fewer on vulnerability management, and practically none on cyber risk management. We are churning out legions of cyber warriors but precious few cyber defenders.

My relocation from Washington, DC, to Colorado (I pulled the cliché COVID ripcord once we decided not to use our corporate office any longer) further opened my eyes to these digital realities. Perhaps getting out of the "Beltway bubble" provided some much-needed clarity.

My rapid integration into my new small community illuminated the lack of cyber sophistication and the lack of resources at the local municipal level. My growing pro bono work thrust me into the gaping hole of support for cybercrime victims at the individual level. Our work in election security illustrated massive gaps in prioritization and resources at the local level.

It was in my new home that I devised a plan to technically modernize, measure, and optimize the water in the Colorado River. The Colorado River supplies water and resources to approximately 40 million Americans across eight states. It is responsible for subsidizing the resources that power a quarter of the U.S. GDP. Yet, we have managed much of this river in a vacuum manually. When talking with Andy Mueller, a wonderful civil servant and the general manager of the Colorado River Water Conservation District, I learned the reason we keep the Colorado River off the grid: We are afraid of cyberattacks from foreign countries. Mueller quickly acknowledged that we could drive better water outcomes for the downstream constituents if we had modern water management. This is especially important when it is widely known that the demand for water from the Colorado River is much greater than the current supply. Together with colleagues from the Grand Junction Economic Partnership (GJEP), Colorado Mesa University (CMU), the city of Grand Junction, and Mesa County, we launched the Resilient Adaptive Protection of Industrial Devices and Systems (RAPIDS) initiative. RAPIDS, which just launched with its first tranche of state funding, aims to provide a reference architecture and framework for deploying industrial devices for the management of water systems with cybersecurity as the backbone, starting with one of the most important national pieces of infrastructure, the Colorado River.

This fear of foreign governments interfering with the operation of our industrial systems is warranted. Many municipalities do not have the talent or resources to defend their current systems—let alone new advanced OT systems—from foreign actors. Further, we aren't sure from whom we are protecting these systems. Are we fighting ransomware gangs, Russian intelligence, North Korean hackers, Iranian cyber vandals—or possibly all of them? In recent months, there has been a buzz about China's infiltration of our critical infrastructure and telecommunications systems. Our headlines have been full of all capital letters trumpeting ransomware victim after ransomware victim.

The motivations of China, Iran, and North Korea are simple to digest. Their sophistication, while formidable, has been demonstrated as moderate to date, with China taking pole position. These country's attacks have been tactical in nature and mission-driven. Iran wanted to deface websites to show support for their proxy armies in Syria and Lebanon. North Korea wanted to steal cryptocurrency to fund its heavily sanctioned regime or punish Sony for making fun of their supreme leader in a movie. What worries me more is the one nation-state that seems to relentlessly attack under various guises and methods for years at a time: Russia.

Andy Greenberg discussed Russia's concept of *informatsionnaya voyna* or "information warfare" in his acclaimed book

Sandworm. Much of that book resonated with me. My team and I were near the Malware Room in iSight Partners and had drinks with John Hultquist and his iSight colleagues in the famous bar in their office around the time the book was being penned. We provided iSight customers with white-labeled dark web intelligence at the time and had been tasked to chase select cybercriminals down their dark web rabbit holes. Attribution is difficult, but we kept ending up in the same place.

Russia's concept of information warfare is more holistic than information systems warfare. *Informatsionnaya voyna* is an ongoing cycle of disrupting the enemy (all enemies) using misinformation, false flags, third parties, and proxies. When Russia first entered Georgia and before their five-day war began in August 2008, they sent in soldiers with no insignia; these soldiers became known as "Little Green Men." They did the same in Donbas in Ukraine before that war, which started in February 2022. It was Russia that repeatedly carried out distributed denial-of-service (DDoS) attacks in Estonia. It was Russia that used misinformation to interfere in elections around the world, from France to Ukraine, Georgia, Moldova, and the United States. Russia repeatedly attacked Ukraine citizens, companies, and critical infrastructure, successfully shutting down their national power systems multiple times. It was Russia that infiltrated and successfully carried out advanced espionage on U.S. companies and governments via the SolarWinds supply chain attack in 2020. As I alluded to earlier in this book, I believe the Russian state also has its hands firmly in the ransomware economy.

We saw clear signs of crossover from cybercriminal ransomware activity and nation-state sabotage with the release of the NotPetya malware in June 2017. Considered one of the most damaging cyberattacks in history, NotPetya caused tens of billions of dollars in damage and halted the operations of global companies. The NotPetya payload, delivered in part by a modified U.S. cyber weapon, encrypted the files of machines using modified ransomware code.

The cyber weapon in question was from the alleged hack of the National Security Agency (NSA) by the hacker group known as the Shadow Brokers. The Shadow Brokers are believed to be a division of Russia's foreign military intelligence agency known as the GRU. This was another example of where the United States developed some of the most powerful cyber weapons in the world, lost control of them, and did not take the necessary steps to protect ourselves or our allies *against* those very weapons.

Russia recently announced that it was using Bitcoin in foreign trade transactions. This is concerning considering the Kremlin's previous hesitance to bless cryptocurrency use. I believe there are two primary reasons they made this charge, which I also believe was always part of their plan: sanctions and their vast BTC holdings. The anonymity afforded wallet owners and the ease of laundering cryptocurrency gives Russia a formidable tool for evading international sanctions, and as of December 2024, it is believed the Russian government controls over $210 billion in BTC, with the capacity to mine another $3 billion a year.

When Putin threw Mikhail Borisovich Khodorkovsky—perhaps the most powerful oligarch in Russia—in jail for tax evasion, he first put him in a small cage and invited the media to observe. The other oligarchs saw their friend and respected peer in a small cage and wondered if they were next. In a meeting at the Kremlin shortly after Khodorkovsky's arrest, the oligarchs reportedly asked Putin what they would have to do to stay out of the cage. His alleged response: "*Half.*"

Of course, Putin has long denied any direct involvement with the ransomware trade. But when he hunted down the leaders of the Revil gang and threw them in jail, did a similar conversation occur? Russia's amnesty for the ransomware gangs is an accepted fact in the cybersecurity community. I have long suggested that there is a quid pro quo for that amnesty. At a minimum, we should assume that the FSB or GRU receives a copy or gets direct access to any data stolen during a ransomware attack, which means Russia has petabytes of our data. They have our employee rosters, our salaries, our personally identifiable information (PII), and more—in droves. They have architectural drawings of our buildings, maps of our roads, and plans for our bridges, trains, and airports. They have our confidential documents, classified material, and top-secret manuals for weapon systems. You might be skeptical, but I have seen it *firsthand*. I think we can also safely assume they have *our money*.

Russian hackers were linked to the Mt. Gox BTC exchange heist, where tens of millions of dollars (now worth billions) of BTC disappeared from the exchange. The BTC-e exchange that laundered the stolen Mt. Gox BTC was run in Russia and was later linked to funding parts of the war in the Donbas region of Ukraine.

The cyber plague emanating from Russia far exceeds the efforts of any other country. Why wouldn't Russia foster the continued operational damaging and economically harmful practice of attacking the U.S. and NATO allies while it fills their digital coffers with BTC? The alignment with *informatsionnaya voyna* and the plausible deniability it provides is too perfect.

Volatility in cryptocurrency continues, but crypto is here to stay. While I do not identify as libertarian, I believe there is inherent good in the cryptocurrency concept. I believe there is a balance between a decentralized system and regulation of using that system. I believe that much of the noise that has put a bad rap on crypto will eventually subside, and more legitimate use of the blockchain and the coins that rely on it will emerge. Yet, as I write this book's final chapter, I read articles referring to the U.S. government investing in a Bitcoin reserve and simultaneously read of Russia's use of BTC to evade sanctions. I cannot help but wonder if we are, yet again, enabling our opponent.

What Does That Mean for *Us*?

Since its formation, the United States has always been about individualism. From our states rights movement to municipal authority to the first and second amendments of the Constitution, this country is built on the individual's right to say what we want, take care of ourselves and our families, and defend ourselves from harm. Divisive politics aside, the concept of individual responsibility and self-reliance is woven into the fabric of our country.

Our approach to cybersecurity and technology use should be no different. At a national level, the United States realized the vulnerability of the foreign-sourced manufacturing of the majority of our computer chips and processors is a national security concern. Congress enacted the CHIPS and Science Act of 2022 to remedy this risk. Take this statement from the CHIPS and Science Act website: "America invented the semiconductor, but today produces about 10 percent of the world's supply—and none of the most advanced chips. Instead, we rely on East Asia for 75 percent of global production." It is for this reason I am pushing my RAPIDS project to drive national awareness of the vulnerability of our industrial control systems (ICSs) to cyberattack and pushing Congress to take a serious, tangible, and focused approach to securing the rest of our critical infrastructure.

Informatsionnaya voyna or not, cyberattacks are causing clear, tangible damage to U.S. citizens. We have foreign actors breaking into our systems, taking our data, and causing sometimes fatal operational disruptions. They are taking our money and using it against us. *This has to stop.*

Legislators need to understand that making ransom payments illegal will not make this go away. I can only hope they will provide a third option for those who are below the cyber poverty line. Ideally, they will provide victims with the resources to protect themselves, prevent future attacks, and recover if an attack is successful. Holding foreign nations accountable for the immunity they provide these cyber actors is also key, if for no other reason than Russia is engaging in information warfare as a constant operation. We are at war *now*, and we are *losing that war*.

I have an entreaty to my fellow cyber people: Give back as much as you can. You have a gift that can quite literally save the United States from harm. Volunteer in your communities, teach your family members all the best practices, and provide pro bono support to those around you. Speak up when you see something that is wrong—does your company make a medical product but not bother to secure it? Do you work at a research university with government-funded programs that have poor cybersecurity? Speak up! Lead by example!

> I was once in a bar in Colorado waiting on a friend and member of the economic development team working on RAPIDS. A well-dressed gentleman approached me and said, "Excuse me, are you that cyber guy?"
> "I think I may be the person you are referring to," I replied.
> "I heard you give a keynote at the university. I run a local bank. Can I buy you a drink?" he asked.
> I asked if he implemented any of the changes I suggested at my keynote talk at his bank. "I did!" he said. "We implemented multifactor and an enterprise password manager because of you."
> "Then, sir," I said, smiling broadly, "I will buy *you* a drink."

Now, a request for my fellow citizens: Protect yourselves! We cannot easily make our government protect us from the cyber invaders. We cannot force Russia to obey international law. Further, we cannot make our software providers do a better job of securing their code. We can't make the coffee shop better secure its Wi-Fi, and we cannot make the telecommunication companies jettison the faulty systems that enable wiretaps on our cell phones. We can, however, protect ourselves by making cybersecurity a fundamental part of our lives. Technology underpins nearly every aspect of our lives, and if we are going to lean into this paradigm, we must accept the responsibility that comes with it. I have long stated that good cyber hygiene at the individual level is a form of patriotism or at the very least a civic responsibility. Tap deep into that sense of stoic self-reliance and embrace Stephen Covey's "7 Habits" sphere of influence. Use token-based multifactor authentication (MFA) everywhere possible; use passphrases when possible; use a password manager; use encryption at rest and in motion; and update your systems as soon as an update is offered. And stop . . . clicking!

I have been lucky to fall into the trenches of this messy conflict. Before I knew it, I was shoulder-deep in the digital muck of a clandestine cyber war. Our understanding of the enemy accelerates our ability to win a war, digital or in person, or to make peace. The world of cyber espionage and cyberthreat actor engagement has put me digitally face to face with those opponents, and they are human. They feel as justified in their actions as you do in yours. These humans have families and futures and want to protect both, just like you and I do. Our ability to apply empathy in our approach will only strengthen our likelihood of getting out of this alive.

Empathy may not seem like an effective weapon, but it is precisely what enables us to understand the motivations and vulnerabilities of our adversaries. Empathy is not sympathy, and it does not mean excusing the actions of cybercriminals. It means understanding them well enough to anticipate, outmaneuver, and neutralize the threat—but this is still not enough. To better secure ourselves and our country, we must hold accountable those who enable these attacks and threats. We must be accountable for our own security. The time to act is *now*. Together, we can secure our future.

If you want to make a difference after reading this chapter, educate yourself, strengthen your defenses, volunteer, and jettison the habits and systems perpetuating this conflict.

Cyber Recon Leader Profile:

Beau Woods

Current Role: Founder, Strategos

Other Affiliations: Cyber Safety Advocate, I Am The Cavalry initiative; Founder, Hackers on the Hill; Co-Founder/Board Member, Aerospace Village; Track Co-Lead, BSides Las Vegas; Coauthor, *Practical IoT Hacking*

Beau's Bio

Beau Woods is a leader with the I Am The Cavalry grassroots initiative, is founder/CEO of Strategos Security, is a Cyber Safety Innovation Fellow with the Atlantic Council, leads the public policy space at DEFCON, and runs the I Am The Cavalry and Public Grounds tracks at BSides Las Vegas. In addition, Beau helped found the ICS Village, Aerospace Village, Hack the Sea, and Biohacking Village: Device Lab. His work bridges the gap between security research and public policy communities to ensure that connected technology that can impact life and safety is worthy of our trust. He formerly served as Senior Adviser with US CISA, Entrepreneur in Residence with the Food and Drug Administration, and Managing Principal Consultant at Dell SecureWorks. Over the past several years, Beau has consulted with the energy, healthcare, automotive, aviation, rail, and IoT industries, as well as cybersecurity researchers, U.S. and international policymakers, and the White House. Beau is a published author, public speaker, and media contributor.

Beau's Mission

I want to leave the world better than I found it. To stay curious and open, getting to truly know the people and the world around me. It is essential to see content within context and appreciate the actions and reactions in a more systemic view. I want to question ideas, assumptions, and my own beliefs, strengthening what holds up and letting go of what doesn't. To be an ambassador and translator, allowing others to glimpse other views and build tools to better contribute toward common goals.

Goals

- Be a true ambassador of who I am and what I stand for.
- Always listen with an open ear and an open mind.
- Never let "certainty" get in the way of discovery.
- Look at the bigger picture—see context, not just content.
- Understand where others are coming from, and what can be done about it.
- Strive for quality over quantity, and always keep things as simple as possible.

YouTube, LLC

YouTube URL: https://youtu.be/H4DaEALEHlo?si=BJC0-P97ivApjBmX

Index

A

AI (artificial intelligence)
   analyzing intelligence
      data, 216
   HUMINT operations, 215
   pattern finding in large data
      sets, 216
   threat actor use, 213–214
analysis
   AI usefulness, 216–217
   intelligence cycle
      functions, 25
anonymity
   sock puppets, 62
   tools, 120
Antoinetti, Heather, 135–136
authenticator apps, 199
automation, AI usefulness, 217

B

bad actors. *See also* threat actors
   categories, 92–94
   defenses employed by, 20
   engaging with, 27
   environment giving rise
      to, 86
   ethics, 149–150
   increase in capabilities, 13
   motivations, 88
   profile, 83–84
Banks, L. Taylor, 210–211
BEC (business email
      compromise), 202–203
Bevilacqua, Max, 188–189
Bitcoin, advantages to
      criminals, 220
Bitcoin Mixers, 221

246 INDEX

blockchain
   advantages to criminals, 220
   traceability, 221
blockchain intelligence tools, 221–222
blue teams, 122–123
breach consultants, 143–144
breach data, collecting, legal considerations, 156–157
business decisions based on values, 168–170
Burkey, Joanna, 104–105
burner phones, 122
business email compromise (BEC), 202
business negotiation, compared to hostage negotiation, 174–175

C
chat interactions, ransomware, 180–182
CIA (Central Intelligence Agency)
   intelligence sources, 13
   role in defense strategy and budget, 13
CISOs (Chief Information Security Officers), strategies and tools, 14
cloud services, shadow IT, 54–55
collection
   AI usefulness, 216–217
   intelligence cycle functions, 22–23

tools
   browser plug-in, 78–79
   wholesale feeds, 79–80
commercial cyber espionage operations, 11
compartmentalization, data protection, 112–113
compromised non-clients, contacting, 161–163
connectivity, effect on financial crime, 88
core values, adherence to, 77
cost of goods scenario, ransomware, 48–49
counterfeit markets, 52
COVID-19, cybercrime markets, 49–53
credentials
   markets, 51–52
   policies, 195–197
credit card markets, 50
crisis communication plans, 205
cryptocurrency markets, 53
cryptography, quantum computing, 224–226
CTI (cyberthreat intelligence), challenges, 14
cyber defense
   critical infrastructure and telecommunications, 235
   cyber hygiene, 194–203
   HUMINT evolution, 17–19
   local and small-scale needs, 234–235
   profiling criminals, 90–94
   questions to ask, 13

scrapers, 19–20
United States, strengths and weaknesses, 233–234
cyber espionage
  AI usefulness, 218
  language skills, 63
  non-core mission issues, handling, 76–77
  sock puppets, 61–63
cyber hygiene, 194–203
cyber incidents
  breach consultants, 143–144
  compromised non-clients, contacting, 161–163
  data recovery companies, 144–145
  ethics, 150–152
  insurance companies, 147–148
  law firms, 147
  reaction advice, 206–207
  responding to, 143, 204–209
  security leaders, 149–150
  security researchers, 145–146
  threat actors code, 149–150
  use of stolen data, 208–209
cyber intelligence
  intelligence cycle, 22–26
  partner selection, 38
  SaaS (software-as-a-service), 11
Cyber Intelligence Advisories, AI use, 215–216
cyber poverty line, 193, 231
cyberattack tabletop exercises, 206

cybersecurity
  OPSEC examples, 116–120
  policy recommendations, 239–241
  talent deficit, consequences, 193
cybersecurity product and service market, evolution, 13

D
Daniels Fund, 139
dark web, 38
  marketplaces, 40–48
  ransomware website design, 180
data
  compared to information and intelligence, 17
  processing, 25
data recovery companies, 144–145
data recovery scams, ransomware, 184–186
datasets, wholesale collection, 79–80
device isolation, 121
digital attack surface, expansion, 232
digital currencies, advantages to criminals, 220
digital extortion, 138–140
  resource constraints, 140–141
Digital Millennium Copyright Act, 43
digital risk artifacts, 35

digital risk protection services (DRPSs), 196–197
digital tools, OPSEC, 120–122
DiMaggio, Jon, 58–59
Discord, 39
disruption service markets, 52
dissemination function, intelligence cycle, 26
documentation, personas, 67–68

E
email
　business email compromise, 202–203
　OPSEC considerations, 121
encryption, OPSEC considerations, 121
espionage, 153–154
　AI usefulness, 218
ethics, personas, use of, 73–74
event cleaning, 122
exit scams, 40
exploit markets, 52
extortion, overview, 138–140
extremists, online gaming and, 54

F
false documents, 49
financially-motivated cybercrime, 88
five-stage OPSEC cycle, 113–116
fuzzing passwords, 197

G
generative AI. *See* AI (artificial intelligence)
Google dorking, 56

H
hackers. *See* bad actors; threat actors
hacktivists, 125
hostage negotiation, compared to business negotiation, 174–175
HUMINT (human intelligence)
　AI, suitability of, 215
　evolution of, 17–19

I
IAB (initial access broker), 44–45
　advertisements, 47
　ransomware sales, 48
　trusted personas, benefits, 70
IAM (identity and access management), 198
incidence response plans, 191–192, 205
industry-specific PIRs, 37
infiltration, sock puppets, 62
information, compared to data and intelligence, 17
information analysis, 19–20
information warfare, 235–238
infostealers, 45–49, 70–71
Ingalls, Jason, 227–228
initial access broker (IAB), 44–45

Index

insurance companies, cyber incidents, 147–148
IntCO (intelligence consumer organization), 35–36
intelligence
    collection sources, 38–39, 40–49
    compared to data and information, 17
intelligence advisories, acting on, 27–28
intelligence cycle, 22–26
intelligence data collection, sourcing, 20–21
intelligence gathering, value of, 34–35
IR (incident response)
    crisis communication plans, 205
    engaging IR firms, 204
    incident response plans, 204–206

K
Kaplan, Maureen, 158–159

L
language skills
    cyber espionage, 63
    persona creation, 63–67
law enforcement
    dark web market takedowns, 41–43
    personas and sock puppets, 71–74
law firms, cyber incidents, 147
least privilege, 112–113
living trusts, OPSEC, 134
LLCs, OPSEC, 133
LockBit, disruption of, 43
log cleaning, 122
logs
    market for, 46
    trusted personas, 70–71

M
mailboxes, OPSEC, 134
malware markets, 52
marketing, AI use, 215
marketplaces
    accessing, 44
    dark web, 40–48
    pandemic fraud, 49–50
    ransomware, 44
    specialized, 49–53
mental health, safeguarding for team members, 77–78
MFA (multifactor authentication), 198–199
misinformation
    orphaned accounts, 74–76
    sock puppets, 63
money laundering markets, 53
morals, as basis for business decisions, 168–170
multifactor authentication (MFA), 198–199

N
nation-state cybercriminals, profile, 86

negotiations
  business compared to hostage, 174–175
  ransomware, 166–168
  transparency, 183–184
network access, public and private organizations, market for stolen, 46–47

O
Ocepek, Steve, 81–82
OFAC (Office of Foreign Assets Control), 44
online gaming, grooming extremists, 54
OPSEC
  AnonymOS, 133
  cybersecurity examples, 116–120
  daily routines and practices, 128–129
  digital tools, 120–122
  five-stage cycle, 113–116
  hacktivists, 125
  living trusts, 134
  LLCs, 133
  mailboxes, 134
  personal, 125–127, 131–132
  personal digital surface, 132
  PO boxes, 134
  principles, 112–113
  public spaces, risks, 107–112
  scams, 129–130
  security researchers, 123–125
  social media, 130–131
  sock puppets, 63
  teams, 122–123
organized criminal activity, drivers of, 86
orphaned accounts
  passwords, 198
  spread of misinformation, 74–76
OSINT (open source intelligence), 13
  sock puppets, 63
  tools, 57

P
password managers, 195, 197–198
password policies, 195–197
paste sites, 54–55
patch management, 199–200
payment
  evolution of methods, 219–220
  ransomware
    business impact considerations, 170–173
    legal considerations, 166–167
    what to ask for from threat actors, 182
personal devices, OPSEC, 131–132
personal digital surface, OPSEC, 132
personal OPSEC, 125–127
personas, 14–17, 19, 49, 61–64. *See also* sock puppets
  creating legitimacy, 68–69
  documenting, 67–68
  law enforcement, 71–74

OPSEC considerations, 121
orphaned accounts, spread of misinformation, 74–76
selecting for infiltration, 27
trusted, 70
infostealer logs, 70–71
PhaaS (phishing-as-a-service), 52
PIR-Zero
AI usefulness, 217
collection targets, 36
goals, 35–36
value of, 34–35
VIP protection, 36
PIRs (prioritized intelligence requirements), 22–24
PO boxes, OPSEC, 134
prediction, AI usefulness, 217
privacy, sock puppets, 62
production function, intelligence cycle, 25–26
profiling criminals, 90–94
AI usefulness, 218
TTPs
analyzing findings, 97–103
limitations and challenges, 95
program support, AI usefulness, 217
proxy servers, 120–121
public spaces, OPSEC risks, 107–112

Q
quantum computing
capabilities, 224
cryptography, 224–226

R
ransomware, 44
attacker operating procedure, 171
business model, 48
chat interactions, 180–182
damage assessment questions, 171
dark web website design, 180
data recovery scams, 184–186
defense strategies, 194–203
extortion overview, 138–140
government policy response to, 192–193
harm to US economy, 186–187
incidence response plans, importance of, 191–192
negotiating strategies, 88–90, 166–168
overview and examples, 174–178
professional negotiators, 178–180
transparency, 183–184
negotiators, selecting, 204
payment (ransomware)
business impact considerations, 170–173
core-value considerations, 168
legal considerations, 154–155, 166–167
what to ask for in return, 182

ransomware (*continued*)
  post-incident monitoring, 171
  profiling criminals, 90–94
  ransom demand notification example, 176–178
  reaching out to ransom actor, 173–174
  reaction advice, 206–207
  response ethics, 142
  response resource constraints, 140–141
  Russian information warfare, 235–238
  timing from contact to close, 182
RAS (remote access software), 201
Ravattine, Brye, 31–32
reconnaissance, sock puppets, 62
red teams, 122–123
remote access software (RAS), 201
requests for intelligence (RFIs), 79
research computers, 122
RFIs (requests for intelligence), 79
risk, assessing, 208
Russia, information warfare, 235–238

S
SaaS (software-as-a-service)
  compared to tech-enabled services, 19–20

cyber intelligence programs, 11–13
  limitations as defense, 21–22
sales, AI use, 215
sandboxes, 122
sanctioned entities, ransomware payments, 167
Satoshi Nakamoto, 220
scams, OPSEC, 129–130
Scott, Jax, 9–10
scrapers, 19–20
security leaders, cyber incidents, 149–150
security researchers, 123–125
  cyber incidents, 145–146
security solution tools, limitations, 193
security subject matter expertise, acquiring, 229–231
security-focused organization culture, 200–202
shadow IT, cloud services, 54–56
SHARKS report, 74–75
SIGINT (signals intelligence), 13
situational awareness, OPSEC, 111–112
social media
  OPSEC, 130–131
  sock puppetry, 63–64
sock puppets. *See also* personas
  creating, 63–64
  documenting, 67–68
  law enforcement, 71–74
  OPSEC considerations, 121
  trust, 62
  use cases, 16, 19, 62–65

sourcing, intelligence data collection, challenges, 20–21
Stuxnet, 232
surveys, profiling cyber criminals, 93–94

T
tech-enabled services, compared to SaaS, 19–20
technology, effect of evolution in connectivity, 88
Telegram, 39
  illicit online market, 41
threat actors. *See also* bad actors
  AI use, 213–214
  engaging with, 27
    AI suitability for, 219
  ethics, 149–150
  financial activity, tracing, 221–223
  negotiating with, 163–166
  profiling, AI usefulness, 218
  ransomware operating procedures, 171
  tradecraft evolution, 232
TI (threat intelligence), evolution, 14–15
tokens, authentication, 199
tools, digital OPSEC, 120–122
TOR, 38–39, 121
  addresses, 39
training, AI usefulness, 218
translation software, persona development, limitations, 64–67

TTPs (tactics, techniques, and procedures), 95, 97–103
TTX (cyberattack tabletop exercises), 206

U
underground economy, 44–46
undercover ops, sock puppets, 63
United States
  defense budget allocation, CIA role, 13
  economic environment, effect on attitude toward cybercrime, 87
unpredictability, 122
user isolation, 121
user training, 200–202

V
values, as basis for business decisions, 168–170
VC (venture capital), business strategy, 193
vertical PIRs, 37
vulnerability management, 199–200

W
Woods, Beau, 242–243

Z
zero-day markets, 52